Sport, Culture & Society, Vol. 4

Marion Keim

Nation Building at Play

Sport as a Tool for Social Integration in Post-apartheid South Africa

Meyer & Meyer Sport

British Library Cataloguing in Publication Data
A catalogue record for this book is available from the British Library

Marion Keim:
Nation Building at Play
Oxford: Meyer & Meyer Sport (UK) Ltd., 2003
(Sport, Culture & Society; Vol. 4)
ISBN 1-84126-099-1

© 2003 by Meyer & Meyer Sport (UK) Ltd.
Aachen, Adelaide, Auckland, Budapest, Graz, Johannesburg, Miami,
Olten (CH), Oxford, Singapore, Toronto
Member of the World
Sports Publishers' Association (WSPA)
www.w-s-p-a.org

Printed and bound in Germany
by: Mennicken, Aachen
ISBN 1-84126-099-1
E-Mail: verlag@m-m-sports.com

Nation Building at Play
Sport as a Tool for Social Integration in
Post-apartheid South Africa

Marion Keim

Sport for every man, all through life, and an intensification of international efforts in physical training, could have a decisive impact on solving the problems of today's world.

(UNESCO Declaration)

CONTENTS

About the Series – *Sport, Culture & Society*

Physical activities, fitness, and sports can be considered cultural practices reflecting multiple meanings. The *Sport, Culture and Society* series deals with issues intersecting sport, physical activity and cultural concerns. The focus of the book series is interdisciplinary, groundbreaking work that draws on different disciplines and theoretical approaches, such as sociology, philosophy, cultural anthropology, history, cultural studies, feminist studies, postmodernism, or critical theory. The *Sport, Culture and Society series* seeks to reflect both, the variety of research concerns from a multi-disciplinary perspective and discussions of current topics in sport and physical activity and their relationship to culture.

The editors:
Karin Volkwein-Caplan (USA), Keith Gilbert (Australia), and Otto Schantz (France)

For further information about the book series or the submission of proposals please contact:

Karin Volkwein-Caplan, West Chester University, Department of Kinesiology, West Chester, PA 19383, USA, e-mail: kvolkwein@wcupa.edu

Keith Gilbert, Deakin University, Burwood Campus, 221 Burwood Highway, 3125 Burwood/Victoria, Australia, e-mail: keith@deakin.edu.au

Otto Schantz, University Marc Bloch, 14, rue descartes, 67084 Strasbourg, France, e-mail: schantz@umb.u-strasbg.fr

KEY TO ABBREVIATIONS

ANC	African National Congress
BVA	Bundesverwaltungsamt
BMI	Bundesministerium für Inneres
CACE	Centre for Adult and Continuing Education
CODESA	Convention for a Democratic South Africa
COSATU	Congress of South African Trade Unions
DED	Deutscher Entwicklungsdienst
DET	Department of Education and Training
DHPS	Deutsche Höhere Privatschule Windhoek
DP	Democratic Party
DSE	Deutsche Stifung für Internationale Entwicklung
DSH	Deutsche Schule Hermannsburg (Natal) DSP
	Deutsche Schule Pretoria
DSJ	Deutsche Schule Johannesburg
DSK	Deutsche Schule Kapstadt
DSR	Department of Sport and Recreation
FA	Freedom Alliance
FAZ	Frankfurter Allgemeine Zeitung
FES	Friedrich-Ebert-Stiftung
FASA	Football Association South Africa
GNU	Government of National Unity
GTZ	Deutsche Gesellschaft für Technische Zusammenarbeit
HSRC	Human Science Reearch Council
IDASA	Institute of a Democratic South Africa
	(seit 1994 Institute for Democracy in South Africa)
IFP	Inkatha Freedom Party
NGO	Non-Governmental Organisation
NOCSA	National Olympic Committee of South Africa
NP	National Party
NSC	National Sports Council
PAC	Pan Africanist Congress
PRAESA	Project for the Study of Alternative Education in South Africa
RDP	Reconstruction and Development Programme
RSA	Republic of South Africa
SACOS	South African Council of Sport
SADTU	South African Democratic Teachers´ Union
SANEP	South African National Education Policy
SANROC	South African Non-Racial Olympic Committee
SAPSSA	South African Primary School Sports Association
SAOCGA	South African Olympic and Commonwealth Games Association
SAONGA	South African Olympic and National Games Association
SARFU	South African Rugby Football Union
SASA	South African Sports Association
SASSA	South African Secondary Schools Sports Association
TBCV-States	Transkei, Bophuthatswana, Venda, Ciskei
UCBSA	United Cricket Board of South Africa
USSASA	United School Sports Association of South Africa
WCED	Western Cape Education Department

FOREWORD

By the Most Reverend Desmond Tutu
Anglican Archbishop Emeritus of Cape Town

I often find myself thinking about joy. What is it? Why does it happen? Is it complicated? Is it simple? Why do some seem to have it and others not? Have we in South Africa been too weighted down by our past to recognize the joy that exists for us each day? If so, how do we recapture it? We have all, I hope, spent many hours in serious discussions about how we might overcome a past of division and hate. We all, I hope, include our children and our students in these discussions. But they are difficult and often painful discussions with little opportunity for laughter or joy.

The author, Dr. Keim, reminds me today of a remark I made at my 70th birthday celebration at St. George's Cathedral in Cape Town. Appreciating beauty is an important task for all of us, because, she heard me say, appreciating beauty prepares us for heaven and teaches us to see God. Now is not the laughter of children playing together in a game of soccer, volleyball, rugby, netball or any sport or recreational activity something of beauty, something that is about joy? Is not teamwork something beautiful to behold in our new South Africa when the team is made up of different colours? I like Dr. Keim's book because I like beauty I laugh out loud – as many who have heard me know well – when joy is upon us. Dr. Keim shows us another road to a future of equality and democracy for all South Africans, a road not filled with the hurt of our long discussions that carry us into the night, but equally important in its capacity to heal. She maintains that through properly organized sport we can learn to play together with respect and with laughter, we can learn to all be on the same team, and in the process, we can contribute to building a new South Africa that is a just nation for all.

Dr. Keim's book was born of her PhD dissertation which was acknowledged by her examiners at the University of Heidelberg as the first scientific study examining the social integrative ability of sport in South Africa. Her findings from a multicultural sample group of 1 144 individuals should make us all sit up and pay attention. Sport in itself, she contends, does not necessarily contribute to breaking down the walls of colour and class. In fact, she found, it is possible that poorly organized sporting activities can strengthen the divisions between us and reproduce the cultural inequality that we are trying so desperately to overcome. South Africa is a complex nation with a heritage of deep divisions in the playing of sports. Coordination of sport activities, whether within or between schools, in neighbourhood sport clubs or in the professional leagues must be sensitive to language, class, facility location and choice, transport problems, cultural heritages and a number of other social, institutional and epistemological factors if these activities are to be successfully integrative experiences for players and observers. Yet her conclusion – and her commitment – is as clear as it is strong. Sport does have a meaningful and powerful role to play in the social transformation of South African society if care is taken to provide the necessary conditions for success. She offers us those conditions and at the conclusion some carefully though out recommendations for providing a level playing field for all our futures.

Dr. Keim chose South Africa as her home in 1990 when she came from Germany to be the first teacher of a multicultural classroom at the German School in Cape Town when it opened its doors to black students. She came not as an outside expert who "knows better," she tells us in her book, but as a learner whose most important lessons were found in failure and confusion. "Having tried in vain to promote social integration between black and white students both inside and outside the classroom," she writes, "I latched onto positive experiences during physical education lessons and have tried to build on them in other contexts." She has been doing so in many contexts ever since.

In 1998 Dr. Keim received the Community Development Award from the University of the Western Cape for the program she initiated for integrating marginalized groups in disadvantaged communities in the Western Cape. Her community work continues to target children and youth, women, street children and teachers. In 1999 she received the Metropolitan Life Award for Community Involvement in Southern Africa for her in-service training program for physical education teachers from disadvantaged areas. As Associate Professor at the Institute for Social Development of the University of the Western Cape where she has taught since 1995, Dr. Keim doesn't simply write about South Africa. She has made real contributions to our transformation and continues to do so today. We are happy indeed that she has made South Africa and the University of the Western Cape her home.

I am happy to commend this book to as wide a readership as possible. It deserves to be read widely.

Desmond M Tutu, Archbishop Emeritus
Cape Town
14 December 2002

❶ INTRODUCTION
Personal Background, Motivation and Aims of the Study

CHAPTER 1

1.1 From Separate and Unequal to... Equally Separate?

*I*t is common cause that, seven years after South Africa's first democratic election, social transformation is lagging far behind the political process. Legislation passed during the transitional phase has greatly improved the legal and political framework within which most South Africans lead their lives. But most observers agree that the social divisions of apartheid persist, and are likely to do so for years to come. Despite the scrapping of discriminatory laws, the "racial character" of most residential areas has remained more or less intact. If Black, White and Coloured adults[1] mix, this usually occurs in the work-place. Except in the highest echelons of society, social mixing is still very limited, and even existing occasions for "mixed" recreation and entertainment are often avoided. For instance, soccer administrators are disappointed that White fans have been staying away since the sport has become predominantly Black. A time when South Africans of different backgrounds not only work together, but also play together seems a long way off.

1.2 Open Schools = Open Minds?

For the youth, things are a bit different. Since the scrapping of apartheid and the overhauling of the legal framework of education, all schools are theoretically open, and many are so in practice. But this process has not been without problems or set-backs, occasionally leading to violent confrontations, one notable example being Vryburg High School. In addition to this, many schools in predominantly Black areas will for all intents and purposes remain "Black" schools, if only for geographic and demographic reasons. If South Africa is to become one society, and if South Africans of different backgrounds are to live together as one nation, this process cannot be left to chance. Conscious efforts must be made to overcome the social and human divisions of apartheid.

My first personal experience of the difficulties in bringing together Black and White youths in South Africa dates back to early 1991. Having grown up in

---

[1] At this point, it is important to remember the difference between "Black" in the "ethnographic", restrictive sense of the word, and "Black" as a political, more inclusive term. In the former sense, "Black" here refers to the Bantu-speaking, indigenous population of Southern Africa and is more or less synonymous with "African". In the wider, political sense of the term, "Black" refers to all victims of apartheid discrimination, and includes all those whom the apartheid system grouped under the term "Non-White", i.e. "Indians", "Coloureds" and "Africans". In the book these terms are used (and will be used without quotation marks) to illustrate the inequalities caused by the apartheid system.

Germany, I had studied English and Physical Education at Heidelberg University. I was teaching at a vocational training college near Heidelberg when I saw an advertisement for a teaching post at the German School in Cape Town.

For the first time, the school was taking in Black pupils, and the successful applicant was to be actively involved in attempts to make them feel at home. Immigrant minorities had been represented in my classes in Germany and in the United States, where I had taught (at Brighton, New York) in the late eighties, and I looked forward to this new challenge. South Africa was just then very much in the news: the ANC and other opposition movements had been unbanned, Mandela was free, and the country was clearly undergoing major change. I applied, got the post, and left for South Africa in early 1991 – excited, but also somewhat apprehensive.

It did not take long for me to realise that my task would not be an easy one. While the German government, through its funding, exerted pressure on the school to accept Black and Coloured pupils, many White parents opposed this, which inevitably must have influenced their children to some extent. Under the best of circumstances, White kids born and raised in apartheid South Africa would have needed some time to get used to the idea of sharing "their" school with Coloureds and Blacks: they had shared virtually nothing in the past, and their living conditions were very different. Just how different, became clear to me when I helped to prepare Black students in Langa township for their admission to the German school in Tamboerskloof. The contrast between these residential areas, and the schools that served them, could hardly have been greater. Such gaps take time to bridge.

Consequently, the initial "intercultural interaction" in my classroom was not much to boast about. The German-speaking White kids kept pretty much to themselves, as in fact did the Black and Coloured newcomers. There were endless meetings among troubled staff to devise ways and means of promoting "interaction" and "integration" between the pupils.

1.3 Where Work Fails, Try Play

But there was also a less complicated, more promising side to the story. In addition to my duties as class teacher, I also took the grade (consisting of two classes) for Physical Education (PE). The PE lessons became an eye-opener. What failed to occur in the classroom, gradually started to happen on the sports field: interaction between children from different backgrounds. In this process, I was more of a learner than a teacher. The kind of integration which eventually occurred, differed widely from what we as staff had anticipated or set out to achieve; nevertheless, it was true social interaction with which all the pupils appeared to be comfortable[2].

---

[2] What exactly is meant by "integration" in this context will become clearer in Chapter 4: Conclusions and recommendations.

This development confirmed what I had experienced in multi-cultural classrooms in the United States and in Germany, but had failed to formulate clearly: that sport could possibly succeed as a vehicle for social interaction where other means failed. Believing that this might be even more so in extra-mural sports projects than within the constraints of PE lessons, I began to devote more time and energy to such ventures. – Chapter 3.1 Scoring a first: *Experiences in a multi-cultural classroom in the early nineties* reflects the experiences of the first 18 month-period I spent in South Africa.

In August 1992, I had to resume my teaching obligations in Germany, but by now I wanted to pursue my South African impressions in a more systematic and sustained way. I shared my ideas with Professor Hermann Rieder of the *Institut für Sport und Sportwissenschaft* (Institute for Sport and Sport Science) at the University of Heidelberg, who encouraged me to pursue a thesis on *"Sport als möglicher Integrationsfaktor im neuen Südafrika"* ("Sport as a possible tool for social integration in the new South Africa") as a doctoral candidate. A scholarship from the DAAD (Deutscher Akademischer Austauschdienst) and study leave from my post in Heidelberg enabled me to return to South Africa in October 1993.

1.4 Dropping in on the "Drop-outs"

Meanwhile, most German Schools in South Africa and Namibia had instituted "integration programmes", partly in response to pressure from the German government, and partly in anticipation of changes in South African educational policy. Despite minor differences in these programmes, they had two things in common: they involved the active recruitment of promising candidates from the disadvantaged communities, and they all had a disturbingly high proportion of "drop-outs". Given the amount of time, energy and money spent on the "integration programmes", the German schools were naturally eager to discover the reasons for their limited success. Since this tied in perfectly with my field of study, I started off by visiting the German schools in South Africa (and one in Namibia). With their assistance, I traced Black and Coloured students who had "dropped out" of these schools and tried to find out why. Chapter 3.1 Failing at integration: Hearing the "drop-outs'" Stories reflects the results of this research.

The basic assumptions and aims underlying the "integration programmes" of German schools in Southern Africa, and their effects on non-German-speaking pupils, are briefly examined in Chapter 4 Conclusions and recommendations. Though perhaps not of immediate concern to the present readership, I believe that the experiences gathered at these schools nevertheless add a further dimension to current South African debates around integration, access to opportunities, cultural rights, nation-building, and mother tongue instruction versus the promotion of a common lingua franca.

1.5 Widening the Scope

After my return to Cape Town, I soon realised that the German schools were not alone in struggling with the problems of "integration". My scholarship allowed me to include South African government schools which had recently opened their doors to pupils from disadvantaged communities. This gave me some idea of which problems might be specific to the German schools, and which were of a more general nature. In order to understand the pupils recently admitted to "model C" schools, I extended my research to the township schools where they had come from.

Over a twelve-month period, I involved 1144 learners, teachers and trainers from different communities and different cultural backgrounds in my research. They included 496 students from the primary schools in Khayelitsha and Langa, 101 pupils from primary schools in the traditionally "Coloured" or "mixed" areas Mitchells Plain Athlone and Woodstock, and students at formerly White schools in Pinelands and central Cape Town.

In order to inform myself on the broader context of sport and education in South Africa, I spoke to a wide range of prominent role players in the fields of politics, education, sport and religion. My interview partners included the then Archbishop of Cape Town and Chairperson of the Truth and Reconciliation Commission, Desmond Tutu, the then Minister of Sport (and late Minister of Safety and Security) Steve Tshwete, Ngconde Balfour (then Head of Sports Administration at the University of the Western Cape, now Minister of Sport), Dr. Dr. Neville Alexander (Director of the Project for the Study of Alternative Education in South Africa, at the University of Cape Town), Muleki George (President of the National Sports Council), Rudolf Rode (Subject advisor for German in the Western Cape Department of Education), and many others.

I would like to thank each and every one of these interview partners, as well as all the pupils, teachers and trainers involved in the research, for the time, energy and insights they have contributed to this study. While acknowledging their contributions, I wish to make it clear that they are in no way to be blamed for any shortcomings in this study, for which I am solely responsible.

The current book is based on my doctoral thesis, which was written in academic German for academic purposes. The present adaptation for a wider readership obviously required significant changes, not only in perspective, but also in style. Some of the information and many explanations for the benefit of a German readership, as well as most footnotes and many tables and graphics have been omitted from the present version. Readers who wish to obtain the original research data are welcome to address their requests to me (via the publisher).

At this stage, a word on the purpose of the present publication may be called for. It is aimed at teachers, trainers, sports officials and organisers, social workers and church workers, and anybody who, in professional or voluntary community work, experiences difficulties in bringing together young South Africans from different cultural and social backgrounds. I hope that this book will help them to unlock the potential which sport undoubtedly has as a means of overcoming the divisions of the past.

Lastly, I wish to anticipate possible misgivings about academic studies in general, and studies on South Africa by non-South Africans in particular. There is a ready and understandable antagonism towards "experts" from "outside" who, on the basis of limited experience in South Africa or, worse, non-relevant experience in other parts of the world, believe they have patent solutions to South African problems. The initiatives described in this study were born, not from "knowing better", but rather from a sense of failure and confusion: having tried in vain to promote social integration between Black and White pupils, both inside and outside the classroom, I latched onto positive experiences during PE lessons and tried to build on them in other contexts.

This brings me to a second, more general objection against academic studies of this kind. Researchers, it is claimed, "exploit" the "objects" of their studies by using them to gain academic laurels, and then leave them to their own devices; the men, women and children behind the "case studies" seldom benefit. I do not believe that such an objection applies to this study. As an integral part of the research, several projects were launched which were of direct benefit to the participants and their communities, as can be clearly gathered from the relevant parts of this book (Chapter 3.6: Dancing across the barriers: The extra-mural dance project and Chapter 3.5 Sport beyond the PT class: The Pinelands project). In addition, an in-service training programme for PE teachers, a programme for street children, and a women's programme were established as a direct consequence of the research described here. Far from reducing them to lifeless "objects" of investigation, all of these programmes involved their participants as active subjects in an open-ended process of investigation and transformation. May this book contribute towards promoting such processes on a larger scale.

II HISTORICAL BACKGROUND AND EDUCATIONAL CONTEXT

CHAPTER 2

2.1 Apartheid, Struggle and Transformation in South African Sport and Education

2.1.1 Education

W hen South Africans think about the history of education in their country, certain catch phrases like "Bantu education" and "Soweto 1976" come readily to mind. Still, in order to establish the context of this study, a brief recapitulation of developments in this sector may be helpful.

Although separate educational institutions for Black and White South Africans existed since the early 20th century, racial segregation was not enforced by law. Up to 1953, the four provincial Departments of Education (of the then Union of South Africa) were responsible for providing primary and secondary education to all population groups, but education was not compulsory. In the first half of the century, many Blacks received no schooling at all, while a small number of African and Coloured children enjoyed a superior education at Mission schools throughout South Africa. Among these children there were many future leaders in politics, society and trade.

In 1953, the Nationalist government passed the infamous Bantu Education Act (Act 47 of 1953), which transferred control over education for Africans from the provinces to the Minister of Native Affairs, a post held at the time by Dr. H.F. Verwoerd, one of the main architects of apartheid. Dr. Verwoerd openly stated the purpose of the new law as providing for an education which would prepare Blacks for inferior and subordinate positions in society:

> By blindly producing pupils trained on a European model, the vain hope was created among Natives that they could occupy posts within the European community despite the country's policy of 'apartheid'.

> There is no place for him (i.e. the Black South African) in the European community above the level of certain forms of labour (...) For this reason it is of no avail for him to receive a training which has as its aim an absorption in the European community, where he cannot be absorbed (cf. Rose & Tunmer, 1975, p. 261 and 266; Sparks, 1990, p. 196 and Hopfer, 1999, p. 154 note 79).

Verwoerd here refers to White South Africa as "the European community"; this alone indicates how poorly the apartheid architects were adapted to Africa.

The overwhelming majority of mission schools was not prepared to bow to this aim of providing a restrictive, second-rate education for Blacks, and most of them were forced to close down. Of the mission schools which existed in 1953, only 3 % were still operational in 1977.

Meanwhile, the apartheid government was extending the principle of segregated education to other "population groups". The Coloured Persons Education Act no. 47 of 1963 put education for Coloureds under the supervision of the Department of Coloured Affairs, while the Department of Indian Affairs assumed control over education for "Asians" with the Indian Education Act no. 61 of 1965. The provincial Departments of Education retained responsibility for the administration of schools for Whites. Educational policy was determined by the Minister of National Education, assisted by the National Education Council.

Following the segregation of administrative structures, separate curricula were developed for the children of the four officially determined "population groups". Education was compulsory only for Whites, while only Black and Coloured children had to pay school fees (though many White schools also introduced school fees in order to maintain buildings and infrastructure).

In the sixties and seventies, Black education was gradually upgraded, especially in the so-called homelands. Not only did the apartheid government feel the need to train a political and administrative elite to run the "homelands"; there was also industry's increasing demand for skilled labour. However, the high growth rate among the Black population, coupled with continued disparities in the per capita spending on education for the various "population groups", offset the gains made by Black education and ensured the continued superiority of education for Whites[1].

The so-called Tricameral Constitution of 1983 ("Constitution of the Republic of South Africa Act", Act 10 of 1983) further entrenched apartheid in this sphere by declaring education an "own affair" of each of the four officially recognized "population groups". As such, it was placed under the control of separate government departments for the various groups. The Department of Education and Training now took charge of Black education, while Indian learners were catered for by the Department of Education and Culture, House of Delegates. The Department of Education and Culture, House of Representatives, assumed control of Coloured education, whereas the Department of Education and Culture, House of Assembly was charged with education for Whites. These "own affair" departments were put under the overall supervision of the

---

[1] In 1971, the pro capita spending on the education of a White child was 18 times higher than for a Black child; by 1985, the ratio had been reduced to 8:1. This disproportion was further reduced by 1986, but according to Schlemmer and Bot (1987), only 29% of the entire education budget for that year was spent on Black education, with White schools still receiving a massive 56% of the total.

Department of National Education. In addition, the four "independent homelands" (TBVC states) had their own autonomous education departments; so did the six "self-governing" homelands.

All in all, there were therefore 17 different departments of education under the auspices of the Department of National Education – a proliferation of administrative structures which existed until 1995. The differentiation at bureaucratic level reflected far-reaching differences in the provision of education for the various "population groups".

Within the apartheid framework, White schools had the function of ensuring the continued supremacy of Whites and of educating the future leadership. Comparatively speaking, these schools offered education of a high quality, not only in the formal class room situation, but also in terms of extra-curricular sport and cultural activities. These included the so-called "school cadet" system as preparation for military training for the boys.

The disastrous effects of the apartheid system can perhaps be most clearly seen in the educational disadvantagement of the Black majority. The traditional education of Black South Africans was rooted in the culture and values upheld by family, clan and tribe. Respect of authority, obedience and self-control were just as much part of this education as philosophy, religion and knowledge of the community's social structure; certain rituals, such as initiation, also played an important role (cf. Booteng, 1984).

The arrival of European settlers disrupted the social structure of Black communities, which in turn resulted in alienation from traditional culture, and from educational values in particular. The 1976 uprising not only indicated that Black youths were no longer prepared to submit to White authority; it also challenged traditional patterns of respect and obedience within Black communities themselves.

With the establishment of mission schools in the 19th century, formal European-style education for Blacks was introduced to selected areas within South Africa. The central aims of this education were to convert Blacks to Christianity and to acculturate them to European civilisation. Historians critical of this education point out that it had the effect of reinforcing the colonial myth of Black inferiority as opposed to White superiority (cf. Chanaiwa, 1980, p. 227f). Whereas the more liberal English-language mission schools strove to integrate and assimilate Black pupils to Christian, European culture, the Calvinist Dutch Reformed Church rejected the notion of equality between the races, and aimed to maintain racial segregation in virtually all spheres of life.

The mission schools catered only for a small minority of the Black population. Even before the concerted apartheid legislation of the fifties and sixties, career opportunities for Blacks with a high level of schooling were extremely limited, restricting the choice to minister of religion, teacher, nurse, or interpreter in a court of law or in some other government institution. In 1945, for instance, only 7.7% of the Black population received schooling, while industry provided for its own skilled labour needs through in-house, on-the-job training (cf. Christie & Collins, 1982).

In 1949, the newly-elected Nationalist government appointed a commission of enquiry into Black education, with specific reference to its contribution towards race relations (cf. Ticlly, 1993, p. 10). Chaired by the Chief Inspector of Native Education in Transvaal, Dr. Van Eiselen, the commission submitted its report in 1951. It criticised the alleged lack of clarity in the formulation of aims and objectives for Black education and deplored a perceived neglect of cultural aspects in the curricula.

In seemingly contradictory recommendations, the commission suggested that Black learners be made aware of their own culture with a view to preserving it; furthermore, that the Christian character of state-sponsored education for Blacks be maintained. In this, the commission reflected the aim of successive apartheid governments to restrict Africans to "their own" geographical, political and cultural space, while at the same time maintaining overall ideological and political control over the segregation process. Furthermore, the commission recommended the establishment of a National Department of Education to plan, coordinate and oversee education at a national level. As for the curricula, the commission recommended that Black learners should be proficient in their mother tongue and in one of the two official languages (English and Afrikaans); furthermore, the emphasis was on basic hygiene and health care and basic skills for agriculture and crafts.

The report of the Eiselen commission had a profound influence on Black education up to the late seventies. For the present study, two of its effects are particularly relevant. Firstly, the emphasis on the mother tongue and on traditional culture tied in with the general aim of apartheid, which was to perpetuate and enhance perceived or real cultural differences between the various "population groups". It is true that, under the new democratic dispensation, there is also a concerted attempt to protect linguistic diversity and to enhance the profile of the indigenous cultures[2]. But whereas the promotion of indigenous languages under apartheid often served the ulterior motive of restricting Blacks to a cultural, linguistic and political ghetto, the new democratic government strives to promote African culture within the

---

[2] For instance, the new Constitution recognises 11 official languages, nine of them indigenous; by contrast, the succession of apartheid Constitutions (the 1910 Union of South Africa Act, the Constitution of the Republic of South Africa of 1961, and the so-called tri-cameral Constitution of 1983) concurred in reserving official status for the two South African languages of European origin, i.e. English and Afrikaans. – By contrast, under the new democratic dispensation, the public profile of the indigenous cultural heritage is also enhanced by the performance of praise singers at occasions such as the inauguration of Presidents Mandela and Mbeki, the opening of Parliament, etc.

framework of a unitary state; furthermore, to counteract the potentially divisive effects of cultural pluralism, the government simultaneously promotes English as a national *lingua franca*.

Secondly, the Eiselen commission's emphasis on agriculture and crafts clearly indicates that it saw Black education as a means of providing subordinate labour for White farmers and White industry. This means that, in addition to the unfortunate effects of limited resources, there was a deliberate attempt to restrict the educational advancement of Black South Africans. The long-term effects of this policy continue to obstruct and retard progress in the new South Africa.

The Eiselen commission also made recommendations on education in what were to become the "homelands". In the view of the commission, schools in these areas had the function of training the future homeland leadership; education therefore had to be less restrictive than in the Black schools in so-called White areas. The higher educational standards of the homeland schools were also to serve as an incentive for Blacks to remain in – or even move to – the homelands.

The Bantu Education Act of 1953 remained in force until it was replaced by the Training and Education Act (Act 90 of 1979). This law, which came into effect in 1981, created a new "Department of Education and Training (DET)" to oversee Black education. While still committed to segregation in education, this law undoubtedly introduced certain improvements: it provided for the gradual introduction of compulsory education (at the request of local school committees), free education and text books, and the co-ordination of curricula and examinations with those of other Education Departments.

In 1980, the government appointed a commission of the Human Sciences Research Council (HSRC) under the chairmanship of Professor De Lange to investigate the entire educational system. Its brief was to make recommendations on improving the organisation and infrastructure of education, with due reference to the composition of the population, prevailing economic conditions and the resources available. Not surprisingly, the so-called 'De Lange Report' noted substantial disparities between the educational systems for the various population groups. While accepting many of the commission's recommendations, the government rejected its call for a single, unified Department of Education charged with developing a uniform schools system with equal opportunities for all. If implemented, this reform would have spelt the end of apartheid in education.

In 1983, a new Constitution established the so-called Tricameral System, which attempted to co-opt Coloureds and Indians as junior partners in government while continuing to exclude the Black majority. Under this system, the Coloured and Indian electorate were to elect representatives to separate and smaller chambers of parliament, while the all-White House of Assembly continued to wield real political power. In keeping with this principle, the 1983 Constitution established three separate Departments of Education for Whites (Department of Education and Culture, House of Assembly), Coloureds (Department of Education and Culture, House of Representatives) and Indians (Department of Education and Culture, House of Delegates); Black education continued to be the domain of the Department of Education and Training.

Based on the White Paper of 1983, the government promulgated the "National Policy for General Affairs Act" (Act 76 of 1984), which defined the "education of each population group" as an "own affair which falls within the cultural and value framework of each group" (South African Communication Service, 1994, p. 281). The competencies of the Minister of National Education were restricted to formulating criteria for curricula, examination standards and qualifications, as well as the qualifications and salaries of teachers (cf. Sanep Report, 1985, Act 76, 1984, sec. 2 (1)). Standards for the matriculation examination, which applied to all schools, were to be laid down by the Joint Matriculation Board, a function which has since passed to the South African Certification Board.

Thus, towards the end of the apartheid era, a general trend in educational policy emerged: despite the gradual convergence of criteria and standards laid down for pupils from all population groups, the administrative structures and, most importantly, the schools themselves remained segregated along "racial" lines. The system pointedly prevented any interaction between young people of different "population groups" in formal education.

Under the new democratic government, serious efforts are being made to improve the educational situation of the Black majority. But a number of factors continue to hamper progress in this direction. Not only are most township schools poorly equipped and overcrowded; the pupil:teacher ratio is also much higher than in the traditionally White schools. Both factors are, of course, closely related to the shortage of funds available for education, given the equally enormous backlogs in areas such as housing and health. In addition, and as part of the apartheid legacy,   Black teachers are often far less qualified than their White counterparts; to compound this disadvantage, the medium of instruction from level 6 upwards is English, which for many Black teachers is their third or fourth language[3]. The combined effect of these problems is often a lack of motivation on the part of the educators, to the extent that the new Minister of Education recently saw fit to criticise teachers in public for their lack of commitment.

---

[3]   The medium of instruction is indeed a complicated matter: while prolongued mother-tongue instruction could separate Black pupils from the mainstream of South African political and economic life, which is conducted in English, instruction by means of a language unfamiliar to teachers and pupils alike may also hamper eductional progress. The current solution of mother-tongue instruction up to grade 5, and English as medium of instruction from grade 6 onwards, is probably the best possible compromise solution to a complex problem.

Given these overwhelming obstacles, a generally low pass rate in township schools is hardly surprising. But academic failure is not the only reason why many Black pupils fail to complete their schooling. The inability to pay school fees, the need to contribute to the family income, teenage pregnancies and the lax enforcement of compulsory education – all of these are contributing factors. Ironically, certain progressive changes away from apartheid and towards equality may – at least initially – aggravate conditions at township schools. For instance, the introduction of uniform examination standards may at first have led to a further deterioration of the pass rate in township schools. Secondly, the scrapping of apartheid has also meant that Black pupils can now legally enrol at formerly White schools. Since it is usually the academically better qualified Black students who benefit from this opportunity, the learning environment for pupils at township schools becomes even less stimulating and enriching.

Like other areas of education, teacher training was also affected by the iniquities of apartheid. Black teachers were paid less than their White counterparts.

In 1986, the Department of Education and Training (DET) reported that 17% of all Black teachers had no qualification at all, while 55% were not educated beyond grade 10; 56% had no matriculation certificate. In 1988, the percentage of Black teachers with a matriculation certificate had risen to 64%, but this still compared poorly with the figure of 75% for Coloured teachers, not to mention the 100% matriculation rate for both Indian and White teachers (cf. Statistisches Bundesamt, 1991, p. 51f).

The educational system devised for Coloureds and Asians under apartheid reflected the overall position which the system allotted to these "populations groups" – a position inferior to that of Whites, but superior to that of the African majority. Like their African counterparts, most educated Coloureds in the 19th century owed their schooling to missionaries. After the Union of South Africa was founded in 1910, a separate Department of Education for Coloureds was created in the Cape Province, where the majority of this "population group" was concentrated. In accordance with the apartheid policy, and echoing the administrative structures put in place for "African education", the responsibility for "Coloured education" was transferred to the Department of Coloured Affairs. This shift was effected through the Coloured Persons Education Act (Act 47 of 1963). By contrast to the Bantu Education Act of 1953, the 1963 Act did not specify any particular educational aims or objectives reserved for this "population group".

To a certain extent, compulsory education for Coloureds has been in place since the forties, and has been gradually expanded since then; however, only in 1980 was legislation passed which made education compulsory for all Coloured children between the ages of 6 and 16 (cf. Statistisches Bundesamt, 1995, p. 57). School fees were scrapped, and books were provided free of charge, as in White schools (Malherbe, 1977, p. 252f). Nor do the similarities end there: the types of schools provided, and the division of pupils' educational careers into different phases (e.g. primary, secondary, senior secondary etc.), as well as the provisions for the co-ordination of curricula and examination standards, were exactly the same as for White schools. The medium of instruction was either English or Afrikaans, depending on the linguistic preferences of the school community. As in the case of White schools, great importance was attached to so-called "extra-mural activities", although both the funds made available for this purpose and the range of choice compared poorly with those of most White schools. Though in theory, curricula provided for differentiation, limitations on resources and on the number of subjects offered often meant that this aim could not be achieved in practice.

In 1968, the Coloured Representative Act (Act 52 of 1968) conferred limited decision-making powers on the Coloured Representative Council, i.a. regarding "Coloured education"[4]. This included not only schools, but also institutions of tertiary education reserved for the "Coloured population", such as the University of the Western Cape (founded in 1960), the Peninsula Technicon, and a number of teacher training colleges. Under certain circumstances, Coloured students had the option of studying at one of the English-language "open" universities, particularly in the case of courses not offered at "Coloured tertiary institutions".

In 1980, the Department of Coloured Affairs and the Department of Indian Affairs were reduced in status to mere Directorates within the Department of Internal Affairs, into which the formerly separate structures were now incorporated. As indicated above, this administrative structure was once again altered under the so-called "Tri-Cameral" Constitution of 1983, when "Coloured and Indian education" became the responsibility of the Ministers of Education attached to the respective legislative bodies, viz. the "House of Representatives" (for Coloureds) and the "House of Delegates" (for Indians).

The problems experienced in the "Coloured educational system" closely resembled those in schools for Africans, e.g. the high number of drop-outs, which Niven (Niven, 1982) attributes to low levels of income and to a lack of opportunities for further training. In addition to this, the absence of the opportunity for Coloureds to participate on an equal footing with Whites in the economic, social and political life of apartheid South Africa occasioned a complex negative response, in which apathy tended to alternate with outbursts

---

[4] The Coloured Representative Council (CRC) was elected by Coloured voters and had limited legislative powers. Through the Department of Coloured Affairs, the all-White House of Assembly (and ultimately the National Party government) exerted control over the CRC, not least through ultimate control over its budget. This explains the "boycott politics" which more progressive organisations, supported by growing numbers of Coloured voters, adopted vis-à-vis CRC elections.

of resistance. Lastly, schools in residential areas traditionally reserved for Coloureds have been particularly hard hit by the pervasive influence of gangsterism, a phenomenon often attributed to the disruption of communities and a breakdown of social relations as a result of the forced removal of whole communities under the Group Areas Act. In several instances, pupils have been killed in shoot-outs between rival gangs on or near school premises.

To complete this brief overview, a few words on the education reserved for South Africans of Indian extraction. Here, too, the earliest providers of education were mostly members of Christian missionary societies. However, members of the Indian community soon started to contribute to the educational process. Because of the high regard in which the community held education, the introduction of compulsory schooling for Indian children in 1973 was, for all intents and purposes, a mere formality, since school attendance had already reached 99% the previous year (Malherbe ,1977, p. 293f).

Up to 1965, responsibility for "Indian education" rested with the administration of the province Natal, where the "Indian population group" was concentrated. In line with developments in "Coloured education", the Indian Education Act (Act 61 of 1965) then put the Department of Indian Affairs in charge of "Indian education". As in the case of "Coloured education", no group-specific educational aims or objectives were formulated for Indians, except for the stipulation that the pupils' awareness of Indian culture and languages was to be raised through "extra-mural activities". English was to be the medium of instruction. Curricula, examination standards etc. were modeled on those for White pupils.

As indicated above, the Department for Indian Affairs, like that for Coloured Affairs, was reduced to a Directorate and integrated into the Department of Internal Affairs in 1980. With the introduction of the "Tri-Cameral" Constitution in 1983, the responsibility for "Indian education" (primary, secondary and tertiary) was conferred on the Minister of Education and Culture attached to the relevant chamber of parliament, viz. the "House of Delegates".

Compared to the other "population groups" defined as "Non-White" under apartheid, the educational, economic, social and political conditions of South Africans of Indian extraction was more advanced, which occasionally sparked conflict between Indians and Africans. Nevertheless, having been denied equality with Whites and full citizen rights under apartheid, many South African Indians committed themselves to the struggle against apartheid (cf. Niven, 1982 and Werschdener, 1990, p. 71).

This brief overview demonstrates the administrative and structural fragmentation, as well as the qualitative differences in the education of the various "population groups" in apartheid South Africa. The system was designed to emphasise and strengthen the (assumed or real) cultural differences between these "population groups", to avoid - as far as possible - all opportunity for social contact between the school-going youth of these "groups", and to reinforce and perpetuate the social stratification and political divisions within South African society. For a post-apartheid South Africa striving for nation-building and equality, the legacy of the apartheid educational system is a heavy burden. Sport may be one of several means needed to overcome this handicap.

Education in the Post-apartheid Era

For the first time, South Africa now – since 1996 – has a constitution which guarantees all its citizens equal rights and access to education. One aim of the *Reconstruction and Development Programme (RDP)* is that

> *education and training should form part of a national human resource strategy based on the principles of non-racism, non-sexism, equity and redress, and be committed to the goal of life-long learning.*
> *(South African Communication Service, 1995, p. 341)*

Other aims in the educational field include free (i.e. state-sponsored) compulsory schooling up to grade 10 for all South Africans, and improvements in formerly neglected areas, such as pre-schooling, ongoing teacher-training, adult education, and equal educational and training opportunities for girls and women.

The Government's White Paper on Education, which was published in March 1996, distinguishes between two categories of schools: *public schools,* which include all community, farm, church, Model C, state and state-aided schools; about 99% of all schools fall into this category. Private schools, on the other hand, belong to the second category, viz. *independent schools.* Suggestions for curricular changes include the proposal that all pupils should be taught through the medium of at least two of the eleven official languages in grades 4 to 6. The history curriculum is be completely overhauled, and is to do justice to the country's aboriginal inhabitants, such as the Khoi and the San.

Despite the changes which have already been effected, or which are already in the pipeline, education remains an area of political contention, and many of the apartheid inequalities still persist. Formerly African schools continue to be plagued by stark inequalities, both in the provision of equipment and in staffing. Even those pupils at African schools who successfully take the matriculation examination, often subsequently discover that this does not necessarily provide them with access to tertiary institutions, or with the necessary skills for higher education. A further cause of discontent are the fees for tertiary education, which African students are often unable to pay. Frustration over attempts to expel students for non-payment of fees regularly leads to marches and boycotts reminiscent of the "struggle years".

In theory, tertiary institutions formerly reserved for Whites are today open to African students; in practice, many African students still find that they are excluded on account of inferior schooling. This is reflected in the relatively low enrolment figures for African students at tertiary institutions in the Western Cape:

Table 1: Number of registered students by population group as on 10 March 1993 (Department of Education, p. 17).

Institution	Whites	Asians	Coloureds	Blacks	Total
University of Cape Town	9 232	676	1841	2 438	14 187
University of Stellenbosch	13 144	26	960	115	14 245
University of the Western Cape	180	634	7 002	4 693	12 509

Furthermore, there have been a number of race-related disturbances at educational institutions. In January 1996, a primary school in Potgietersrus (Northern Province) hit the headlines when White parents resisted the admission of African pupils. A few months later, several universities were plagued by interracial incidents (cf. Sunday Independent of 19 May, 1996). From 23 July 1997, the Cape Times published a series of articles dealing with difficulties experienced by pupils and teachers at multicultural schools (Cape Times of 23 and 30 July and 6 August, 1997).

These problems are exacerbated by retrenchments and cut-backs in the educational sector. In the Western Cape alone, 6 000 teaching posts were scrapped between August and September 1996, at a time when schools in predominantly African residential areas desperately need qualified teachers. The end of the educational crisis is not yet in sight. Education will be plagued by the apartheid legacy for a long time to come. Until recently all educational institutions were strictly segregated along racial lines, with significant differences between the schools reserved for each of the different "population groups" in terms of material equipment, subjects offered, teacher-pupil ratios, and teachers' qualifications.

Naturally, these differences ultimately led to concomitant differences in the average educational level attained by these groups, the gap being particularly noticeable between Africans and Whites. Discontent with these conditions still erupts occasionally.

Despite the last few years' attempts to put African and Coloured education on a par with White education in terms of curricula, examination requirements, etc., it is obvious that, the above-mentioned problems indicate that neither equality of educational opportunities nor any true integration has so far been achieved. Wide-ranging and sustained measures will be needed to meet these goals, and to overcome the after-effects of apartheid.

2.1.2 Sport

Towards the end of the 19th century, British settlers brought their sport culture to South Africa, where it took root within the framework of existing social relations. In general terms, this meant that sport practised by the White population group could flourish and grow unhindered, gradually developing its own structures, institutions and social traditions. This is not to say that "non-White" South Africans were completely excluded from sport as we know it today. As Archer & Bouillon (1982) point out, Black South Africans started to practise the modern sport disciplines shortly after these had been introduced to South Africa. By the turn of the century, regional and national associations for "Black" soccer, rugby and cricket already existed. But whereas the "White" sport structures generally experienced the kind of continuity which is conducive to development, progress and growth, the history of "Coloured" and "African" sport was an unhappy one of oppression, interference and forced relocations, particularly in the 20th century. In keeping with the overall distribution of resources between the various officially defined "population groups", White schools, clubs and municipalities had generous and easy access to sports grounds and other facilities, while little or no provision was made for Blacks (cf. Watson as quoted in Archer & Bouillon, 1982, p. 39). Watson cites the example of the African township Langa in Cape Town, where 36 soccer clubs had to share a single stadium without seating or flood lights. The situation in Coloured and Indian townships was not quite as desperate, not least because in contrast to "Africans", "Coloureds" and "Indians" (and clubs registered in their name) were legally entitled to own land in so-called "White" South Africa, i.e. all land outside the "homelands", the "self-governing territories", and other areas reserved for Africans. Nevertheless, apartheid legislation such as the "Land Act" and the "Group Areas Act" also affected Coloureds, Indians and Whites, since their application restricted sportsmen and –women to competing within their own "population groups", and thus prevented the emergence of non-racial sport, and of contacts across the enforced "colour line".

Although racial segregation was only applied to sport by way of legislation in 1948, most sport was already segregated as early as the thirties. Due to the increasingly stringent nature of Afrikaner nationalism, a similar separation gradually occurred between the two White language groups, Afrikaans and English speakers:

> For the most part, sport remained segregated, not only between the races, but between the white communities – as the effort of Hofmeyr to take cricket to the Afrikaaners demonstrates. Afrikaaner nationalism was naturally antagonistic to all such aspirations. At the end of the 1930s and during the 1940s, the nationalists were forming their exclusive Afrikaans-speaking cultural organizations all over the country (Archer & Bouillon, 1982, p. 31).

What few sporting contacts were allowed to exist between Black and White South Africans mainly occurred in the so-called "non-contact sports", such as cricket. On the other hand, sporting contacts between the three "non-White" population groups increased, and it was not unusual for African or Indian players to be included in predominantly Coloured teams, and vice versa. Before 1948, so-called "Inter Race Boards" existed which regularly organised cricket and soccer matches or tournaments between Indian, Coloured and African teams.

After the National Party came to power in 1948, however, even this limited measure of integration in sport came to an end. The newly-appointed Minister of Internal Affairs, Eben Dönges, soon promulgated a whole body of legislation in terms of which sports matches and contests between members of different "population groups" were declared illegal. Among these laws were the "Urban Land Act", which reserved sports facilities for the exclusive use of one "population group" only; the "Separate Amenities Act" (1953), which enforced racial segregation in public places such as sports stadiums; and the "Native Laws Amendment Act" (1957), which prescribed racial segregation for organisations such as sport clubs and associations, schools and churches. In addition, the "Group Areas Act", coupled with the "Pass Laws" (amended 11 times between 1952 and 1978) had the effect of making it practically impossible for "Blacks" to attend sports meetings (or, for that matter, any other social events) held in areas reserved for Whites.

Furthermore, the "Liquor Amendment Act" (1963) made it illegal for "Indians," "Coloureds" and "Whites" to consume alcohol in the presence of "Africans", which severely restricted the opportunities for members of the various "population groups" to meet and mix socially. All these laws had a detrimental effect on the development of sport in South Africa.

From the 1950s onwards, African spectators were either restricted to segregated sections of stadiums, or totally excluded from attending sport events. Hains described how, in 1966, this regulation affected the players and fans of the Pretoria soccer club to which he belonged:

> The carnival atmosphere engendered by their enthusiastic support disappeared. But crowds of Africans still gathered outside the grounds, listening to the matches. Others tried to watch from the trees adjoining the ground: this so angered local white residents that in September 1966 police dogs were used to drive them from their vantage points (Hains, 1971, p. 40).

The 1965 proclamation prohibited "Africans" from attending sport and other social events attended by members of other "population groups". The same proclamation empowered sport organisers to prohibit matches on privately owned grounds if the players belonged to different "population groups". If clubs or other institutions who owned stadiums wished to admit spectators from different "population groups", they were compelled by law to build separate entrances and toilet facilities. Schools and their sports grounds were similarly affected by legislation: sports meetings and matches between participants from different "population groups" were no longer possible:

When the National Party took power in 1948 (...) the rights and opportunities of black people were reduced in all domains, and therefore in sport as well (...) from the beginning apartheid laid hands not just upon the playing of matches but on the social and economic environment which conditions and makes the playing of sport possible and enjoyable (Archer & Bouillon, 1982, p. 43).

The aim of the apartheid government was clearly to suppress all social contact between members of different "population groups". Although initially no laws specifically prohibited non-racial sport, it fell victim to a whole barrage of laws dealing with other aspects of social life: when residential areas, education, public transport and similar services, even hospitals and toilets had been segregated, non-racial sports meetings simply became impractical. Without explicit prior permission, Africans were not allowed to use the same buses as Whites to travel to sports grounds; once they got there, they needed further explicit permission to use toilets and change rooms. Conversely, Whites, Coloureds and Indians were required to apply for permission to enter "African residential areas" (or "townships"). Finally, members of all "population groups" needed explicit permission to compete, on the sports field, against members of any of the other "population groups", or to watch sports matches attended by spectators belonging to any of the other "population groups" (cf. Ramsamy, 1982, pp. 19 – 23; Archer & Bouillon, 1982, p. 45; Archer, 1987, p. 229ff).

In this way, non-racial sport fell victim to general laws regulating social relations between different racially-defined "population groups". At national and even at regional level, sportswomen and -men in South Africa could thus only compete against fellow-members of their own "population group". For each sports discipline or game, there were thus up to four associations or controlling bodies at national level. Apart from the enormous waste of financial and administrative resources and capacities, the participants themselves bore the brunt of this policy. Because they were not allowed to compete against the best available opposition, South African sportswomen and -men could not develop their own full potential, and were restricted to an artificially and unnecessarily low level of competence. In an attempt to prove the supposed superiority of White sportsmen and -women, the National Party government reserved the best facilities for the exclusive use by members of this "population group". Like virtually all other spheres of life, sport in apartheid South Africa was subjected to the policy of separate development.

Resistance Against Apartheid in Sport

In 1956, the Minister of Internal Affairs, Eben Dönges, issued a proclamation which was clearly intended to restrict the growing influence of "African sport bodies and organizations", and to thwart their attempts to be officially recognised, both locally and internationally (cf. p. 27 of this chapter for a summary of the contents of this proclamation). Up to that stage, only "White sport associations" had attained international status and recognition. African sportswomen and –men therefore had to overcome enormous legal, political and organisational obstacles if they wanted to be recognized in their own right, and to overcome the effects of apartheid in sport. Not surprisingly, the 1950s witnessed a growing number of protest actions by African sport enthusiasts.

The first victory against the sport policy of the apartheid government was achieved in 1950, when the International Tennis Association first refused membership to the all-White South African Tennis Union, and then accepted the South African Tennis Board as a member, because this latter association refused to apply apartheid policies. However, it was not easy for African or Black sport bodies to establish relationships with international organisations, many of which had contacts with the White South African sport bodies, often dating back to colonial times. In some cases, South Africa had been one of the founding members of the international controlling body, and could therefore not be expelled constitutionally. In some cases, Black South African sport organisations pointed out to the world body that the racial exclusivity of White sport organisations violated the principle of equality as enshrined in the Olympic Charter. However, having made this point, these organisations were then faced with the difficulty that they themselves could not claim to represent the whole South African sporting community, since they themselves were forced to function, under apartheid legislation, on the basis of racial exclusivity. In this sense, the apartheid laws often succeeded in preventing non-racial sport, since very few Whites dared to challenge these laws by joining what the government called "non-White" sport organisations.

In the course of the 1950s, "Black" sport bodies in South Africa gradually gave up their attempts to supplant their "all-White" counterparts as members of international associations and controlling bodies: effectively, the situation created by apartheid legislation restricted them to agitating for the exclusion (or expulsion) of the "Whites only" bodies from the international sporting community.

On the other hand, the government and the "all-White" sport bodies countered these attempts by claiming that South African sport was free of racial discrimination. They did this by pointing to the fact that no legislation had been passed which explicitly prohibited matches or competitions between teams representing different "population groups". In addition, the "White" sport bodies took great care to ensure that their constitutions avoided any reference to racial exclusivity. However, this "cosmetic" measure had no effect on the racial composition of their membership, nor did it prevent the disastrous consequences of apartheid practices in sport.

In 1956, a number of "Black" sport organisations applied for membership of the respective international bodies (soccer, cricket, weight-lifting and rugby). In response, the Minister of Internal Affairs, Eben Dönges, promulgated the following principles, which remained in force and guided official policy until 1971 and beyond:

1) Whites and Non-Whites must organize their sport separately.

2) No mixed sport would be allowed within the borders of South Africa.

3) No mixed teams would compete abroad.

4) International teams competing in South Africa against White South African teams must be all-White according to South African custom.

5) Non-White sportsmen and -women from abroad could compete against Non-White South Africans in South Africa.

6) Non-White organisations seeking international recognition must do so through the already recognised White organisations in their code of sport.

7) The Government would refuse travel visas to "subversive" Non-White sportsmen who sought to discredit South Africa's image abroad or to contest the Government's racial policies (cf. Archer & Bouillon, 1982, p. 46).

With the knowledge of hind-sight, it can today be stated that the apartheid government's interventions in sport had the unintended effect of strengthening the non-racial sport movement in South Africa. For instance, in 1959, the Minister of Internal Affairs withdrew the passports of the South African table tennis team, thus preventing the players from participating in the World Championships in Germany. Likewise, the Minister refused to issue travel documents to representatives of the South African Football Association and the non-racial Boxing Association.

The result was that the affected players and organisations joined forces in their opposition to apartheid, and founded an "independent Black sport movement". Up to that stage, there had only been one "all-White" umbrella body in sport, i.e. the South African Olympic and Commonwealth Games Association (SAOCGA), which changed its name to the South African Olympic and National Games Association (SAOCGA) when the country left the Commonwealth on becoming a republic in 1961.

Towards the late 1950s, the opposition against apartheid in sport had gathered enough momentum for the Black sport associations to found an umbrella body of their own. The first body of this nature, the Coordinating Committee for International Recognition in Sport (1956), only enjoyed a brief existence. But only two years later, in 1958, the South African Sports Association (SASA) was founded, with the support of eight associations (athletics, cycling, cricket, soccer, weight-lifting, tennis, softball, netball and baseball) with a combined membership of 70 000.

In his opening address, Alan Paton, chairperson of the Liberal Party, described SASA's aims as follows:

"To co-ordinate the non-white sport, to advance the cause of sport and the standard of sport among non-white sportsmen, to see that they and their organisations secure proper recognition (in South Africa) and abroad, and to do this on a non-racial basis" (quoted from De Broglio, 1970, p. 3).

SASA gave new impetus to sport organisations at national level to join their forces, and it demonstrated that the majority of Black sportswomen and –men were opposed to apartheid. SASA supported its member organisations' struggle against apartheid and advanced the interests of "Black" sport in a sportsmanlike way, but it was not non-racial. For instance, SASA did not demand the integration of their member organisations with their "all-White" counterparts to form a unified, non-racial body for each code or discipline. Instead, it merely demanded its own recognition, and that of its member organisations, and it insisted on the right of Black sportswomen and –men to represent South Africa as members of a national team (Springboks), and to do so on the same basis and conditions as Whites. In other words, SASA did not campaign for non-racialism, but merely for the right of Black sportsmen and –women to participate in international meetings and competitions, within the framework of existing separate sport institutions and facilities.

From 1958 onwards, SASA concentrated on building structures for the effective administration of "Black" sport, and on building its lobby in the IOC and other international bodies. Internationally, SASA established links with foreign and international sport bodies; locally, i.e. in South Africa itself, it organised protest meetings against discrimination in sport. Internationally, SASA was able to chalk up a number of successes. In 1961, FIFA suspended the "White" Football Association of South Africa (FASA). In 1962, the IOC, acting on SASA's request, demanded that the South African Olympic and National Games Association (SAONGA) denounce its racist sports policy before the IOC's next meeting in October 1963, or face expulsion. This campaign not only resulted in South Africa's gradual isolation from world sport, but also, in 1970, in its expulsion from the Olympic movement.

Locally, SASA suffered a number of setbacks at the hands of the authorities. In 1961, SASA chairman Dennis Brutus was served with a banning order in reaction to SASA's launching of the SONREIS (Support Only Non-Racial Events in South Africa) campaign.

In the wake of the Sharpeville massacre, the early 1960s saw a more ruthless form of repression being challenged by ever-increasing levels of resistance. As a result of SASA's actions, the opposition against sport in apartheid grew steadily. After many Black leaders, including Nelson Mandela, had received heavy sentences in the Rivonia Trials, SASA founded the South African Non-Racial Olympic Committee (SANROC) in 1963. This organisation demanded that the selection criteria for international teams be "completely non-racial", and that team members be chosen "purely on merit" (Draper, 1963, p. 104). SANROC headed the campaign which eventually, in 1970, led to the IOC's expulsion of the all-White South African Olympic and National Games Association (SAONGA). However, success was a long way off and came at a high price. By 1965, so many leading SANROC and SASA members had been either detained or banned that SASA had to suspend its activities, and SANROC was forced into exile. SANROC president Dennis Brutus, who had already been banned in 1961, was arrested in 1963 and imprisoned on Robben Island. After his release from prison, he was served with another banning order.

When Brutus was arrested, John Harris, a "White" teacher from Johannesburg, succeeded him as SANROC president. Following a bomb blast at Johannesburg station, Harris was arrested, and in July 1964 he was found guilty of sabotage. The next year, he was sentenced to death and executed.

Despite the detention or banning of many of their prominent members, SASA and SANROC achieved some success in their efforts to co-ordinate the campaign to isolate apartheid South Africa from international sport. The campaign enjoyed the diplomatic support of various African states – and the moral support of a growing number of people and institutions worldwide.

The reaction of the South African government was an attempt to undermine the non-racial movement by separating Indian and Coloured sportsmen and –women from their African colleagues. Despite this, the "White" associations for netball, cross-country running, pentathlon, gymnastics, judo and weight-lifting were expelled from their international umbrella organisations in 1969; tennis followed in 1970.

Rugby remained the only major sport in which South Africa was still represented at international level, and even here, it ran into serious difficulties. During the Springbok rugby tour of 1969/1970, each match was disrupted by thousands of demonstrators, whose actions reverberated on TV screens and in newspaper headlines around the world. Finally, in 1970, South Africa became the first country in history to be expelled from the international Olympic movement. South Africa's "White" sport establishment now realised that it had its back against the wall. Desperate to find a way out, "White" sport associations initiated negotiations with their "Black" counterparts, anxious to find a compromise that would satisfy apartheid opponents, both at home and abroad, and which the South African government would allow to function unhindered.

After lengthy discussions behind closed doors, the South African government finally revealed its new "multi-national" sports policy in 1976. The then Minister of Sport, Dr. Piet Koornhof, described the principles guiding this policy as follows:

1. "Multi-cultural" (i.e. racially mixed) teams from abroad would be allowed to visit South Africa, where they would compete against racially segregated "White" and "Non-White" teams.

2. "Black" South African sportsmen and –women belonging to "White" sport bodies would be allowed to compete as individuals in international sport meetings outside the country. However, within South Africa itself, all competitions would be racially segregated.

3. At provincial and club level, no contact between "White" and "Non-White" sportsmen and –women would be tolerated (cf. Archer & Bouillon, 1982, p. 330).

The wording of this statement was deliberately misleading, in the sense that the term "multi-national" (or "multi-cultural") did not imply that players of different "population groups" would be allowed to train or practise together, or to belong to the same team; the intention was merely to allow "homogenous" teams, each representing one "population group", to compete against one another. This step must be regarded as a concession to the pressure of anti-apartheid groups, both at home and abroad, which made it inopportune for the South African government to ban the unofficial non-racial sport organisations, although these openly opposed racial segregation in sport. By contrast to the repression meted out to political organisations by the apartheid state, "Black" and "non-racial" sport bodies were allowed to organise and to join forces in their campaign for "non-racial" sport.

The official "White" sport organisations recognised (and subsidized) by the South African government were those which accepted – or even supported – the segregationist principles of apartheid. The "non-racial" sport bodies therefore had little difficulty in proving that these "White" organisations defied the non-discriminatory, egalitarian principles of sport's international controlling bodies, and to demand their expulsion from these bodies.

South Africa's expulsion from international sport presented the country's government with an intricate problem, since sport played, and continues to play, an important role in South African public and social life. On the one hand, many "White" voters blamed the government for the loss of international sport links, which they experienced as a loss not only of entertainment and excitement, but also of respect and prestige. On the other hand, any real and meaningful integration on the sport field would have had wider social implications, and there can be little doubt that the majority of voters would have rejected these effects outright. Organised sport in South Africa was usually practised in racially segregated clubs, which tended to play an important role in their members' spare time and social lives. To insist on any significant changes to the segregationist practices of these clubs would have had far-reaching social consequences. This was the main reason why so many "White" South Africans were opposed to "non-racial" sport. As for school sport, the government unequivocally stood by its segregationist views.

In the wake of the Soweto uprisings, however, Minister of Sport Piet Koornhof felt compelled to extend the principles of "multi-nationalism" or "multi-culturalism" downwards to include provincial and club level. His successors F W de Klerk (1978-1979) and Janson (1979-1980) upheld this change.

SACOS

The organisation which was perhaps the most consistent and vociferous in its rejection of this "multi-national" sport policy, was the South African Council of Sport, SACOS. This organisation was founded in Durban in September 1970 by representatives from eight sport associations, and it saw the light of day as the South African Non-Racial Sport Organisation". About two and a half years later, on 13 March 1974, it adopted the name which was to become almost synonymous with the struggle against apartheid in sport, i.e. SACOS. Whereas all "Coloured" sport organisations opposed to apartheid joined SACOS, the "African" sport organisations failed to form an umbrella body of their own, and some of them chose to become SACOS members.

SACOS' Aims

SACOS recognised the principles of the Olympic Charter, the IOC, and the international umbrella bodies for the various sport codes and disciplines. However, SACOS did not apply to be officially recognised by the IOC, pointing out that it was impossible to practise "normal" sport under apartheid laws. "No normal sport in an abnormal society" was a central SACOS principle. According to SACOS, no sport organisation in South Africa could claim to fulfil the most important prerequisites for any legitimate organisation, i.e. "representivity and non-racialism".

The number of sport bodies and organisations affiliated to SACOS grew steadily: from eight in 1973 to 13 in 1975, and even 26 in 1980. All SACOS' member organisations had to subscribe to its non-racial principles, and SACOS reserved the right to expel any organisation found to violate these principles.

Initially, SACOS' role was to represent the interests of non-racial sport, to unite the non-racial sport movement, and to act as a co-ordinating forum for its member organisations. By contrast to those sport bodies which were officially recognised, neither SACOS nor any of its member organisations received any subsidies from the South African government.

Apart from a growing number of sport organisations, two other important bodies belonged to SACOS: the South African Primary School Sport Association (SAPSSA) and the South African Secondary School Sport Association (SASSA). Between them, these two bodies represented about 20 000 young sport enthusiasts throughout the country, and each of them made valuable contributions to the non-racial movement. Unfortunately, very few "African" schools belonged to either of these two associations. Because of their political sensitivity, and especially after the Soweto uprising of 1976, "African" schools were closely monitored by the apartheid government, and they were deliberately isolated from their "Indian" and "Coloured" counterparts.

In 1983, the Ministry of Sport was dissolved, and sport became the responsibility of the Minister of National Education. If anything, this administrative arrangement tended to align, and reinforce, sport segregation by the segregation entrenched in education. Despite this, no umbrella organisation for sport in "African" schools was established which could have played a role comparable to that of SAPSSA and SASSA in respect of "Coloured" education. Teachers at "African" schools knew from experience that any form of mobilisation would inevitably lead to a crackdown by apartheid security forces. – Racial segregation in school sport was such an established tradition that most "White" schools refused to compete against teams from those private schools which admitted small numbers of "Non-White" pupils (Davies, 1989, p. 354).

In 1982, the Transvaal Education Department (TED) introduced a new sport policy, which resulted in splitting the "White" school league into two components: one league for exclusively "White" schools, and one for those private schools which admitted "Black" pupils, plus those "White" schools which had no objections against competing against these "mixed" private schools. According to Davies, the Cape Province and Natal applied a similar two-tier school league system, though they did so unofficially. Meanwhile, the government rejected a suggestion by the Human Sciences Research Council (HSRC) that the under-utilised sport facilities of poorly attended "White" schools be made available to pupils of all "population groups".

A further HSRC suggestion, viz. that the departments of education serving the different "population groups" be combined to form a single, unitary department, was also rejected. The government's motivation for rejecting both proposals was that these amounted to transgressions of existing legislation, and that they would entail an "unacceptable infringement of the "Group Areas Act" (op. cit., 46; cf. also White Paper, 1983, p. 5f and Davies, 1989, p. 356). The HSRC report on sport indicates just how unequal the distribution of sport facilities under apartheid really was.

It found that "White" schools possessed 72.4% of all school sport facilities, including 79.9% of facilities for athletics, 88,6% for cricket, and 87.7% of all rugby grounds (cf. HSRC 1982, 18 and 88). Another HSRC study concluded that there was one sport field for every 3 000 pupils in the Cape Province (cf. CAPE TIMES of 3 May, 1983). The report also criticised the lack of qualified physical education teachers and sport instructors at "Black" schools. In 1984, sport (or Physical Education) ceased to be a subject of instruction at Black schools:

> *The new curriculum introduced by the government devaluated African (and also Indian and Coloured) education in the interests of separate development, which required Africans to be unskilled. It also removed most of the elements of organized sport and physical education (UNESCO, 1972, p. 63f, as quoted by Archer in Baker & Mangan, 1987, p. 239).*

SACOS' Policy

a) Resistance against "permits"

Towards the end of the 1970s, the government introduced a new system of "permits" in order to facilitate the introduction of its new "multinational" sport policy[5]. SACOS' answer to the concept of "multinationalism" was its principle of "non-racialism", which was defined as the "non-reference to race or skin colour, but to people participating in activities as sportspersons" (cf. Robert , 1988, p. 6).

As indicated above, the concept of "multinationalism" indeed differed greatly from true "non-racialism": far from "race" or "colour" having no effect on the selection and/or composition of sport teams, "multinationalism" did not allow for racially mixed teams, but only tolerated sport contests between "racially homogenous" teams, each of which was thus to represent one particular "population group". Thus "African" teams were now allowed to compete against "Coloured" or "Indian" teams, but – as far as the government was concerned – any truly integrationist contact over "population group" barriers remained illegal.

From the outset, SACOS made no secret of its unwavering opposition to this new system. As a result, SACOS sportspersons were now regularly interrogated by the police; in many cases, they were arrested and detained.
In 1978, SACOS issued a pamphlet to explain its stance on the "permit" system:

> People who live in houses where they require permits, or people who work under permits or have children educated under permits have no option but to do so. There are laws governing these things – although we detest them. But sportsmen and others who play and attend sport under permit are not forced to do so. They do it from free choice, voluntarily. In other words they are collaborating in their own humiliation... Sportsmen should refuse to play sport because it ... injures their human dignity and deprives them of their right as South Africans.

> There is only one way to equality and that is to abolish all which militates against the playing of sport in a truly non-racial manner in a democratic society" (Ramsamy, 1977, p. 21).

---

[5] SACOS' opposition to the Government's „multinational" sport policy may require some explanation. In order to counter its bad press abroad, the apartheid government introduced the term „multinational" for its sport policy. This suggested a certain degree of integration, although no such thing was intended. The same intended ambiguity marked the term „interracial", which was also at times used to describe the new sport policy. SACOS was acutely aware of the insincerity of this verbal window-dressing, and hence rejected the „multinational" concept in no uncertain terms: "We need to remember that whatever movements are made by the white sports bodies are only to safeguard their own positions and add more camouflage for overseas. The same thing is happening in the political arena. Everyone is saying we are moving away from discrimination, which is not true, and I must challenge white administrators because I feel there is no sincerity in their approach" (SACOS Report, 1975, p. 70).

By defending their own rights, the SACOS sportsmen and –women called attention to the infringement of human rights which affected all South Africans.

Sensitive to the bad publicity of the "permit system", both at home and abroad, the South African government shied away from brutally suppressing the protests at home and applied a more lenient policy to the granting of permits. Government spokespersons and representatives of "White" sport organisations now claimed that the issuing of "permits" was a mere formality. However, in the experience of "Black" and "non-racial" sport organisations, the "permits" continued to be a legal requirement, which the authorities could grant or withhold at will. This fact pointed to a problem of vital importance for an organisation such as SACOS: the problem whether, under apartheid, it was practically possible to live by the principles of "non-racialism" at all. No organisation could exist and function under apartheid without, to a certain extent, compromising these noble principles, or without making certain concessions to the powers-that-be.

A totally uncompromising adherence to SACOS principles would simply have meant that no sport at all could be practised in or by "Coloured", "Indian" and "African" communities in South Africa. Hassan Howa, then president of the South African Cricket Board of Control, conceded that apartheid often imposed a contradictory course of action on its opponents:

> *If we were non-racial purists, we should stop playing cricket altogether. I have said this before at a school debate where children said we were racists, we are. We are forced to be racialists by the laws of the country (Howa as quoted by Odendaal, 1977, p. 277).*

Further problems were brought about by the so-called "double standards resolution", the matter of sponsorships, and the moratorium.

b) The "double standard resolution"

On 6 April 1977, the SACOS executive released what soon became known as the "double standard resolution". This resolution was taken against the background of a serious dispute within the South African Cricket Board of Control regarding its relations with the "White" Cricket Board, and forbade all SACOS members to have any relations with sport organisations practising racial discrimination or participating in "multinational" sport.

At SACOS' third AGM, this resolution was extended to include not only sport organisations, but all official institutions. More than any other SACOS principle or policy, this "double standard resolution" was criticised by political and sport organisations alike for its political and dictatorial nature. For the overwhelming majority of the "African" population, who were bound by law to live in townships or homelands, apartheid laws made it simply impossible to abide by this resolution. If it had been applied strictly, hardly any "African" sportsperson could have remained a SACOS member.

c) Sponsoring

SACOS' stand on commercial support (or sponsorship) was an equally intractable problem. SACOS was committed to the struggle against apartheid, but the companies who sponsored sport events profited from the system, and therefore supported it. Whereas SACOS rejected sponsorships from such companies, many of its member organisations could simply not afford to adopt such a principled stand. Many SACOS members therefore did not give effect to the organisation's 1979 call to reject all sponsorships from companies with links to the apartheid government; in fact, many members continued to launch discreet requests for financial support.

d) The moratorium

SACOS called on the international community to suspend all sport links with South Africa until such time as apartheid would be scrapped. This moratorium policy strengthened the "non-racial" movement, while at the same time weakening the position of apartheid supporters in sport. This policy was not without sacrifice, since even the non-racial sport bodies were called upon to suspend all international tours, and to uphold the moratorium.

The road to unity in South African sport

The NSC

Partly in reaction to the problems described above, a number of SACOS members founded the National Sports Congress, NSC, in 1989. Since they not only represented different sport codes and disciplines, but also all four of South Africa's official "population groups", these founder members (e.g. Ngconde Balfour, Muleki George, Krish Naidoo, Krish Macerdugh and Bill Jardine) could claim to be fully representative. The idea was to form an "umbrella sports body, bringing together all sport disciplines for the mutual benefit of all South Africans" (NSC pamphlet, no date given).

Many years later, one of the founder members (and a subsequent Minister of Sport) Ngconde Balfour described the NSC's aims as follows:
- (To adopt) A forward-looking, future-oriented approach to sport
- To move away from the principle of 'no normal sport in an abnormal society', and from the "double standard resolution"
- To try to unite all sports bodies across the apartheid divide as SACOS had not managed to embrace all our communities, especially the African townships (interview with N. Balfour on 9 November 1996).

The NSC was to concentrate on three points of focus: firstly, the "unity programme" was intended to unite sportspersons from all "population groups". Secondly, especially sportspersons from previously disadvantaged "population groups" were to benefit from the "development programme". Thirdly, after a protracted period of international isolation, a "preparation programme" was meant to prepare South Africa's sportspersons for international competition.

In 1990, the National Sports Congress, as it was then called, also assumed the role of the National Olympic Congress (NOSC) and gave attention to South Africa's position in the international Olympic movement. Its first "unity programme" was aimed at uniting the country's various Olympic organisations, i.e. the NOSC and the bodies working in exile, viz. SANROC, SACOS, SANOC, and COSAS (Confederation of South African Sports). This process led to the formation of the Interim National Olympic Committee of South Africa (INOCSA), after which the NSC withdrew from the Olympic arena, and once again concentrated on its role as National Sports Congress.

In 1991, South Africa was readmitted to the Olympic Games and, having shed its "interim" character, INOCSA transformed itself into NOCSA, the National Olympic Committee of South Africa. Between 1991 and 1994, most racially segregated associations joined up with their respective counterparts to form one united, non-racial body for each sport code or discipline. For instance, the SACOS-affiliated South African Cricket Union joined up with the White South African Cricket Board (SACB), in 1989, to form the United Cricket Board of South Africa (UCBSA). In 1991, the unified South African Rugby Football Union (SARFU) was jointly formed by the SACOS-affiliated South African Rugby Union (SARU) and the "White" South African Rugby Board (SARB). By the end of 1994, this unification process in South African sport was almost complete.

In 1994, the National Sports Congress and the Confederation of South African Sports (COSAS) combined to form the National Sports Council of South Africa (NSC). In order to facilitate cooperation between the government and the various sport associations, the same year saw the creation of the National Sports Forum, in which the NSC, NOCSA and the Department of Sport and Recreation enjoy equal representation.

In 1999 the Sports Commission was formed out of the amalgamation of part of the Department of Sport and Recreation and the National Sports Council. It functions as an as umbrella organization and is a legislated body governed by the South African Sports Commission Act 109 of 1998 as amended.

Despite this process, it needs to be stressed that there are still many sport associations where, in practice, little has changed, and where the top decision-making positions continue to be occupied by "Whites". Examples of sport disciplines where this is the case are rugby, cricket, athletics, and swimming.

USSASA

In 1991, the South African Primary School Sport Association (SAPSSA) and the South African Secondary Schools Sport Association (SASSA) amalgamated to form the United School Sports Association of South Africa (USSASA), the first united school sport organisation in South African history.

Summary

Undeniably, sport in South Africa has been politicised. The blame for this state of affairs must be put squarely at the door of the apartheid ideology, which resulted in decades of social segregation. Initially intended to guard "White" control over politics and the economy, the apartheid minority government gradually extended and applied its policy of "separate development" to all spheres of life, including sport. Through the extension of existing rules and regulations, as well as the introduction of new laws, the government gradually assumed an ever more relentless control over people's lives, including their recreation, sport and entertainment.

However, it became apparent that segregation in sport caused the government greater problems than, for instance, legislation dealing with the trade unions or, for that matter, with "mixed" (i.e. inter-race) marriages. The resistance of "Non-White" sport associations, and of SACOS in particular, resulted in victory over segregation in sport. Simultaneously, a whole array of factors forced the government to modify its stand: firstly, the principle of equality in international sport (enshrined in the statutes of the International Olympic Committee, which prohibit all discrimination on the basis of race, religion or creed), secondly, the great social importance of sport to "White" South Africa, and, last but not least, SACOS' effective campaign for the international isolation of South Africa's racially exclusive "White" sport associations. Still, unity in South African sport was only achieved in 1994. For the first time, the new democratic Government's "(Draft) White Paper" on sport assured access to sport to all sportsmen and –women, regardless of skin colour:

> In the apartheid era more than 30 million South Africans were never taken into any serious account when it came to sport and recreation. A new era has now dawned in which the fortunes of those 30 millions need seriously to be recognised in concrete terms. ... As South Africa enters into a new democratic dispensation the need to entrench that new democratic ethos in sport as part of the transformation process for the upliftment of the quality of life for all South Africans cannot be over-emphasised (DSR: White Paper (Draft), 1995, p. 2).

Admittedly, developing countries often do not offer their sportsmen and -women the same kind of access to sports facilities as industrialised countries do. However, in the South African case, the abundance of excellent facilities for

White sport persons, and the high levels of competitiveness achieved by this privileged group, combined with the whole population's enthusiasm for sport, made Black South Africans acutely aware of the second-rate status and the limitations inflicted on them. South Africa was the only country in the world which officially denied access to equal opportunities to the majority of its population on the grounds of race; it was also the only country to have applied this ideology to the realm of sport.

The political demise of apartheid

The scrapping of the race laws

The South African Government was very slow in responding to international pressure and political unrest at home; it did so by gradually dismantling the apartheid system. Early steps in this direction were the granting of limited political rights to "Coloureds" and "Indians" in 1984, and the scrapping of the "Mixed Marriages Act" the following year. Next, the government of P. W. Botha scrapped the infamous "Pass Laws", which had treated Black South Africans as citizens of various "homelands", and hence as aliens in South Africa proper.

For many South African and foreign observers, the "shift of the repressive apartheid regime towards a free, democratic political system" began with President De Klerk's 'Rubicon speech' of 2 February 1990. In this speech, he announced the release of Nelson Mandela and other political prisoners, and the start of constitutional negotiations with all parties, on the basis of equal rights for all South Africans" (Karpen, 10 March 1996, p. 10).

On 11 February 1990, Nelson Mandela was released after 27 years in prison. The next year, the De Klerk government dismantled all race laws. Of particular importance was the scrapping of the "Group Areas Act" on 6 June 1991, which made it possible for "Africans", "Indians" and "Coloureds" to move into residential areas formerly reserved for "Whites". The last law to go, on 17 June 1991, was the "Population Registration Act", which meant that newly-born babies and immigrants were no longer to be classified in terms of race. However, existing racial registers were not destroyed and continued to exist. Complete equality before the law was only to be achieved with the passing of a new constitution, which, among other rights, conferred the vote on Black South Africans.

The ensuing years were marked by consultations, negotiations, compromises, and first drafts for a new constitution. The "Convention for a Democratic South Africa (CODESA)", which first met in Johannesburg on 20 December 1991, demonstrated that a rapprochement between the various political forces in South Africa was possible: in addition to the government, the ANC under the leadership of Nelson Mandela, and the Inkatha Freedom Party, no fewer than 17 political organisations took part in these deliberations.

The decision of CODESA to reintegrate the four nominally independent homelands, i.e. Transkei, Ciskei, Bophuthatswana and Venda into South Africa, and to recognise their more than 10 million inhabitants as South African citizens, was seen as an important step in dismantling apartheid. There was also agreement that multi-party democracy, proportional representation, the separation of powers, and a charter of human rights should all be basic elements of the new political system. Nevertheless, the negotiations on the composition of a transitional government became deadlocked in May 1992 on account of irreconcilable differences, partly on the issue of a federal versus a centralist system of government.

On 17 May 1992, President F. W. de Klerk called on "White" voters to endorse his concept of a negotiated settlement in a referendum. The result – 68,6% of votes in favour of negotiations, 31,2% against - showed that the majority of "White" voters favoured the government's reform policies. Still, in April 1993, the assassination of SACP leader Chris Hani by White right-wing fanatics brought the country to the verge of a civil war.

In November 1991, CODESA reached an agreement on a new constitution, including a Bill of Rights. On 22 December 1993, this constitution was passed into law by an act of Parliament; for the first time, all South Africans enjoyed the right to vote, regardless of race or skin colour. The first democratic elections, held from 26 to 29 April 1994, proceeded peacefully and with a high voter turn-out, although White right-wingers attempted to create chaos in the run-up to the elections. They planted several car bombs, which claimed several casualties. The African National Congress (ANC) won the elections, with 62.6% of all votes cast. In order to secure the participation of the Inkatha Freedom Party (IFP), considerable concessions had been made to the province KwaZula-Natal, among them constitutional safeguards for the continued existence of the monarchy of the Zulus' King Zwelithini. On 27 April, South Africa's new, democratic transitional constitution came into power, ending 342 years of White domination. Nelson Mandela, Chairman of the African National Congress and veteran fighter against apartheid, became the country's first democratically elected president, with Thabo Mbeki (ANC) and F. W. de Klerk (NP) as vice-presidents.
    After the inauguration of Nelson Mandela as President on 10 May, 1994 in Pretoria, the new "Government of National Unity" (GNU) assumed its responsibilities. The era of apartheid, which had been imposed on the country by a White minority government for 40 years, had finally come to an end.

"Since the first democratically elected Parliament was constituted in 1994, constitutional negotiations have proceeded well. Exceptional as it may seem, the provisional constitution of 27 April 1994 contains 34 constitutional principles, which are binding on the authors of the final constitution. The principles have been integrated into the draft of December 1995, which is now on the table." (Karpen, 10 March, 1996, p. 10). In terms of this transitional constitution, South Africa has eleven official languages. English functions as lingua franca, while most of the other languages are of regional importance. Since May 1994, there is a 400 member strong National Assembly and a Senate consisting of 90 representatives, 10 from each of the nine provinces. On 8 May, these 490 elected representatives adopted the new transitional constitution with the required 2/3 majority, thereby fulfilling the first task which the voters had set them on 27 April 1994.

From the first democratic elections until June 1996, the African National Congress (ANC), the National Party (NP) and the Inkatha Freedom Party (IFP) co-operated as members of a Government of National Unity (GNU). On 1 July 1996, De Klerk's NP withdrew from this government to become the then official opposition, i.e. the strongest party opposing the government. Thereafter the government has been formed by the two remaining parties, the ANC and the IFP.

On 10 December 1996, the last significant symbolic step on the road to the new South Africa was taken, when President Nelson Mandela signed the new Constitution in Sharpville, thereby passing it into law.

2. 2 Drawing Educational Consequences: First Attempts at Integrating Private Schools

2.2.1 Opening up the Schools and Universities

Officially, apartheid in South Africa was abandoned when all race laws – among them corner stones like the "Group Areas Act" and the "Population Registration Act" – were scrapped in 1991. In practice, rapprochement and narrowing the gaps between the population groups is fraught with difficulties. Friction and occasional flare-ups at many of the country's schools and universities attest to this (cf. the Sunday Independent of 19 May 1996).

In many spheres of life, e.g. the appearance of residential neighbourhoods, standard of life, job opportunities, etc., the effects of the apartheid past are still being felt. But especially in education, the legacy of alienation brought about by apartheid is still firmly in place. A telling symptom of this are the differences in state expenditure on the education of children belonging to different population groups. In the 1988/1989 school year, roughly four times as much money – R 3 082 – was spent on the education of a White child as on that of an African child (R 765); a Coloured child cost the state about half as much as a White child (R 1 370), while the average Indian child's education cost the state two-thirds of the expenditure for a White child (R 2 227) (cf. Statistisches Bundesamt, 1991, p. 47).

Before 1994, South Africa had 17 different education authorities, according to ethnic-racial and regional differentiation; a single, democratically legitimated department of education was only formed after the first democratic elections. However, first attempts to rectify the situation had already been made in the late eighties and early nineties, when the old dispensation was still in place.

In 1989, the government announced a number of important changes in educational policy, which were designed to promote the gradual dismantling of apartheid in education, and to reduce the extreme inequality. As part of these changes, subsidies were to be granted to private schools wishing to admit Black pupils, provided that 90% of the White parents agreed. This was to pave the way for the cautious integration of African, Coloured and Indian pupils into formerly White schools. However, the prevailing strong opposition of White parent-teacher-associations thwarted the scheme.

In 1990, the government introduced a new scheme to allow White parents to admit Black pupils to "their" schools; this time, the prerequisite approval rate of (White) parents was set at 72%. From 1991 onwards, the F. W. de Klerk government and the ANC jointly worked towards the unification of the formerly racially segregated education departments. The same year saw the beginning of the opening of state schools to pupils of all population groups; private schools had been opening up since the early eighties.
     In January 1993, the Minister of Education published an "Education Renewal Strategy". Among the measures advocated in this document, were the formation of a unitary educational system for all South Africans, as well as the introduction of compulsory schooling for nine school years. Up to that stage, school education was only compulsory for Whites (since 1953), Coloureds (since 1980) and Indians (since 1979). The urgency of this measure, particularly for the African population, is demonstrated by the fact that there are at present approximately 1,7 million African children between the ages of 6 and 17 years who receive no schooling (cf. Statistisches Bundesamt, 1995, p. 55).

The inequality in education, caused by the disparity in funding, is visible in the furnishings and equipment of schools, the teacher-pupils ratios, the training of teachers, and consequently in differences in the quality of education provided. This in turn perpetuates differences in the levels of university training and of professional qualifications achieved and held by members of the different population groups (cf. Statistisches Bundesamt, 1995, p. 53ff). – Another factor is the need for additional schools, partly as a result of the introduction of compulsory schooling for Africans, and partly as a result of the natural growth of the population. In 1991, for example, approximately one million African children could not attend school for lack of facilities; simultaneously, many schools for White children were under-utilised and had surplus class rooms. According to an estimate by the South African Foundation, 177 225 African children could have been accommodated at under-utilised White schools in 1990 alone (cf. Statistisches Bundesamt, 1991, p. 52).
     The following table provides a breakdown of educational institutions in the "old South Africa" according to population group. The House of Assembly used

to be responsible for "White" education, the House of Delegates for "Indians", "Coloured" education was administered by the House of Representatives, and "African" education was the responsibility of the Department of Education and Training.

Number of Educational Institutions, 1993

Table 2: Number of educational institutions; date: 1993 (South African Communication Service, 1994, p. 282).

	Public Ordinary school education	Special school education	Private ordinary school education	Technical college education	Teacher training	Technikon	University
House of Assembly Education and Culture	3112	82	278	68	11	8	11
House of Delegates Education and Culture	465	18	54	3	2	1	1
House of Representatives Education and Culture	1988	60	16	12	11	1	1
Education and Training	8151	51	106	24	13	1	4
National states	6587	15	23	21	33	3	-
TOTAL	20 303	226	477	128	70	15	17

Since the demise of apartheid in the early nineties, the government has made a concerted effort to overcome the inequalities in education. However, it will still take a long time before the apartheid heritage is overcome. This is partly due to limitations on funds available for this purpose, and partly to the slow pace at which mental patterns change. This applies not only to the former apartheid perpetrators, but also to the victims, some of whom struggle to overcome the effects of their previous educational disadvantage.

As indicated above, private schools in South Africa had led the way to the integration of schools: many of them had opened their doors to pupils from all population groups from the early eighties onwards. I shall now proceed to describe and analyse my own experiences at one such school, the Deutsche Schule Kapstadt (DSK), the German School, Cape Town. Admittedly, this school differed (and differs) from South African state schools, in that it consciously seeks to maintain and preserve the cultural links of a German-speaking community to its country of origin. Nevertheless, I believe that the particular perspective arising from this endeavour, plus the relatively early stage at which the school attempted to overcome apartheid in education, are able to shed additional light on the matter, and are therefore worthy of consideration.

2.2.2 The German Schools' Concept of "Opening up" to all Population Groups

There are five German-language schools in Southern Africa which are partly funded and staffed with aid received from the German Federal Government. They are the *Deutsche Schule Hermannsburg (DSH)*, the *Deutsche Schule Johannesburg (DSJ)*, *Deutsche Schule Kapstadt (DSK)*, *Deutsche Schule Pretoria (DSP)*, and the *Deutsche Höhere Privatschule (DHPS)* in Windhoek, Namibia.

With the exception of the DHPS, formerly *Kaiserliche Oberrealschule,* and the DSH, a mission school, all these schools were founded as confessional schools, and they are among the oldest surviving schools in South Africa.

Mission schools and church-affiliated schools, as well as the German-language private schools, took the lead in opening their doors, from the early 1980s onwards, to pupils from all population groups. I shall use my knowledge and personal experience of the *Deutsche Schule Kapstadt (DSK)* as an example of this process, and of the thinking that informed it.

2.2.3 The Deutsche Schule Kapstadt (DSK)

The *Deutsche Schule Kapstadt (DSK)* began its existence as the D*eutsche Martini-Schule* in 1883, when it was founded by the largely German-speaking Lutheran *Martini* congregation. Six years later, the then Cape Education Department obtained authority over the school, and its name changed to *St. Martin's Public School.* Since 1930, the *Deutsche Schulverein Kapstadt* has been the governing body of this school; its 1975 constitution binds this body to ensure that "children of German extraction receive well-founded instruction and a German education, regardless of their religious affiliation" (Constitution of the Deutsche *Schulverein Kapstadt,* 23 April 1975). In 1961, a bigger, new school building was erected with the financial support of the German Federal Government, and the present name was adopted. A hostel attached to the school was also opened at this time.

In September 1997, the *DSK* had 660 pupils and a teaching staff of 63, a quarter of which – including the school principal – were seconded by the *Zentralstelle für Auslandsschulwesen* (Central Office for German-language schools abroad) in Cologne. The rest of the teaching staff are recruited locally. (In 1999 the DSK had 704 pupils and a teaching staff of 83.)

As a private school, the DSK depends on support from the German Federal government (staff and finance), subsidies from the South African government, and contributions from pupils' parents.

According to the constitution of its governing body, the *Deutsche Schulverein,* the *DSK* aims "to offer German-speaking children a thorough education, in accordance with local curricula, so that they may become good and respectable citizens of this country. Furthermore, the school aims to educate its pupils, regardless of their religious orientation, in a Christian spirit, and to impart to them a thorough knowledge of the German language and culture[1]."

In short, the *DSK* aims to offer its pupils a South African qualification, coupled with German language skills, and a synthesis of German and South African educational orientations. – In 1988, the *DSK* opened its doors to pupils of all population groups. Like the other four German-language schools in Southern Africa, the *DSK* today sees itself as an "(intercultural) meeting place", with the declared aim of making a meaningful contribution to mutual understanding and tolerance.

The school career of pupils at the *DSK* consists of the following phases: "foundation" phase (grade 1 to 3), "intermediate phase" (grade 4 to 6), "secondary phase" (grade 7 to 9) and "senior secondary" (grade 10 to 12). In 1988, the "German mother-tongue" stream at the *DSK* was supplemented, at "junior secondary" level, with a "foreign-language" stream covering grades 8 to 12 (thus leading up to matric). This "foreign-language" stream is open to pupils from all population groups, provided they have successfully completed a "preliminary course" in grade 7.

Up to grade 6, i.e. in the "foundation" and "intermediate" phases, curricula resemble those used in Germany, except in the subjects English and Afrikaans. From grade 7 onwards, the orientation of curricula veers more strongly towards the curricula of the Western Cape Education Department. With a view to the matriculation examination, i.e. the entrance qualification for South African universities, instruction in the "senior secondary" phase is based on South African curricula. However, the German component is maintained throughout, and pupils willing and able to do so may take the German university entrance examination (the so-called "Abitur") after completing an optional 13th year of schooling.

In the "foundation phase", the language of instruction is German. English language instruction begins with two periods of English per week in grade 2; this is complemented by two periods of Afrikaans per week in grade 4. Since the matric examination requires a mother-tongue level of proficiency in English, English is used as medium of instruction for all examination subjects from grade 8 onwards.

2.2.4 The Integration Concept of the German-language Schools in Southern Africa

Towards the end of the 1980s, the German Federal Government made it clear that it wished German-language schools in Southern Africa to open its doors to learners from all population groups. On account of differences in local

---

[1] Constitution of the Deutscher Schulverein Kapstadt, dated 23 April 1975

conditions, each of the German-language schools developed its own model in response to this request. The *DSK*, for its part, had already decided in 1978 to institute extra-mural German language courses for pupils of all population groups. The aim behind this model was that gifted, but disadvantaged pupils would attend these language courses for three or four years, after which they could enrol as DSK pupils from grade 9 or 10 onwards. The first of these courses, which were predominantly attended by Coloured pupils, was launched in 1979.

The idea of "opening up" the school met with some resistance, not only from pupils' parents who, through the governing body, exerted control over the school, but also from other interested parties. One reason for this resistance was that the German-language schools in Southern Africa had until then regarded – and legitimated their function as – schools for the exclusive use of a linguistic minority. Furthermore, there were fears that the high educational standard of the German-language schools would be compromised if "Coloured" children, and particularly "African" children, were admitted. In an article entitled *"Lieber Schweine als Schwarze" ("Rather pigs than blacks")*, Schweizer described the attitude prevalent at the *DSH*, where it was believed that the very existence of the school would be threatened if pupils from "other racial groups" were to be admitted (Schweizer, 1982, p. 38). Like the other German-language schools, the *DSK* felt the pull of opposing political forces. On the one hand, the German Federal Government exerted pressure for the school to be opened; on the other hand, the *DSK* had to comply with the apartheid rule of the Cape Education Department, which allowed for a maximum of 4 % of pupils from "other race groups" at "White" schools.

After heated discussions, contending DSK interest groups formulated the "language school model" described above as the institution's first response to these conflicting demands. However, this model failed to achieve the target of opening the school to all population groups. One reason for this was that very few pupils successfully completed the extra-mural language courses in order to qualify for admission to the school; it was felt that these low numbers did not justify the massive institutional and educational effort required for their integration. Consequently, in 1985, it was agreed that a "preparatory stream" would be instituted for non-German-speaking pupils at the DSK, with the aim of fully integrating successful candidates into the (German-language) "main stream" from grade 10 onwards. At a meeting of the principals of German-language schools at the *DSK* in 1986, participants were urged to institute changes which would allow their schools to admit greater numbers of Coloured and African pupils.

All models presented for consideration at this conference amounted to the creation of separate "foreign-language streams" for Coloured and Black pupils at "junior secondary" level; pupils successfully completing this phase were to be integrated with the "mother-tongue stream" at senior secondary level.

The *DSK* and the *DHPS* (Windhoek) introduced preparatory classes in 1987, instituting their first full "foreign-language stream" (F-stream) classes the following year (1988). The *DHPS* dropped this concept in 1991 and has been taking in "foreign-language" pupils (i.e. non-German-speakers) directly (i.e. without preparatory classes) ever since. The German-language schools in Pretoria and Johannesburg took a bit longer to move forward. The DSJ opened preparatory classes in 1988, and first group of "foreign-language" stream pupils was admitted in 1989; deviating from the other German-language schools in this respect, the DSJ teaches Art and Physical Education to integrated groups of "mother-tongue" and "foreign-language" pupils from grade 5 onwards. 1988 also saw the institution of a preparatory course in 1988; the following year, successful participants from this course were selected to form the first class of F-stream learners from 1990 onwards. The first fully integrated class of mother-tongue and foreign-language learners at this school was the grade 10 class of 1992. The *DSH*, for its part, took a different line, dispensing with preparatory classes altogether and forming an F-stream class of mostly African pupils, at grade 8 level, from 1987 onwards.

Despite the differences between these models, all five schools strive to transform themselves from "minority language group schools" into "intercultural meeting place schools", in accordance with the aims set by the German Federal Government for all the German-language schools beyond German borders.

What importance the German Federal Government attaches to this "intercultural meeting place" concept, and particularly to the integration of Black and White pupils at these five schools, can be seen from the level of its financial commitment, which increased from DM 296 300 in 1983 to almost DM 2.4 million in 1995, and is set to rise even further. It is doubtful that all other role players are equally committed to the integration concept: The executive of the *DHPS* governing body made no secret of its opinion that the "integration venture would be definitely under threat if the Federal Republic of Germany should reduce its subsidy" (Marteson, 1993, p. 33).

2.2.5 Transforming a "Minority Language Group" School into an "Intercultural Meeting Place": the Example of the Deutsche Schule Kapstadt (DSK)

The *DSK* took the first practical step to give effect to its new "F-stream" model by admitting two classes of learners, at grade 7 level, to a preparatory language course in 1987. Apart from equipping these learners, within one school year, to become a fully-fledged "foreign-language stream" grade 8 class, the preparatory course had the aim of familiarising these pupils with their new German-speaking environment and acquainting them with the curricula and teaching methods used. A further aim was to give teachers a reliable impression of the learners' skills and level of proficiency.

Since Cape Town's African townships were in the grip of political unrest at the time, prospective candidates for the preparatory course were at first recruited from schools in "Coloured" areas, from where they had to be bussed to the *DSK*. Once learners successfully completed the course, a final decision on their admission to grade 8 was taken by the school principal, on recommendations from the head and teachers of the "F-stream". Grade 8 was chosen as entry level, because the South African school system provided for a change from primary to secondary school at this stage. Successful participants in this process started their *DSK* career as members of a separate English-medium class.

The *DSK* has guidelines on curricula differentiation, and on the time-frame for integrating the "mother-tongue" and "foreign-language" streams. These can be adapted on a year-to-year basis to the conditions and needs of each group of learners, leading to a variety of integration paths. For instance, in January 1991, five gifted African children were promoted from the preparatory course to the grade 7 "mother-tongue" class. In January 1992, 19 additional candidates, among them three Africans and six Coloureds, were divided between two grade 8 "mother-tongue" classes, thus doing away with the "F stream" and achieving a fully-integrated "mother tongue" course.

This trend was reversed in 1994, when a totally separate "F-stream" class of successful "preparatory course" candidates was formed at grade 5 level; this class even took PE lessons separately from the "mother tongue" stream. In the same year, newly-enrolled "F-stream" learners at grade 7 level were also kept separate from the "mother-tongue" stream, except in the subjects Art and Physical Education. Unfortunately this was reversed later again and even after 2000 some German schools continue to keep learners separated in subjects like Physical Education.

The introduction of "foreign-language streams" at German-language schools in Southern Africa initiated a complex and difficult transformation progress, intended to change these schools into "intercultural meeting places". German Federal authorities made it clear that only schools which successfully embarked on this process, could expect subsidies by the German government to continue. A Federal report on German-language schools abroad (dated March 1990) urges that this policy should be pursued vigorously, particularly in Southern Africa, and that it should be based on a broad definition of "cultural interaction", which incorporated not only social interaction, but also familiarisation "with cultures, traditions, languages, historical developments, and an engagement with the values of free and democratic societies".

According to a circular from the Auswärtiges Amt (i.e. the Federal German Department of Foreign Affairs), the German-language schools in Southern Africa had embarked vigorously on this venture, as indicated by the academic success of African and Coloured children at these schools (*Auswärtiges Amt, Rundbrief of 20 August 1990*).

2.2.6 Personal Observations: The Problems of "Integrating Hearts and Minds"

As a teacher at the DSK in 1991 and 1992, and particularly as class teacher of the **first multi-cultural class** (consisting of four African and eleven Coloured pupils, the rest of the class being White), I gathered valuable insights into the situation of the "foreign-language" pupils ("F-pupils", for the sake of brevity). My second extended stay (1993/1994) gave me the opportunity to check, confirm or revise these impressions. My remarks are based on observing pupils' behaviour and on talking (or rather listening) to African and Coloured pupils at the DSK, either individually or within small groups. I also spoke to many so-called "drop-outs", i.e. pupils who left the "F-stream" before its impending full integration with the "mother-tongue stream". All these sources confirmed my impression that there remained unsolved problems regarding the **integration of the hearts and minds of these pupils,** which contributed to the fact that they did not feel quite at home, or fully accepted, at the German-language schools.

At this stage, it may be helpful to remind ourselves of the complex nature of the problem, i.e. the integration of "pupils from the previously disadvantaged population groups" (frequently referred to as "non-Whites") into formerly White schools.

South African schools

Many South African schools, both private and Model C schools, had at that stage (the early nineties) only admitted small numbers of African and Coloured pupils. Reasons cited for this state of affairs included long distances, lack of public transport, school fees, and high admission criteria. In some cases, the conservative attitude of management or parents constituted a problem, which manifested itself in a fear of "lowering standards", or even in persisting apartheid ideology.

The five German-language schools

In the early nineties, the German-language schools in Southern Africa had no joint model or blue-print for the admission of African and Coloured pupils. Decisions on aspects such as the appropriate stage of admission, composition of "F-stream" classes, time-frame for the integration of the "foreign-language" and "mother-tongue" streams, etc., were taken by each school individually. There were two reasons for this. Firstly, there were differences in the conditions under which each of these schools operated (size, feeding area, number of pupils, etc.); secondly, the integration problem was still in an initial, more or less experimental stage.

Research by the DSK's school psychologist indicated that many more "F-stream" than "mother-tongue stream" pupils "dropped out": more than 30%

of "non-White" pupils left the school after two years or more, despite good academic results. The other German-language schools in Southern Africa recorded similar statistics. (cf Statistics presented by *DSK* school psychologist). Repulsive as it may seem, it is necessary to break up "non-White pupils" into more precise categories, such as African, Asian, Malay, Indian etc., if one wishes to understand the drop-out phenomenon. Firstly, because of apartheid, there were differences in the schooling these pupils had received prior to attending the DSK; secondly, it was noted that pupils normally chose friends and companions from their own "group".

Due to the stringent process followed by the DSK, it can be assumed that only gifted and motivated candidates were admitted. Nevertheless, it soon became apparent that, apart from the quality of previous schooling, other differences between pupils retarded their integration, such as cultural background, living conditions at home, problems of identity, lack of frankness on the part of parents, teachers and pupils alike, etc. The addition of German as a "third language" posed problems, especially for Xhosa-speakers, who were required to learn English and Afrikaans, in addition to their mother tongue.

It is unrealistic to expect any integration programme to succeed immediately under such conditions. Experiences in the USA indicate that it can take several generations for pupils, teachers and parents to overcome social and psychological barriers imposed by deliberate attempts to keep "population groups" apart. Even then, it remains doubtful whether such attempted integration succeeds in the end. Still, the research conducted at German-language schools in Southern Africa is seen as an important step towards understanding the problem of "integrating hearts and minds", and of presenting possible solutions to this problem (cf. Keim, 1992, p. 23ff).

▥ EMPIRICAL STUDIES

CHAPTER 3

3.1 Failing at Integration: Hearing the "Drop-outs'" Side of the Story

*F*or non-German-speakers, admission to one of Southern Africa's five German-language private schools is a long and arduous road. First, they have to be made aware of the possibility of attending a German-language private school. In the case of the *DSK*, this usually happened by the targeted selection of certain primary schools by the German school, where it then advertised its services in order to recruit pupils. Applicants are then carefully screened on the basis of performance at their previous school; they also have to submit to IQ tests. If the results are satisfactory, the applicants are admitted to extra-mural preparatory courses in German, English and Mathematics. The successful completion of these courses – and hence admission the German school – hinges on an entry examination.

Given this elaborate process, which devoured considerable time, effort and resources, it is understandable that the *DSK* should have been alarmed at the limited success of its initial efforts. Research conducted by the school psychologist in January 1991, revealed that more than a third of "Non-white pupils" had left the school between 1988 and 1990, after an attendance of two years or more, despite achieving satisfactory academic results (cf. Statistics: Althof, 23 January 1991). If figures for the years 1991 to 1994 are included, the percentage of "F-stream" pupils leaving the school prematurely, i.e. before the end of their school careers, rises to an alarming 46%. This figure was considered even more damning, since for the first time it included African pupils, whose selection and preparation had been conducted with particular care. Whereas 37 African applicants had been admitted to the "F-stream" between 1991 and 1994, 10 had left the school during that time (cf. Statistics: Althof, 15 February 1991).

These figures prompted me, in April and May 1992, to investigate the reasons for the high drop-out rate. I traced 23 pupils, three of them African and 20 Coloured, who had prematurely left the *DSK* between 1987 and 1992, most of them having been enrolled there for two years. At the time of the research, the pupils' age varied between 13 and 20 years, and 21 of them were attending "opened" South African government schools (i.e. schools where apartheid had been scrapped). The research was conducted by way of questionnaires, which both the pupils and their parents were asked to complete. This is a summary of the findings. (Access to the original data can be obtained on request to the author via the publisher.)

As evinced by the accompanying graphics (Figures 1a and 1b), most parents and pupils chose the German school for its reputation for high academic standards. A contributing factor may have been the wish to escape the difficult situation prevalent at township schools (teacher strikes, violence, occasional loss of class time, etc.). Eight of the 23 pupils cited the supposed advantages impressed upon them by *DSK* representatives, i.e. academic and career advantages, unspecified privileges, a possible journey to Germany). The reasons which the DSK and the Federal Government of Germany may have hoped for, i.e. an interest in the German language and culture, or an emotional attachment on account of German descent) clearly weighed less with the applicants and their parents.

Reasons for choosing the DSK

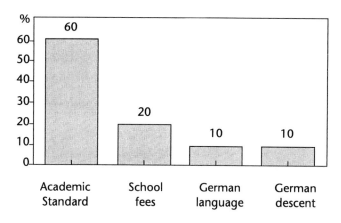

Fig. 1a: Parents' reasons for sending Kids to German school (DSK)

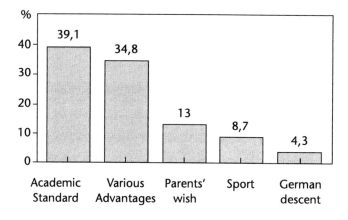

Fig. 1b: Pupils' reasons for choosing German school (DSK)

Despite the long distances to be covered, all 23 applicants had attended the extra-mural preparatory classes in German, English and Mathematics. Ten candidates would have preferred these to be offered at their "old" schools, but the majority (13) appreciated the opportunity of getting to know their "new" school environment and fellow-pupils from other schools. All parents except one regarded this preparation as helpful, while the remaining respondent regretted the lack of interaction with German-speaking pupils. None of the students had serious difficulties with the academic standard of either the preparatory classes or the entry test, or – for that matter – with any subject taught in the "F-stream".

Asked what they particularly liked at the German school, most pupils cited the sports facilities (74%), followed by the school building (61%), the teachers, and the teaching style and methods employed at the school (39% each). Notably less enthusiasm was shown for the choice of subjects (26%) and for the atmosphere prevailing at the school. These answers are borne out by the pupils' responses to a request to list their *dislikes*: whereas the sports facilities and school buildings received only one negative rating each, more than half the pupils (56%) criticised the atmosphere at the school; more than a quarter (26%) disliked the attitude of their German-speaking schoolmates, and quoted instances of discrimination. Parents' responses confirmed these findings: while their children had been favourably impressed with buildings and sports facilities, they had not taken to the school's atmosphere.

Classes at the German school normally consist of 20 to 25 pupils. Thirteen of the 23 respondents indicated that they had found "very many" (i.e. 16 to 20) or "many" (11 to 15) friends at the German school; six pupils indicated "few" (3 to 6) friends, one claimed "no friends", and one did not respond to this question. Asked to characterise their "F-stream" classmates, 76% of the drop-outs underlined positive adjectives, such as "eager to help", "jolly", "friendly" and "open"; on the other hand, characterisations of their White German-speaking schoolmates were mostly (55%) negative, indicating an "arrogant", "mean" or "prejudiced" disposition. Teachers were seen in almost as positive a light as "F-stream" classmates (74%), viz. as "open", "eager to help", or "interested"; only 26% of the drop-outs felt that the "F-stream" teachers had been "strict" or "disinterested".

Twelve of the 22 parents who responded had the impression that their children were happy at the German school, at least "most of the time"; seven felt that their children had "seldom" or "hardly" been happy. Two-thirds of the parents attributed their children's dissatisfaction to the creation of separate foreign-language and mother-tongue "streams", and to the strong feelings of group cohesion within each of these "streams".

As noted above, most of the "drop-outs" (20 out of the 23) were fond of sport and participated in various disciplines. The most popular of these were basketball (52%), athletics and swimming (26% each), and hockey and volleyball (22% each). "Multi-cultural sport", i.e. sport practised jointly with the "mother-tongue" pupils, was rated as "very good" or "good" by 15 of the respondents; of these, 12 said that they had appreciated this opportunity of integrating with their White fellow-pupils, who appeared not to judge them by skin colour on the sports field. Conversely, four respondents disliked joint PE sessions because of alleged "condescension" on the part of the White kids, which had led to tensions. Four respondents found the PE sessions too strenuous and competitive, while three others said they simply disliked sport. Among proposals for improving the PE sessions were calls for a wider choice of disciplines, more teamwork, and a better class atmosphere.

Looking back on their time at the German school, the "drop-outs" listed their "agreeable" and "disagreeable" experiences as follows:

Positive experiences

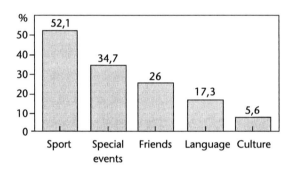

Fig. 2a: Positive experiences of F-stream pupils at the DSK (N=23; multiple responses allowed)

Negative experiences

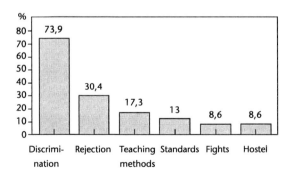

Fig. 2b: Negative experiences of F-stream pupils at the DSK (N=23; multiple responses allowed)

Figure 2a indicates that, even years after the event, many "drop-outs" have fond memories of the sporting opportunities enjoyed at the German school; together with other cultural events, sport encounters rate even above friendships. While some pupils do, in fact, mention the opportunity of getting to know a new language and culture, these pale into insignificance if compared to memories of sport and cultural events.

Regrettably, 17 of the 23 respondents indicated that they had experienced racial prejudices from the White "mother tongue" stream pupils; seven felt "unwelcome" at the German school, and two even came to blows with White school mates. Asked what they had been missing during their time at the German school, eight respondents named friends, six pointed to a lack of cultural activities, and four had longed for some form of community feeling or "school spirit".

In their parents' opinion, the problems their children had to face at the German school were the following:

Parents' views of problems experienced by "drop-outs" at the DSK

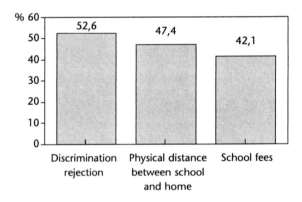

Fig. 3: Parents' views of problems experienced by their children at the DSK

As Figure 3 indicates, parents of the so-called drop-outs were well aware of the problems their children encountered at the *DSK*. Ten of the respondents felt that their children had been exposed to racial prejudices, nine thought the distance between school and home was too great, and eight complained about excessive school fees. Four parents did not reply to this question.

Asked why they had left the *DSK*, or what had prompted them to take their children out of the *DSK*, the "drop-outs" and their parents replied as follows:

Parents' reasons for taking their children out of the DSK

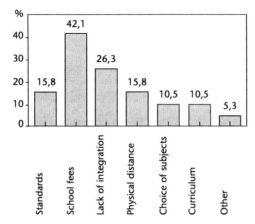

Fig. 4a: Parents' reasons for taking their children out of the DSK (N=19; multiple responses allowed)

Pupils' reasons for leaving the DSK

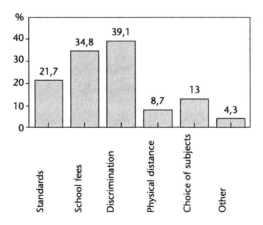

Fig. 4b: Pupils' reasons for leaving the DSK

Figures 4a and 4b indicate a high degree of convergence between parents and pupils on the reasons for dissociating from the DSK. The reasons were not, as many DSK staff members wish to believe, the "high standards" exacted by teachers, or limitations to the choice of subjects (i.e. the absence of commercial subjects from the curriculum), but rather the high school fees charged, and the lack of social integration at the school.

Of the 23 respondents, 21 had switched to a recently-opened Government school. According to 17 of them, the most striking change had been the more positive attitude of their fellow-pupils, and the spirit of co-operation between teachers, parents and pupils at their new school. Eleven "drop-outs" indicated that, at their new school, they had formed "real friendships" with pupils from other cultural groups within a very short time; four prefer the extra-mural societies and sport opportunities at their new schools, and they prefer the facilities; on the other hand, three found the facilities inferior to those at the German school. A further four pupils prefer the teaching methods at the South African schools, while six regret that standards are lower and classes are bigger than at the German school. Almost all of the 21 respondents had found either "many" (i.e. 11 to 15) or "very many" (16 to 20) friends at their new school, while only one failed to answer this question. Thirteen of the pupils reported that they were still in contact with some of their former "foreign language"-stream class mates at the German school, eight had no more links, and one did not answer the question.

Given the general view of White South Africans as the prejudiced perpetrators of apartheid, the "drop-outs'" favourable comments on finding friends among this group is significant. Apart from pressure exerted by the German Federal Government, proponents of opening German-language schools to Black South Africans probably believed that these schools would develop a model which, in time, could be adopted by English and Afrikaans medium South African schools. The findings of this study suggest otherwise.

Looking back at their children's time at the German school, 13 of the 19 responding parents felt it was good for their children to go through this experience, although only ten indicated that the children had gained by it. On the other hand, four believed that the experiment had been a waste of time. As ways of improving conditions at the school, parents suggested the integration of the "foreign language" and "mother tongue" streams into combined classes, as well as a change of attitude towards Africans and Coloureds. It was also felt that English-medium instruction should not be delivered by German teachers, since this led to misunderstanding and confusion. Parents also believed that school fees needed to be reduced. In view of the long distances travelled, some parents suggested hostel accommodation for "foreign language" pupils.

At the insistence of the German Federal Government, German-language schools in Southern Africa had admitted African and Coloured pupils since the mid-eighties. Given this fact, it is surprising that, up to now, no research has been conducted to explain (and prevent any recurrence of) the high drop-out numbers. The present study suggests the main reason for "dropping out" of the German school: the "foreign language" stream pupils simply did not feel at home there. The situation was probably aggravated by the fact that, with few exceptions, "foreign language" and "mother-tongue" pupils were taught in separate classes: there was hardly any opportunity to move beyond prejudice and preconceived ideas into the realm of personal acquaintance or even friendship. As Figure 3 above indicated, the pupils' parents were acutely aware of these problems; they, too, criticised the separation into two different "streams" for reinforcing group sentiments in each of the two groups, thus making integration even more difficult. Given this fact, it is even more remarkable that sport temporarily broke down these barriers. On the sports field, too, there occurred problems which the "F-stream" pupils attributed to the German-speakers' misplaced sense of superiority. However, two important points should be remembered in this context. Firstly, it is not unusual for tensions to arise between members of groups who hardly ever mingle. Secondly, despite the reported difficulties, three quarters of the "foreign-language" pupils were in favour of joint PE classes with the "mother-tonguers".

3.2   Learning to Integrate – Integrating to Learn: Opinion Polls among Pupils at Integrating Schools

Having questioned the "drop-outs" on their recollections of being enrolled at the *DSK*, I was curious to know the feelings and thoughts of pupils currently enrolled – not only at the *DSK*, but at all five German-language private schools in Southern Africa. The sample consists of 287 pupils who were enrolled at these schools in grade 8 in 1992 – 192 of them in "mother-tongue" classes, and 95 in "foreign-language" classes. The distribution of these pupils among the schools surveyed was as follows:

Table 3: Numbers of grade 8 pupils at German-language schools in Southern Africa who participated in opinion survey.

German Schools	DSP	DSJ	DHPS	DSK	DSH	TOTAL
Mother-Tongue stream	38	68	54	17	15	N= 192
Foreign-language stream	18	18	26	24	9	N= 95

Of the original sample, three did not respond to any questions. The remaining group of 284 consisted of 164 girls and 120 boys between 13 and 14 years of age. A break-down of participating students according to population group reads as follows:

Population Group	Number absolut	%
White	193	67,9
Coloured	53	18,7
African	38	13,4
Total	284	100

Table 4: Break-up of 284 grade 8 students at German-language schools who participated in opinion poll (three members of initial sample of 287 submitted no replies).

"Mother-tongue stream" learners at the DSP, DHPS and DSJ were separated from "foreign-language" learners in class-time, except for the *DSJ's* 8c class, who joined the "F-stream" learners for PE classes. At the *DSH*, "foreign language" and "mother tongue" pupils were jointly instructed in "non-verbal" subjects such as Art, Music and PE, whereas the *DSK* group constituted the first "fully integrated" grade 8 class at the school, four African pupils having been admitted in 1991, and 15 Coloured pupils at the beginning of 1992.

Asked why they were attending a German-language school, the most frequent answer given by "mother tongue" pupils was that this had been their parents' wish. In order of frequency, this was followed by references to the pupils' German extraction, and to the school's high academic standards. Just over half of the "foreign-language" pupils (55%) said the German-language school had been their own first choice of high school, the opportunity of a good education in an environment free from township troubles being the most frequently given reason given for this choice. The second-most frequent reason cited by this group was the fact that they had been recruited by the German-language school, with prospects of reduced school fees and a wider choice of subjects. It may be interesting to note the emotional state in which the "foreign language" pupils joined their new school: 48% confessed to "mixed feelings", 31% looked forward to the experience, and 14% were apprehensive. The answers of African pupils to this question were more polarised than those of Coloured children, possibly because the privileged private school was even further removed from their previous schooling than for the Coloured children: while 45% of the African kids "looked forward" to their new school, 25% were apprehensive. By contrast, 51% of all Coloured respondents had indicated "mixed feelings".

Both "mother tongue" and "foreign language" pupils were asked what they particularly liked at the German school, multiple responses being allowed. In order of preference, "mother-tongue" pupils mentioned their class mates (68,8%), sports facilities (36,5%), the school atmosphere (25%), and the choice of subjects (11,9%). "Foreign language" pupils, on the other hand, were particularly impressed with the sports facilities (60,9%), followed by class mates (44,6%), teachers (36,9%), the choice of subjects (31,5%), and the school atmosphere (23,9%). – Information on the pupils' dislikes indicated a certain potential for tension at the schools, but also implied that "non-White" pupils reacted more graciously to the newly-established "integrated" social environment than their White counterparts. The second-most frequent dislike named by "mother-tonguers" was the fact that their school had opened its doors to members of other "groups" (26%), and that these qualified for a reduction in school fees; other "thumbs down" reactions were reserved for the teachers (29%), the school building (18%), and methods of instruction (13%). Especially those "mother tongue" pupils whose classes are totally separate from the "foreign language" stream, even in non-verbal subjects such as PE and Music, appear to find it difficult to accept "non-White pupils at their school, as is the case at the *DSP, DSJ* and *DHPS*: although 36% of the "mother-tongue" pupils said they like the school atmosphere, 25% of "mother-tonguers" at the mentioned schools rejected the admission of "foreign language" pupils. By contrast, the "foreign language" pupils were much more reticent about their dislikes: of 91 respondents, only 47 replied to this question, furnishing a total of 48 replies. Of these, most indicated a dislike for teachers (12), followed by methods of instruction (9), and discrimination on the part of "mother tongue" pupils (8). Asked what they had missed since switching schools, the pupils were more forthcoming: 38% said they missed friends, both "old" friends at their previous schools and new acquaintances at the German school, followed by the games and sport they had known at their "old" schools (23%); 20% of respondents indicated that they missed their previous school and its teachers, while 12% indicated a longing for their parents.

Social contacts among pupils

Friendship patterns among "mother tongue" pupils did not change greatly within one school term after the admission of "foreign language" pupils. Surprisingly, this also applies to the DSK and the DSH, although "foreign language" pupils at these two schools did not form separate classes, but were directly admitted to the "mother tongue" class.

Of the 190 "mother tongue" candidates who answered this question, 42% said they had "very many" (i.e. 16 to 20) or "many" (10 to 15) friends in the class/at school, 24% had "a few" (6 to 10), 31% indicated they had "few" (3 to 6) or "very few" (1 or 2) friends, while 2% had none. Divided into "population groups", the friendships of "mother tongue" pupils at the five German-language schools indicated the following pattern:

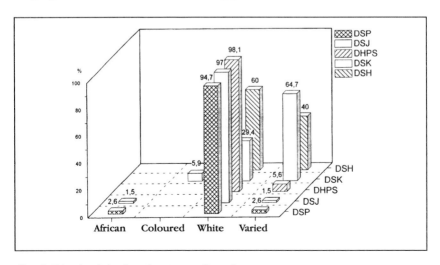

Fig. 5: *Friends of the "mother-tongue" pupils*

The overwhelming majority of participating "mother tongue" pupils indicated that their friends predominantly belonged to the White group. Few pupils (i.e. one each at the *DSP* and *DSJ*, and three at the *DHPS*) indicated they had "Black" friends, or friends among the "foreign language" pupils. Furthermore, Figure 5 shows that hardly any friendships across "colour lines" occur at schools where the "mother tongue" and "foreign language" streams are kept totally separate; at integrated or partially integrated schools, on the other hand, friendships between pupils of different population groups begin to take shape. For instance, one "mother tongue" pupil at the DSK said she had eleven friends, most of whom were Coloured; six DSH pupils stated they had friends among more than one group. Where friendships across the "colour bar" occurred, it was noticeable that White pupils had more friends among Coloureds than among Africans.

Similar questions were put to the "foreign language" pupils. To elicit comparative data, candidates were asked how many friends they had left behind at their previous school. Of the 87 learners who replied to this question (out of a total of 95), 64% indicated that they had "very many" (16 to 20) or "many" (11 to 15) friends; 7% had "several" (6 to 10), 27% had "few", and 1% said they had no friends at their old school. Of the 57 pupils who had attended preparatory courses at their "new" German schools, 37% said they had met "many" new friends among their fellow "foreign language" pupils, 26% had met "several", and 35% said they had met "few"; only 2% had failed to make any new friends at all. – Moving from the preparatory courses on to their "new" classes, 70% of the responding 88 pupils had met "many" or "very many" new friends, 17% had met "several", and 12% had met "few".

The results in Figure 7 indicates a break-down of the "foreign language" students' friends by "population group".

Positive and negative experiences of "mother tongue" pupils at German-language schools

A request to list positive and negative experiences at their schools elicited 135 responses from the "mother tongue" learners, 81 (or 60%) of which concerned disagreeable impressions, and 54 (40%) agreeable ones. These responses confirmed the pupils' earlier statements regarding their likes and dislikes at school. The positive experiences mostly related to class mates, sport, extra-curricular activities, and the good quality of education. The negative impressions, on the other hand, had to do with the school atmosphere, the fact that African and Coloured pupils were admitted to the school, and (partly confirming the previous point, and partly negating it) fellow students' discriminatory behaviour towards the "foreign language" students.

Positive and negative experiences of "foreign language" pupils at German-language schools

Of the 29 responses submitted by "foreign language" pupils to this question, 21 (or 72%) regarded disagreeable experiences, and the remaining 8 (or 28%) were of a more positive nature. While the school as a whole and school sport was seen as agreeable, the most frequently mentioned disagreeable experience related to the discriminating attitude of "mother tongue" students, which in some cases even led to physical confrontations between "foreign language" and "mother tongue" pupils.

The relationship between "mother tongue" and "foreign language" pupils at German-language schools

187 "mother tongue" and 93 "foreign language" students indicated whether they found it easy or difficult to foster friendships across the divide of the "colour bar". Figure 6 illustrates their responses:

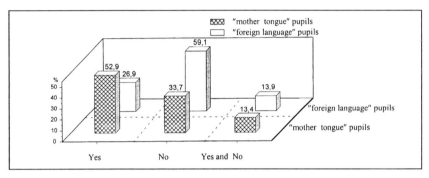

Fig. 6: Answers (in percentages) by "mother tongue" learners (N = 187) and "foreign language" pupils (N = 93) to the question: "Is it difficult to foster friendships with pupils from other cultural groups?"

Figure 6 illustrates an interesting result: "mother tongue" learners and "foreign language" pupils differ significantly from one another in their assessment of obstacles to friendships between these two groups ($p < 0.01$): while the majority of "foreign language" pupils seem to experience no serious difficulties in fostering friendships across the "colour line", "mother tongue" learners seem to regard such friendships as rather difficult to achieve. A break-down of the five schools investigated reveals the following results for "mother tongue" learners:

Table 5: Answers of "mother tongue" learners at the five German-language schools, both in absolute numbers and in percentages, to the question of whether it is difficult to foster friendships with pupils from a different cultural group.

Mother tongue learners	DSP	DSJ	DHPS	DSK	DSH	No.	%
Difficult	14	46	31	4	4	99	2,9
Not difficult	17	12	14	9	11	63	33,7
Unsure	6	9	6	4		25	13,4

These results confirm the interpretation suggested by Figure 5, viz. that it is easier for members of multi-cultural school classes to foster friendships across the "colour line", than it is for pupils from totally separate "mother tongue" classes. The only result which runs counter to this interpretation is that of the segregated "mother tongue" class at the DSP, where the majority of pupils sees no grave impediments to multi-cultural friendships. – Perceptions of obstacles to such friendships must therefore be rooted either in the institution of separate "streams" at these schools, or in the social environment, e.g. students' homes, parents' views, etc.

This assumption is confirmed by the reasons given for their answers to the previous question: 107 "mother tongue" learners (i.e. 60%) thought friendships with "foreign language" pupils were "difficult" because these children were "too different", and "did not really belong in a German school". On the other hand, 48 "mother tongue" learners (or 26%) thought friendships with "foreign language" pupils should pose no problems, since these children were so "friendly" and "open".

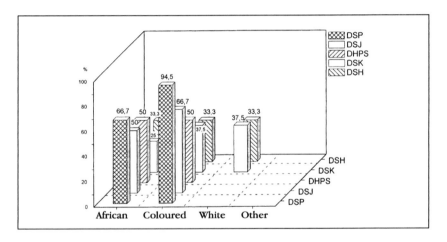

Fig. 7: Breakdown of "foreign language" pupils' friends by Population group; multiple responses allowed in the case of DHPS

Figure 7 illustrates the lack of social interaction between "mother tongue" and "foreign language" pupils – especially at those schools, where the two "streams" are totally separate. Consequently, no friendships across the "colour bar" were reported by "foreign language" pupils at the *DSP, DSJ* or *DHPS*. Findings differed slightly at the partially integrated schools: of the *DSK's* 24 "foreign language" pupils, nine indicated White friends, a further nine said they had Coloured friends, and six reported friendships with Africans. Of the nine "foreign language" pupils at the DSH, three indicated African friends, a further three Coloured friends, and three reported White friends.

An overall view of the investigated grade 8 classes at all five German-language schools in Southern Africa reveals the following statistics: 88% of all "mother tongue" learners at these schools indicate White friends, while only 11% describe their circle of friends as "mixed" or "varied". 49% of the "foreign language" learners report Coloured friends, 39% say they have African friends, and only 11% have White friends.

> There is a significant difference between "mother tongue" and "foreign language" learners (p < 0.01) with regard to the population groups among whom they choose their friends. Whereas most "foreign language" pupils choose their friends from among their "foreign language" class mates, the "mother tongue" pupils choose theirs almost exclusively from among other "mother tongue" students.

Equally instructive is a detailed analysis of the responses given by "foreign language" pupils regarding the difficulty pertaining to multi-cultural friendships:

Table 6: Breakdown (in numbers and percentages) of assessment of difficulty of inter-cultural friendships by "foreign-language" pupils at the five German-language schools in Southern Africa (N = 93)

Foreign language pupils	DSP	DSJ	DHPS	DSK	DSH	No.	%
Difficult	6	5	7	3	4	25	26,9
Not difficult	3	11	15	21	5	55	59,1
Unsure	9	2	2			13	13,9

The findings contained in Table 6 form an interesting contrast to those of Table 5: opposed to the "mother-tongue" learners, and with the exception of the DSP, most "foreign-language" pupils perceive little difficulty in fostering multi-cultural friendships. Admittedly, the readings for the DSJ and the DHPS are unexpected: despite discriminatory behaviour from many "mother-tongue" pupils at these schools, the responses of "foreign-language" pupils are overwhelmingly optimistic. Overall, 26 (or 35%) of the "foreign-language" pupils thought friendships with "mother-tongue" pupils easy because these were regarded as "friendly" and "open". Eleven of the respondents (14%) only liked some of the "mother-tongue" learners, and a further eleven (14%) regarded sport as the only possible area of social contact.

Of those who were sceptical about inter-cultural friendships, 23 (or 31% of the total sample) said they were intimidated by the negative, arrogant attitude of "mother-tongue" learners.

Next, the pupils were asked how they saw their fellow students in the "other" stream. Candidates could choose one or several of the following terms: jolly, eager to help, open, shy, arrogant, mean. A breakdown of the participants according to the school and the "stream" they belonged to, reads as follows:

Table 7: Break-down (in numbers) of "mother-tongue" learners' (MS) opinions of "foreign-language" pupils, and break-down (in numbers) of "foreign-language" pupils' (FS) opinions of "mother-tongue" learners.

School Pupils Characterics	DSP		DSJ		DHPS		DSK		DSH		No.of responses MS	No.of responses FS
	MS	FS	MS	FS	MS	FS	MS	FS	MS	FS		
Friendly*					20	13					20	13
Jolly	10	5	13	6	7	9	10	10	10	4	50	34
Eager to help	10	4	13	5	9	11	8	10	9	5	49	35
Open	10	4	11	4	5	4	8	12	10	1	44	25
Shy	16	2	11		14	3	7	2	2	3	50	10
Arrogant	6	8	39	2	20	7	1	2	3	1	69	20
Mean	2	9	23	10	9	2	2	3	3	1	39	25
Hostile					2	2					2	2

* Added at DHPS only, by teacher who administered the poll

The 192 "mother-tongue" learners submitted a total of 323 responses to this question (i.e. on characteristics attributed to the "foreign-language" pupils at their school). As appears from Table 7, 163 (or 85%) of these referred to likeable characteristics (friendly, jolly, eager to help, and open), 50 (or 26%) to neutral qualities (shy), and 110 (or 57%) to disagreeable character traits (i.e. arrogant, mean, and hostile). Likewise, the majority of "foreign-language" pupils took a positive view of their "mother-tongue" school mates: of a total of 164 responses, 107 (or 116% of the sample of 92 persons) referred to likeable traits, ten (or 11%) recorded neutral characteristics, and 47 (or 51%) mentioned dislikable characteristics.

If one goes through Table 7 school by school, it becomes clear that the "foreign-language" pupils have an overwhelmingly positive view of their "mother tongue" school mates – with the exception of the *DSP*, where 50% of them see the students from the other "stream" as "mean", and 44% regard them as "arrogant". By comparison, the "mother tongue" learners are quite divided on their views about the "foreign language" students, particularly at the *DSP, DSJ* and *DHPS*. Especially at the DSJ, both groups of learners seem to take a relatively dim view of one another. On the other hand, "mother tongue" learners at the *DSK* and *DSH* have a predominantly favourable impression of their "foreign language" fellow pupils.

In conclusion, and despite the considerable number of disagreeable characteristics cited by both sides, Table 7 shows that roughly two-thirds of each group do not experience any deep-seated aversion against the other. In many cases, what prevents friendships from being formed appears to be nothing more serious than lack of contact, or the influence of the parents. In particular, the "foreign-language" pupils seem to be open-minded and well-disposed towards the "mother tongue" learners.

All the respondents – i.e. pupils from the integrated classes at the *DSK* and the *DSH*, as well as learners from the segregated "mother tongue" and "foreign language" streams at the *DSP, DSJ* and *DHPS* – were subsequently asked whether they felt at ease and at home in their classes. With the exception of the DSP, a significant majority of "mother tongue" learners at all these schools responded in the affirmative: 128 "mother tongue" learners (or 67%) felt at home in their classes, 47 (or 25%) were not happy, and 15 (or 8%) were uncertain; two pupils did not reply. The overall pattern was roughly the same for the "foreign language" pupils: 75 (or 82%) liked being in their classes, 13 (or 14%) disliked it, and four (4%) were uncertain.

A feeling of "group cohesion" or "belonging" clearly prevails in all this classes: 60% of the "mother tongue" learners, and 78% of the "foreign language" pupils motivated their positive assessment of the atmosphere prevailing in their classes by referring to their "friendly" class mates, to the "fun" they had together, and to the existence of such a "group feeling".

Subsequently, we asked pupils with whom they spent their breaks at school. As Figures 8 and 9 indicate, a majority of both "mother tongue" learners and "foreign language" pupils prefer to spend play-time with friends from their own cultural groups:

a) Mother-tongue learners

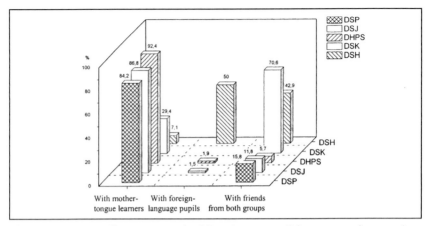

Fig. 8a: Responses (by percentage) of "mother-tongue" learners to the question: With whom do you spend break-time?

b) Foreign-language pupils

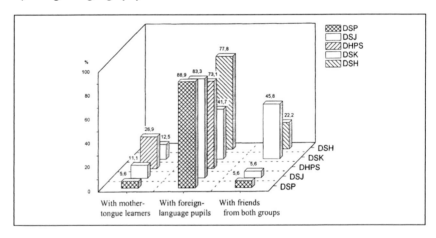

Fig. 8b: Responses (by percentage) of "foreign-language" pupils to the question: With whom do you spend break-time?

On the whole, "mother-tongue learners" and "foreign-language" pupils differ significantly from one another in their choice of company during break-time (p < 0.01).

Next, the pupils were asked whether they wanted "mother-tongue" and "foreign-language" streams at their schools to be integrated into single, combined classes. Figures 9a and 9b demonstrate the responses to this question:

a) Mother-tongue learners

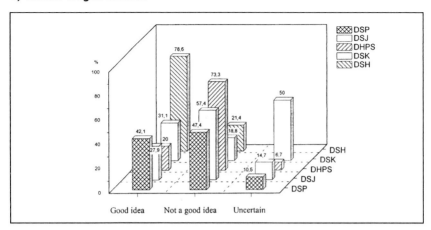

Fig. 9a: *Responses (in percentages) of "mother-tongue" learners to the question: How do you feel about integrating "mother-tongue" and "foreign language" streams at your school into a single, combined class? (N = 181)*

b) Foreign-language pupils

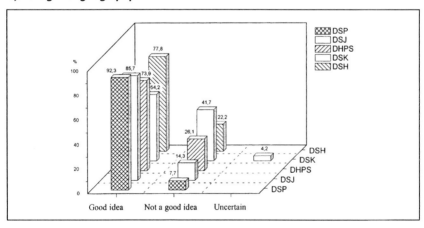

Fig. 9b: *Responses (in percentages) of "foreign-language" pupils to the question: How do you feel about combining "mother tongue" and "foreign language" streams at your school into a single, combined class? (N = 83)*

"Mother tongue" learners and "foreign-language" learners differ significantly from one another in their opinions on combining "mother tongue" and "foreign language" streams at the schools into single, combined classes: while 95 (or 53%) of mother tongue learners opposed this integration, 61 (or 73%) of foreign-language pupils supported it. (Eleven "mother tongue" learners and twelve "foreign language" pupils did not respond to this question.) Of the "mother-tongue" learners in favour of integration, some (17%) wanted more social contact with "foreign language" pupils, or even friendships (22%). Others said the integration of classes would enable students to get to know one another's culture (12%), or to learn one another's language (49%). "Mother-tongue" learners opposed to integration believed this would cause many conflicts, because cultural differences were too great (44%). Others feared a drop in standards (34%), while 21% adopted the attitude that a German-language school was no place for "African" and "Coloured" children; only one pupil (1% of the sample) cited expected language problems as a reason for opposing integration.

The "foreign language" pupils, for their part, motivated their support for integrating the classes by the wish to get to know more "mother tongue" learners, and to learn their language (68%). Others feel that this would promote the social integration they desired, because – according to them – it made no sense to attend a White school, and still be segregated in a "non-White" class; this opinion was expressed by 32%. 58% of the pupils who opposed the integration of their "foreign language" stream with the "mother-tonguers" pointed to their own language problems in a German-language environment; they also criticised their "mother tongue" school mates for frequently speaking German in the presence of "foreign language" pupils. Further criticism was reserved for teachers, who used either German or poor English as medium of instruction, which confused the pupils. Some "foreign language" pupils (23%) said they felt unwanted at the German-language school, and 15% said they had difficulties with some of their school subjects.

Sport and PE at the German-language schools

In response to a question, 166 (or 86%) of the "mother-tongue" learners (N = 192) indicated that they liked sport, as did 81 (or 90%) of the "foreign language" pupils (N = 90). 52% of the "mother-tongue" pupils, and 72% of the "foreign-language" pupils preferred team sports to individual sports.

Asked to name their favourite sport, both groups combined gave a total of 370 responses for 34 different sports disciplines. Among the "mother-tongue" learners, the most popular disciplines were swimming (15%), athletics (13%), and tennis (12%), followed basketball (9%) and volleyball (8%). The "foreign language" pupils, on the other hand, preferred soccer (20%), dancing (14%) and basketball (12%), followed by athletics and tennis (11% each).

Next, the pupils were asked to indicate whether they liked PE classes at school "very much", "much", found it "okay", liked it "not so much", or "not at all". 45% of the "mother-tongue" learners opted for the rather neutral "okay", 42% liked PE, and 13% didn't. Of the "foreign-language" pupils, many of whom had not experienced any PE instruction at their previous schools, most (71%) liked

PE at the German-language school, 26% found it "okay", and a mere 3% disliked it. Subsequently, the pupils were asked how they felt, or would feel, about integrating "mother tongue" and "foreign language" stream learners for joint PE classes; it should be kept in mind that learners at the DHPS, DSK and DSH were already enjoying integrated PE classes, while those at the DSP and DSJ had segregated classes. The following figures indicate the pupils' responses:

Mother tongue learners

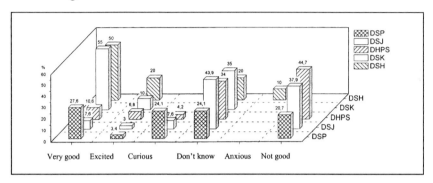

Fig. 10a: *Responses (by percentage) of "mother-tongue" learners at the five German-language schools in Southern Africa to the question: "How do you feel/would you feel about being integrated for PE classes with the "foreign-language pupils" at your school?"*

Foreign-language pupils

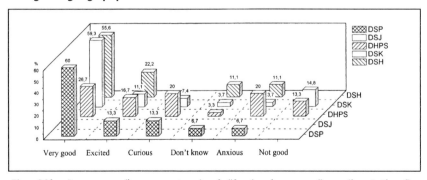

Fig. 10b: *Responses (by percentage) of "foreign-language" pupils at the five German-language schools in Southern Africa to the question: "How do you feel/would you feel about being integrated for PE classes with the "mother-tongue" learners at your school?"*

As Table 10a illustrates, the majority of "mother-tongue" learners feel uncertain about integrated PE classes: 35% have mixed feelings, 34% are opposed, and only 31% in favour of joint PE classes with their "foreign-language" school mates. Table 10b, on the other hand, shows that a majority of the "foreign-language" pupils (74%) were in favour of joint PE instruction, 21% were against, and only 5% were uncertain.

The two groups – "mother-tongue" learners and "foreign-language" pupils – differ significantly from one another in their feelings about participation in joint PE lessons with the other group (p < 0.01).

Summary interpretation of opinion poll findings

The present opinion poll study confirms the initial hypothesis, i.e. that social contact between South Africans of different "population groups" is still very limited. Since all five German-language schools in Southern Africa see themselves as "inter-cultural meeting places", relationships between "mother-tongue" learners and "foreign-language" pupils at all these schools were investigated. With regard to some findings, detailed analysis of the results were believed to be instructive, since each of the five schools developed its own model for "opening up" to previously excluded population groups, and for integrating pupils from these groups. Wherever detailed information was integrated into a more comprehensive presentation of the overall picture, data can be obtained on request from the author via the publisher.

Reasons for choosing a German-language private school

This question highlighted differences in the expectations tied to the attendance of a German-language private school. For the "mother tongue" learners, German descent or nationality, coupled with their parents' wishes to preserve their German language and culture, was often the decisive factor. "Foreign-language" pupils, on the other hand, were often attracted by the prospect of a reputable, interference-fee education at a well-equipped school far away from the troubles and disturbances of the townships.

In the early nineties, when this survey was conducted, it was still quite unusual for Black South Africans to attend schools outside their apartheid-designated residential areas. This explains the nervousness and anxiety with which a quarter of the Black (African or Coloured) children embarked on this educational adventure. Though these apprehensions were perfectly natural, given the history of social, residential and educational segregation in South Africa, many Whites lacked the sensitivity to appreciate or respect these sentiments.

How did the pupils see their schools?

Most of the "mother-tongue" learners feel at home and comfortable at the German-language schools: they usually have numerous friends among their classmates and enjoy the sports facilities. Regrettably, there were pockets of resistance to the admission of "non-White" pupils at all five schools – notably at those, where the "mother-tongue" and the "foreign-language" streams are totally segregated. This can not only be attributed to traditional racism, which many of the answers reveal, or to views held by the pupils' parents; an aggravating factor was undoubtedly the reduction of school fees for "foreign-language" students, which many "mother-tonguers" felt to be unfair. According to this survey prejudices within the German-speaking community still exist. The schools need to address these attitudes on an ongoing basis, although the eventual success of such measures can never be guaranteed.

The impression that the attitude of many "mother-tongue" learners was problematic, was reinforced by the "positive" and "negative" experiences recorded by both groups of pupils: at all five schools, discriminatory behaviour of "mother-tongue" learners towards "foreign language" pupils was criticised, not only by victims of such discrimination, but also by some "mother-tongue" pupils – in fact, 29% of the "mother-tonguers" at the DSP, 16% of those at the DSJ, and 7% at the DHPS castigated their classmates for such attitudes.

The poll indicates that "foreign-language" pupils do not feel welcome at German-language schools. This is clearly the case at the DSP and DSJ, where almost a quarter of the "foreign-language" pupils feel discriminated against by the "mother-tonguers". In addition, some "foreign-language" pupils indicated that they disliked the atmosphere prevailing at the DHPS. It would therefore seem that, especially if "foreign-language" pupils are not integrated into combined classes with "mother-tongue" learners from the very start, at least for non-verbal subjects such as Music, Art and PE, "mother-tongue" learners find it hard to overcome their prejudices, and hostile feelings may arise between the two groups.

In order to gain a better insight into their situation, the "foreign-language" pupils were asked what they missed most at the German school when thinking back of their "old" schools. Many of them must have felt quite lonely, since they were longing for friends or teachers at their previous schools, as well as for their parents. Considering the pupils' age (13 to 14 years), the separation from a familiar environment, coupled with the immersion in unfamiliar surroundings which many experienced as hostile, the situation must have been quite stressful – especially for the "hostel dwellers" among them, who only rejoined their families over weekends.

Pupils also criticised the lack of community spirit and extra-mural activities. What the "foreign-language" pupils did like about their "new" schools, were the sport facilities, their classmates, the teachers, and the choice of subjects. – For both the "mother tounge" learners and the "foreign-language" pupils, agreeable experiences therefore seemed to revolve around their classmates and sport.

Social contact among pupils

As a rule, the "mother tongue learners" had established friendships among their classmates. Even in those schools where their classes were totally or partially integrated with "foreign language" pupils, the "mother tongue learners" chose their friends from among their German-speaking classmates. In fact, both groups, the "mother tonguers" as well as the "foreign language" pupils, tended to seek social contacts within their own "streams" or "groups".

Relations between "mother tongue" and "foreign language" learners

Relations between learners of the two groups cannot be regarded as satisfactory. "Foreign-language" pupils at all five schools complained about the "arrogant and mean" behaviour of "mother tongue learners" towards them. Equally disturbing is the high percentage of "mother tongue learners" (60% of the 107 respondents) who find it difficult to foster friendships with "foreign language" pupils. Apart from typical prejudices, the reasons cited for these difficulties possibly echo views expressed by the pupils' parents, e.g. that Black pupils were "different" and did not belong in a German-language school, etc.

At the *DSH* and *DSK*, inter-group attitudes were more favourable and open-minded than at other schools; there was also a greater prevalence of friendships across the cultural (and language) divide. The fact that the two "streams" at both schools were fully integrated at the time, suggests that such integration produces higher levels of mutual acceptance than either partial integration or, even worse, total segregation. It would therefore seem imperative to at least attempt such integration wherever circumstances permit. Without such integration, it is hard to see how the German-language schools mean to fulfil their chosen role as "inter-cultural meeting places".

Whatever their feelings about the school as a whole, most learners are at ease within their own classes. For instance, pupils in "foreign-language" classes had already developed some form of "community spirit" and "sense of belonging" by the end of the first school term. On its own, this may be positive development, though it does seem to run counter to the aims and aspirations of an "inter-cultural meeting place". This is also reflected in Figures 8a and 8b, which indicate that most pupils spend break-time with friends from their own "cultural group" (Also in this regard, the *DSK* and the *DSH* – with their integrated classes - are welcome exceptions. The same does not apply to the *DHPS* and the *DSJ*, although they are also partially integrated.).

Surprisingly, the two groups differed significantly from one another in their assessment of the difficulties of forming inter-cultural friendships: while the majority of "foreign-language" pupils saw no obstacles to inter-cultural friendships, most "mother-tongue" learners were rather apprehensive.

A possible explanation for this difference is the fact that "foreign-language" pupils at these German-language schools already constitute a "heterogenous" group, consisting of Coloured and African pupils; already having overcome one "group barrier", it is possible that these students are more confident and open-minded about these assumed obstacles. Another explanation are possible differences in the concept of friendship: what rates as a mere "acquaintance" in one context, may be termed "friendship" in another. Asked about friends at their "old" schools, "foreign-language" pupils consistently indicated a higher number of "friends" than their "mother-tongue" counterparts.

A comparison between Figures 8a and 8b suggests that problems originate not so much within the "foreign-language" group, but rather from the "mother-tongue" learners' resistance to "integration" and to the concept of an "inter-cultural meeting place". Surprisingly, many "mother-tongue" learners at the DSP, where the two "streams" are segregated, are quite amenable to the suggestion of integrating both streams. On the other hand, many "mother-tongue" pupils at the DSK, who have first-hand experience of integrated classes, are opposed to integration, citing cultural differences and a fear of "lower standards" as reasons for their opposition. Remarkably, though many "foreign-language" pupils complain about the German-speakers' condescending and discriminatory behaviour, all "foreigners" are in favour of integrating with the "mother-tongue" stream. It is also quite revealing that, according to research conducted at South African schools (roughly at the same time as the present study), White South African pupils were far less opposed to integrating their schools than the German-speaking pupils at the five German-language schools in Southern Africa.

Sport and PE at the German-language schools

Sport appears to be of great importance to both the "mother-tongue learners" and the "foreign-language pupils": many respondents cited it as one of the things they had liked at the German school, and consequently as one of their "favourable" memories. Whereas the "foreign-language pupils" clearly preferred team sports, the preferences of "mother-tongue learners" were divided between team sports and individual sports. As for integrated PE classes, the greater open-mindedness of "foreign-language pupils" was once more evident, as Figures 10a and 10b indicate: three quarters of the "foreign-language" pupils were in favour of joint PE instruction, as opposed to only one-third of the "mother-tongue" learners. The exception were once again learner at the DSK and the DSH, whose experience of joint PE classes had prompted a more open-minded and favourable response. Unfortunately, the "foreign-language" pupils at the DSJ did not answer this question: their answers could have been instructive.

By way of conclusion, it is clear that greater efforts are required, if the German-language schools in Southern Africa are to become true "inter-cultural meeting places". Information workshops to generate a favourable attitude among "mother tongue learners" and their parents appear to be just as necessary as welcoming and introductory functions for the "foreign-language" pupils and their parents. For as many subjects as is practically possible, learners of both "streams" should be integrated into single classes from the earliest possible stage onwards. Joint classes in non-verbal subjects, such as Music, Art and PE, should be compulsory. Possibilities of using sport and PE as tools for social integration need to be investigated, because sport is very popular among both groups of pupils.

Overall, greater efforts are required to create occasions where "mother-tonguers" and "foreign-language" pupils can get to know one another and interact socially, because it is clear that many "foreign-language" pupils are not yet "at home" in their new schools. Without such initiatives, the schools could be faced with a new generation of "drop-outs": there was no significant difference between the unfavourable experiences of the previous "drop-outs" (cf. chapter 3.1) and the more recent intake, or between what both generations of "foreign-language pupils" found lacking, and longed for, after changing to the German school.

The results of the present study confirm the initial hypothesis, i.e. that there is still very little social contact between members of different "population groups" in South Africa, even between children attending the same school. Secondly, they show that the general "atmosphere" prevailing at a school is of vital importance for the decision of African and Coloured children to either continue their education at a particular institution, or to change to a different school.

The research into the "drop-out" phenomenon (chapter 3.1) and into the experiences of learners in the early nineties (chapter 3.2) had a great effect on the planning of the further studies (chapter 3.3 and chapter 3.4). In particular, this applies to the role of sport, which the first two studies had shown to be popular among all pupils. To my knowledge, the following study constitutes the first empirical investigation of the possibility of using sport as a tool for integration during the initial "contact phase" of disadvantaged "foreign-language" pupils at a formerly culturally homogenous school.

3.3 "Where Do these Children Come from?" A Look at the Socio-economic Background to Integration Problems at SA Schools

After speaking to a fair number of "drop-outs" from newly-integrated private schools (cf. chapter 3.1 above), and realising that pupils subsequently admitted to these schools had similar problems (cf. chapter 3.2 above), I was convinced that it was necessary to take one step further back in order to find solutions. If we wanted to make Coloured and African pupils feel at home at the DSK, and help them to "settle in", we first had to take a closer look at these pupils' prior schooling, and at the norms and expectations they brought with them. Why were these pupils, and the African girls in particular, so shy? Was the significance of sport to these pupils such, that one could realistically hope to promote social integration by this means?

Education and training are among the areas where the after-effects of apartheid are most strongly felt. Recent policy changes and controversies surrounding OBE (outcomes-based education) show how difficult it is to transform the inherited education system. A single, unitary administrative structure is a fairly recent acquisition, and the authorities have hardly had the opportunity to deal adequately with the unfortunate apartheid legacy. As late as 1995, institutional segregation in education continued to exist in the form of separate government departments for the various population groups: the Department of Education and Training (DET) for Africans, the Department of Education and Culture (House of Representatives) for Coloureds, and the various provincial Education Departments for the formerly White schools. Though no longer enforced by law, the racial segregation of residential areas has a long tradition, and is deeply entrenched in habit and socio-economic conditions. This, in turn, supports the continued factual (if not legally enforced) segregation of most educational institutions: most children, particularly in the poorer areas, continue to attend the local school, if only to avoid the additional expense of having to travel further to and from school.

However, where schools are geographically accessible to more than one group, the lines of segregation are gradually becoming blurred. The same applies to private schools, and to African and Coloured children from high-income households. Moreover, ever since apartheid in education was officially abandoned in 1991, some government schools in formerly White residential areas have been striving to attract African and Coloured pupils by means of bursaries, reduced school fees, and/or bridging courses.

In order to gain a more accurate understanding of the situation at African and Coloured township schools, I conducted the following research. The sample consisted of 478 pupils at 12 primary schools in the African township, Khayelitsha, and 92 pupils at three schools in the predominantly Coloured residential areas Mitchell's Plain and Zonnebloem. There were 361 girls and 209 boys, all of them enrolled in grade 7. Since I administered the questionnaires personally, a return rate of 100% was achieved.

Like all government schools, the three traditionally Coloured schools in this study have been open to all population groups since 1991. However, no White pupils had enrolled by the time this study was conducted. Neither had any African pupils been admitted to the grade 7 class at Mitchell's Plain Primary School. Zonnebloem Primary, however, had 4 African pupils, or 14% of the total intake, in grade 7 at the time, and Holy Cross Primary's grade 7 class had 14 African pupils (50% of the class).

a) Pupils' socio-cultural situation

1. Age

At the Coloured schools under consideration, all grade 7 pupils were between 12 and 14 years of age, with the following four exceptions: one pupil was 11, two were 15, and one was 16 years old. By contrast, the age of grade 7 pupils at the African schools varied between 12 and 20 years, with the following distribution: 262 (or 61%) were between 12 and 14, 122 (or 28%) were between 15 and 16, 10 (or 7%) were between 17 and 19, and one pupil (0.2%) was 20 years old.

2. Family size

Most African pupils came from relatively big families: 120 (or 27%) had one or two siblings, 201 (or 45%) had three or four, and 90 (or 20%) had five or six siblings; 36 (or 8%) even had between seven and eleven. On average, the Coloured families were considerably smaller: 57 (or 67%) had one or two siblings, 23 (or 27%) had three or four; only three pupils (3%) had five siblings, and one each had six and seven siblings respectively.

3. Transport to and from school

The overwhelming majority of African pupils (76%) walked to school: 68% had to walk 15 minutes or less, a further 24% walked 30 to 45 minutes. By contrast, most Coloured pupils travelled by car (29%), by bus (15%), or by some other means of transport (22%); only 33% walked.

4. Meals

The survey showed that many children, especially among the Africans, lacked a sufficient or balanced diet. Most of the African children had bread (31%) or porridge (40%) for breakfast, some 23% only drank a cup of tea; 15% neither ate nor drank before going to school. Most of the Coloured pupils (87%) did have breakfast, with most (70%) eating oats porridge, while 23% had bread.

The majority of African pupils (86%) had lunch at school, which consisted either of bread and tea (53%), or of a sandwich with egg or fish (20%). Some African pupils went home for lunch (14%), while 5% did not have any lunch at all. As for the Coloured pupils, roughly two-thirds had lunch at school (66.2%), and one-third (34%) went home for lunch. Once again, most pupils had either bread and tea (75%) for lunch, or a sandwich (43%).

Approximately a quarter of the African respondents went without supper, whereas roughly three-quarters had a rice meal (74%). Almost all Coloured pupils did have supper (97%), in most cases (89%) also a meal consisting of rice and meat or fish.

5. Pastimes

Asked how they spent their time after school, the respondents cited a wide range of activities:

Pupils' hobbies/pastimes

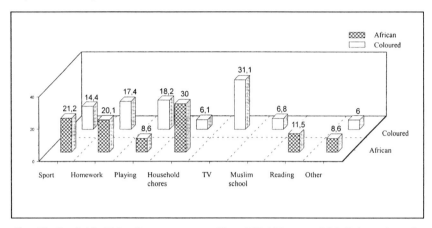

Fig. 11: Pupils' hobbies (in percentages; N = 477 African and 92 Coloured pupils; multiple responses permitted)

As Figure 11 indicates, commuted to percentages, 143 African pupils replied that they performed household chores (i.e. cleaning, washing, doing the dishes) after school, 101 participated in sport (mostly soccer), 96 studied or did their school homework, 55 read, and 41 played in the street. Most of the Coloured pupils, 41 in all, said they spent their time watching TV, 24 played, and 23 did their school homework or studied. 19 of the Coloured respondents practised some form of sport, 9 attended Muslim schools in the afternoon, and 8 performed household chores. Two Coloured pupils each indicated that they spent their time with the following activities respectively: eating, shopping, visiting friends, and chatting on the telephone.

Under this caption, certain gender-specific differences emerged, as did some group- or culture-specific differences. For instance, among the Coloured pupils, only the girls performed household chores, whereas both girls and boys mentioned "sport" and "playing" with roughly the same frequency. Among African pupils, on the other hand, more than one-third of the girls (34%), and slightly less than one-quarter (23%) of the boys performed household chores in the afternoon; more than one-third of the boys (35%), but only 13% of the girls practise sport; 22% of the girls and 16% of the boys did their school homework or studied, and 12% of the girls read in their spare time, as opposed to 10% of the boys.

6. Class size

As far as the size of school classes is concerned, the following data was gathered:

Class size

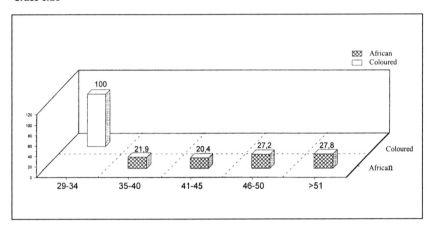

Fig. 12: *Data (in percentages) on the size of pupils' school classes (N = 464 African and 89 Coloured pupils)*

Figure 12 indicates that classes in formerly (and traditionally) African schools were much bigger than in schools in Coloured areas. 18% of African pupils' classes had 51-60 pupils, and 10% had classes of 61-75 pupils.

7. Friends

Many pupils indicated a relatively high number of friends: 35% said they had as many as 10 to 32 friends in their class or at school. Most, however (41%) cited two to five friends, 18% included six to nine persons in their circle of friends, and 6% said they had only one school friend.

b) How did the pupils regard their school?

The following question attempted to establish what pupils liked and/or disliked at their schools.

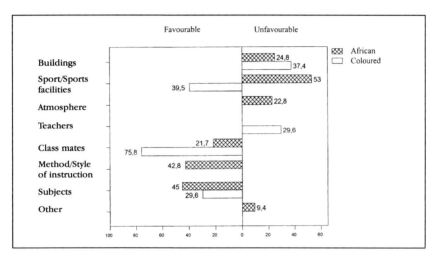

Fig. 13: Pupils' responses (in percentages) to the question: What do you like/dislike at your school? (N = 478 African and 91 Coloured pupils: multiple responses allowed

From Figure 13 it appears that, from among the alternatives offered, African pupils most liked their school subjects and the style of instruction; class mates were cited as a further "favourable". Least popular among African pupils were sport/sports facilities and the school buildings. Under the "other" category within the "unfavourable" field, 9% of African pupils cited corporal punishment. By contrast, the Coloured pupils were most favourably impressed with their class mates, sport, and the school subjects; the least favourable impression was left by the school buildings, and by the teachers.

Asked what was lacking at their schools, and what they missed most, African pupils mentioned (in order of frequency) sport and sports facilities, particular school subjects (e.g. Natural Science, Health Education, Geography), and items of equipment (e.g. books, films, musical instruments). Further desiderata were more teachers and/or more instruction, and improvements/additions to the school buildings and/or facilities (e.g. toilets, windows, showers, school bus, school yard). – Like their African fellow-pupils, the Coloureds mostly wished for sport/sports facilities at their schools. Other wishes included a greater number of friends, improvements/additions to school buildings and/or facilities (e.g. toilets, lockers, school bus), additional school subjects (Natural Science and History), and equipment (books, films).

c) What was pupils' attitude to/experience of sport?

In order to assess their attitude towards sport, the pupils were asked which sport codes or disciplines they liked, where they learnt/acquired skills in these, and which forms of sport they practised outside the institutional frame of the school.

Do the pupils like sport?

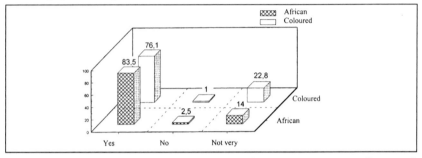

Fig. 14: Pupils responses (in percentages) to the question: Do you like sport? (N = 442 African and 92 Coloured pupils; multiple responses allowed)

Figure 14 indicates that the overwhelming majority of both the African and the Coloured pupils liked sport. Of the African pupils, 62% spend 1 to 2 hours per week on sports training per week outside school structures, 27% train 3 to 5 hours per week, and 10% train even 6 to 10 per week. Most Coloured pupils (77%) practise sport for 1 to 2 hours per week, a further 18% train 3 to 4 hours weekly. The following illustration gives an impression of the pupils' preferred sport codes and disciplines:

Favourite sport codes/disciplines

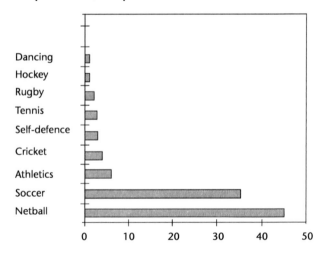

Fig. 15: Pupils' responses (in percentages) to the question: Name your favourite sport. (N = 410)

With African (35%) and Coloured (19%) boys, soccer was the most popular sport, while the African (40%) and Coloured (19%) girls liked netball best. Cricket and tennis were popular with both genders, scoring average approval rates of 18% and 13% respectively. This result confirms the relative popularity of team sports among African pupils, as compared to individual disciplines: 77% of the African respondents said they preferred team sports, as opposed to the 18% who voted for individual sports, and 5% who said they liked both. Among the Coloured students, 70% liked team sports, 25% preferred individual sports, and 5% said they liked both. – The overwhelming majority of the African pupils (89%; N = 397) said they had learnt their skills in these sports at school, either during PE classes or extra-murally, 4% said they had gathered some experience from other areas (e.g. Natal, the Transkei) where they had previously lived, 4% had acquired their knowledge at home, and 1% in his/her congregation. 22% of the Coloured pupils (N = 185) said they had learnt to practise their sport at a sport club or stadium, 19% at school, 16% at home, and 5% in a church group/congregation.

Next, the pupils were asked which sport codes or disciplines they practised outside the institutional framework of the school. In total, 269 African and 91 Coloured pupils responded to this question; of these, 52 African and 49 Coloured pupils said they did not participate in any sport. The rest responded as follows:

Table 9: *List of sport codes and disciplines practised by African (N = 217) and Coloured (N = 42) pupils outside the institutional framework of their school (multiple responses allowed)*

Pupils Sport code	African pupils Number %		Coloured pupils Number %	
Soccer	77	35. 5%	10	23.8%
Netball	46	21.2%	8	19%
Small Games	28	12.9%	2	4.7%
Dancing	14	6.5%	3	7.1%
Body building	14	6.5%		
Basketball	12	5.5%	3	7.1%
Cricket	11	4.6%	6	14.3%
Jogging/running	6	2.8%	4	9.5%
Softball	5	2.3%		
Swimming	4	1.8%	6	14.3%

Table 9 indicates that 45% of the responding African pupils practise some sport in their spare time. Relatively few of them – 18% - belong to sports clubs; 29% of the club-affiliated African pupils played soccer, 3% to cricket, and 2% each of the following respectively: running/jogging, basketball, dancing, and softball. Of the Coloured pupils, 30% belonged to a sports club, where they play soccer (20%), netball (14%), basketball (7%), or dance (7%).

In order to improve access to sport in the townships, 46% of the Africans among the pupils believed that more sports grounds were needed, as did 56% of the Coloureds. Other items on the pupils' wish list were "more coaches/trainers" (44% of the Africans mentioned this, and 41% of the Coloureds), and "more equipment" (37% of the Africans, 54% of the Coloureds). Multiple responses concerning these desiderate were allowed.

d) School sport

Which sport codes/disciplines are practised at township schools?

Sport codes/disciplines practised at school

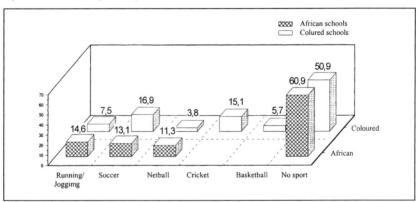

Fig. 16: Pupils' answers (in percentages) to the question: Which sport codes/disciplines are practised at your school? (N = 389 African pupils; N = 27 Coloured pupils)

Figure 16 indicates the high percentage of pupils who enjoy no sport or PE instruction at school, especially in the African townships. The only sport codes practised at African schools in the mornings, i.e. in the course of the school day, are running/jogging, soccer, and netball. Most sports are practised in an unstructured, not systematically planned or organised way, except in the case of players who represent the school as members of the school team; this state of affairs was confirmed in interviews with teachers and pupils at the schools concerned. 27% of all pupils are members of such school teams. **61% of the**

African pupils in the present sample indicated that they did not practise any sport at school. Even for the members of school teams at African schools, netball (43%) for the girls, soccer (33%) for the boys, and athletics (running/jogging – 8%) appear to be the only available options.

At the predominantly Coloured schools, only about half of the pupils have access to sport during normal school hours, with 17% participating in soccer, 15% in cricket, 7% in running/jogging, 6% in basketball, and 4% in netball. At one of the Coloured schools investigated, no PE instruction was offered. 51% of the Coloured respondents indicated that they did not practise any sport at school. 17% of the Coloured pupils are members of school teams, and are coached/trained in the afternoons, mainly in netball (45%) and soccer (26%).

What sports facilities/opportunities/equipment are most sorely missed by the pupils?

Table 10: List of desiderata regarding sports facilities at their schools as noted by African (N = 478) and Coloured (N = 92) pupils (multiple responses allowed).

Pupils Item lacking	African pupils (N=478)		Coloured pupils (N=92)	
	Number of responses	%	Number of responses	%
Swimming pool	292	61.1%	77	83.7%
Showers	180	37.7%	41	44.6%
Bats/raquets/equipment	168	35.2%	22	23.9%
Tennis courts	154	32.2%	40	43.5%
Gymnasium	143	29.9%	16	17.4%
Changing rooms	132	27.6%	37	40.2%
Coaches/trainers	107	22.4%	22	23.9%

Table 10 indicates that pupils' wishes for improving their schools' sports facilities are varied and wide-ranging. Although Cape Town is a coastal town, with both the Indian and the Atlantic oceans lapping the shores of the Cape Peninsula, few African and Coloured children can swim, because the townships offer no opportunities of acquiring this skill. Under apartheid, public swimming pools were racially segregated, and almost all pools were built in White areas, and reserved for use by Whites under the provisions of the Group Areas Act. Many shameful cases of the enforcement of this "petty apartheid" have been recorded (cf. Roberts, 1992, p. 19). As for the beaches, these were also racially segregated, with the best bathing spots reserved for Whites, and Africans and Coloureds often being relegated to unsafe, stony beaches. This background information may explain why a swimming pool takes pride of place in the collective wish lists of African and Coloured students, as illustrated above.

e) What benefits did the pupils gain, or expect to gain, from practising sport?

Most of the pupils (58% of the African and 61% of the Coloured pupils) hoped to improve their health and fitness by practising sport. Others (15% of the Africans, 20% of the Coloureds) hoped to meet more friends through sport. The desire to achieve success indicated an interesting difference between the two groups: while 16% of the African children cited this motivation for participating in sport, only 4% of the Coloured students subscribed to this reason. There were similar differences in the actual gains pupils believed to have gained through sport: while more than one-third (35%) of the African pupils saw the greatest actual advantage in having met and won new friends, Coloured pupils rated an increase in self-assurance as the greatest advantage derived from sport (42%). Conversely, new friendships and social contacts took second place with the Coloured students (18%), while the African pupils relegated the gain in self-confidence to third place (13%), the second place being taken by the acquisition of self-discipline. 10% of the African, and 15% of the Coloured students felt they had actually become fitter by practising sport.

f) What role did the pupils attribute to sport in promoting social integration?

Interestingly, there was a significant difference (p < 0.01) between the two groups regarding their eagerness to participate in intercultural sports, and in their assessment of sport as an agent for social integration.

Asked about the social/cultural composition of the sports class or group they would most like to join, the African pupils (N = 469) responded as follows:

- 75% favoured a multi-cultural group;
- 15% preferred an all-African group;
- 6% favoured a White group;
- 3% favoured a Coloured group.

As reasons for their choices, the respondents named the quest for peace and understanding between different population groups, and the prospect of meeting friends from all groups; 11% mentioned the wish to learn a further language.

By comparison, the Coloured pupils (N = 92) answered the same question as follows:

- 89% wanted to practise sport as members of a multicultural group;
- 4% favoured an all-Coloured group;
- 3% (three African pupils enrolled at predominantly Coloured schools) preferred an African group;
- 3% (one African and two Coloured pupils) favoured a White sport class or group.

These students' choices, too, were mainly motivated by a striving for peace, and by the wish to meet friends from other population groups (83%). A further 9% said they wanted to explore hitherto unfamiliar surroundings, and 3% wanted to improve their English.

Three-quarters (75%) of the African pupils were of the opinion, that sport could help to overcome the divisions between the different population groups in their traditionally segregated residential areas; 5% doubted this, and 19% were undecided. 72% motivated their optimism by saying people would form acquaintances and friendships through sport, since sport made people forget their differences; 8% gave no reasons for their answers. 3%, no doubt from among the sceptical 5%, said that because of apartheid, multi-cultural sport would lead to trouble. More than two-thirds of the Coloured pupils shared the belief that sport could help to bring together people from different cultural backgrounds, one pupil (1% of the sample) doubted this, and 30% were uncertain. As reasons for these beliefs, 78% said sport helped to promote understanding, and thus to build friendships, 8% believed integrated sport groups would give them access to better facilities, and 7% gave no reason for their convictions.

The pupils were then asked which groups could, in their opinion, be induced by sport to form friendships. They responded as follows (multiple responses were allowed):

		African pupils	Coloured pupils
a)	Whites, Africans, Coloureds	82%	84%
b)	The rich and the poor	32%	23%
c)	Men and women	29%	22%

In conclusion, I wish to quote a few of the pupils' statements reflecting or motivating their conviction that sport could be used as an agent for social reconciliation and integration:

- "sports builds us and in sports we must unite"
- "if we play sports together, we get to know each other"

- "sport is for everybody, and in sport we are equal"
- "we will play together and become friends"
- "we share ideas and help each other"
- "new South Africa – in all the years we didn't have a chance to relate".

Summary interpretation of findings relating to pupils in Khayelitsha, Zonnebloem and Mitchell's Plain

The present findings regarding the living conditions of pupils in Cape Town's African and Coloured townships were informed by the author's experiences and observations in these areas.

Variable: socio-economic conditions

Children growing up in South Africa's African townships continue to be the most disadvantaged section of the country's youth, as a comparison with the living conditions of their White and Coloured compatriots readily demonstrates. Many of come from big families and have as many as eleven siblings. Many African children are over age when they enter school, others have to repeat one or more classes before they pass. It is therefore hardly surprising that more than one-third of African children (36%) only leave primary school at the age of 15 to 20 years, whereas most Coloured children reach this educational stage by the age of 12 to 14.

The living conditions of many African children are determined by stark poverty, which manifests itself in an unsufficient and unbalanced diet. More than one-third of the African pupils in the research group take their first meal of the day during lunch-break at school. Even then, this meal often consists only of bread and tea and can hardly be regarded as nutritious or rich in vitamins. (Apart from the physical effects of this unhealthy situation, its emotional and psychological dimension is reflected in the fact that many children were too embarrassed to say that they had gone without breakfast, and claimed to have started the day with a meal of "steak" or "cake".) Roughly a quarter of the African children further indicated that they usually went without supper. Interviews with teachers revealed that poverty and malnutrition were both worse and more widespread than the pupils' responses suggested. By contrast, most Coloured pupils enjoyed a healthier diet, which consisted of porridge for breakfast, a school lunch of bread and tea, and regular meals at supper-time.

Similar differences were evident in pupils' spare time activities: whereas almost one-third of the African children had to perform household duties (washing dishes and clothes, house-cleaning) when they got home from school, half of the Coloured pupils watched television or played games. The only distraction available to many African children – if household chores and school homework allowed – was sport, mostly soccer. The situation of African girls was even less enviable than that of the boys: one-third of them have to perform household duties before they can do their school homework.

These living conditions are typical of an African township (at least, they were, when this study was conducted). Although the unemployment rate is high, low wages usually force both parents to be economically active. Travel between the township home and the place of employment in town often takes longer than an hour in either direction. Since public transport is often unreliable, many parents leave home very early (in many cases before 6.00 a.m.), and the elder daughters are charged with organising breakfast, getting the younger siblings to and from school, preparing lunch (if any), and performing household duties. The parents often come home from work late, leaving very little time for family life.

Nor is school life for African pupils at township schools a bed of roses: more often than not, the situation is marked by huge classes, inadequate class room space and furniture, a lack of teachers, and the use (or abuse) of corporal punishment. Often, the schools possess no sports facilities or equipment, and none of the African primary schools offer PE instruction. Consequently, two-thirds of the African pupils put sports and sports facilities on their school wish list, along with particular subjects, and the provision of teaching materials, such as books and musical instruments.

At the schools in predominantly Coloured areas, the situation is better, though far from ideal. Class sizes are manageable, and basic equipment (class room furniture, etc.) is adequate. Apart from a variety of school subjects and the sports facilities, Coloured pupils particularly like their class mates. Even so, many Coloured pupils regret the limited range of choice open to them in terms of school subjects and sport codes/disciplines and facilities, which one-third of the research group criticised.

Considering that the research focussed on primary school children, it was remarkable to what extent the respondents were aware of the shortcomings at their schools: asked to suggest improvements, many called for the repair or upgrading of school buildings, the provision of equipment, and a wider choice of school subjects. Both the African and the Coloured pupils emphasised the lack of sports facilities and trainers/coaches/instructors.

For instance, in the black township Khayelitsha, where most of the African respondents lived, there were at the time nor more than one stadium and six soccer fields for a population of about 600 000. By contrast, many of the Coloured schools had at least some (albeit insufficient) sports facilities and equipment, such as hard courts and balls.

At the time of this research, hardly any predominantly African primary school offered any PE instruction; there were also many predominantly Coloured schools which could not afford to do so. Reasons for this omission were severe financial shortages in the Department of Education, the lack of infrastructure, the shortage of qualified instructors, the absence of sports facilities and equipment, and a lack of interest and motivation on the part of teachers and school principals.

The provision of extramural sports training and coaching was equally erratic (and often non-existent). As Figure 16 indicates, more than half of the Coloured pupils, and almost two-thirds of the African pupils, had no opportunity of practising sport at primary school. Some sports codes and disciplines were being practised, in an "ad hoc" and unsystematic way, during playtime. Not surprisingly, the lack of equipment and facilities not only severely restricts the number of disciplines practised at school, it also undermines the motivation of teachers to involve themselves in sport.

As a substitute for proper and regular PE instruction, many schools maintain school teams for athletics, soccer (only for boys) and netball (only for girls), which, under the auspices of USSASA, compete with the teams of other, equally under-resourced schools. Athletics coaching usually takes place before school, from 7.00 a.m. onwards, and is often restricted to running (for lack of equipment for other disciplines). A handful of other codes and disciplines (cricket, basketball) are offered at those Coloured schools which are lucky enough to possess the necessary equipment. The poignancy of this under-provision and lack of resources is illustrated by Figure 14, which shows that most African and Coloured pupils valued sport as a means of improving their health and fitness, and as an opportunity to make acquaintances and meet friends.

The present research showed little or no gender-specific differences in the way Coloured youths spend their spare time: both girls and boys named "watching television" as their favourite pastime. By contrast, gender is a determining factor in the spare-time activities of African youths: household chores and reading are much more prevalent among the girls than the boys; whereas boys cited sport as their most important pastime, it occupied fourth place in the girls' list of priorities.

A poignant discrepancy exists between the pupils' favourable attitude towards sport on the one hand, and their actual lack of opportunities to engage in this pastime on the other. This discrepancy affects the African pupils more heavily than the Coloured children, and is worse for girls than for boys, leaving African girls in the least favourable position. This finding must be read together with the gender-specific role prescriptions and expectations to which many girls are still being subjected (cf. the paragraph Variable: gender below).

In order to gain a first impression of the possible role of sport as a tool for social integration, the pupils were questioned on their preferences regarding the demographic composition of sports groups or classes. Three-quarters of the African pupils voted for a "mixed" or integrated group, although none of them had any prior experience of practising sport in such a group. As for the Coloured pupils, the more advanced status of sports facilities at their schools as opposed to the African schools, as well as the greater exposure to television, appears to strengthen the wish for social integration on the sports field: nearly all the Coloured respondents voted for this option.

The present enquiry did not specifically focus on the topic "social integration through sport"; rather, it was intended as a first exploration of the living conditions and attitudes of African and Coloured pupils who had not had any personal experience of integrated schools or sports clubs. For this reason, both the scope and focus of the question does not allow for far-reaching conclusions. Nevertheless, the reasons pupils gave for their wish to be part of an integrated sports group or club were very encouraging.

Appendix: Gender as social factor/variable

In the course of this study, it became clear why sport is such a neglected and rare pastime among (particularly) African girls and women: this phenomenon relates directly to the functions assigned to them within the family and household. If African girls and women only devote little time and energy to sport, this does not necessarily point to a lack of interest on their part; rather, the reasons have more to do with tradition, and with gender-specific roles and expectations. I gained this impression through personal observation, and found it variously confirmed when speaking to pupils, their parents, and to educationists. The following, therefore, is an attempt to characterise the general influence of tradition on the involvement of women/girls in sport.

As a vital phenomenon or element of superstructure, the influence of tradition in African society is pervasive (Seppänen uses the term "superstructural phenomenon" for various determinants of behaviour in African society, such as differentiated social expectations, values and norms etc.; cf. Abel, 1984, p. 142). Many areas of social life, and leisure in particular, are governed by a tradition which assigns gender-specific rights and duties to all members of society, and thus determines to a great extent how leisure time is to be spent (cf. Weische-Alexa, in Abel, 1984, p. 142). Furthermore, this tradition not only ties women to the homestead and household, but also requires their submission to male partners or family members, which makes active participation in competitive sport virtually impossible.

The societal expectations foisted on women, and their position within society, emerged clearly in a number of interviews I conducted with members of the first female soccer club in the African township Gugulethu outside Cape Town. As the leader of the club, Winnie Qhuma, put it:

Women in the townships are expected to do all the domestic chores at home. Men very seldom assist if the women are working during the day. Women are expected to dress conservatively by not wearing clothes that will expose their bodies, and they are not allowed to wear pants or go hatless. Obedience to the wishes of the husband and in-laws is expected. She even has to conform to the traditional 'African body shape', i.e. big hips and buttocks. She is not expected to participate in any physical activities outside the home. (cf. Keim, 1996, pp. 84f)

93

Similar attitudes are widespread in South Africa, particularly in rural areas, and can also be found in parts of Muslim and Afrikaner society. Even where obstacles and prohibitions have been removed or revoked, they often persist as taboos, and instil fear of societal reprisals. As the goal-keeper of Winnie's club, Polisa, said of her family:

> *When they realised that I have less time for cooking and that expenses... have to be covered, they were not so keen anymore (to let me play).*

Pini, another team member, encountered a different problem with her teacher:

> *She didn't believe that I was a girl because of (my) playing soccer, so I had to go to the principal's office, where the misunderstanding was sorted out.*

Against this backdrop, the active participation of girls in sport must still be regarded as a "problem area", i.e. as an area of foreseeable (behavioural) conflict. The situation appears to be comparable to that of Islamic women (cf. Weische-Alexa in Abel, 1984, p. 143).

3.4 Personal Experiences in the First "Multi-cultural" Class at a Private School

At the beginning of each school year, a number of non-German-speaking pupils, or "foreign-language" pupils, are admitted by each of the five German-language private schools in Southern Africa. For these pupils, the first school term is a "familiarization" or "acclimatization" period, during which they acquaint themselves with their new school environment. Each of the five schools has its own regime regarding the "foreign-language" pupils' first two years of instruction: during class-time, they are either fully segregated, as a "foreign-language stream", from the "mother tongue learners", or they are fully integrated with the "mother tongue stream", or they form separate "foreign-language" classes, but take joint lessons with the "mother-tongue learners" in non-verbal subjects, such as Music, Arts and Crafts, and Physical Education/ Sport.

According to the curriculum, PE instruction in the first term is devoted to individual sports, such as athletics and swimming. In 1991, the *DSK (Deutsche Schule Kapstadt/German School, Cape Town)* for the first time admitted 8 African pupils to a single, "integrated" class. The following year (1992), twelve Coloured pupils were also integrated into this class, which by then had reached grade 5 level. All the "foreign language" pupils had attended preparatory extra-mural language and mathematics classes, prior to their admission to the school. Together with 19 "mother-tongue" learners, these 20 "foreign language" pupils constituted two culturally integrated, co-ed grade 5 classes with a combined total of 39 pupils between the ages of 12 and 15.

At the beginning of the school year 1992, I was appointed as PE teacher to this class. For the purposes of PE, the pupils were divided along gender lines into two separate, although culturally integrated classes. The composition of each of these classes was as follows:

a) Girls' class: 16 "foreign language" pupils (eleven Coloureds, five Africans, plus nine (German-speaking, White) "mother-tongue" learners, i.e. a total of 25 girls

b) Boys' class: four "foreign language" pupils (three African, one Coloured), plus ten (German-speaking, White) "mother-tongue" learners, i.e. a total of 14 boys.

As PE teacher of both classes, I had the ideal opportunity to investigate the possible role of sport (and of Physical Education) in promoting social interaction between members of previously segregated population groups. I also had an opportunity to test a further hypothesis, i.e. that team sports promote social interaction (and integration) more effectively than individual sports. The investigation was conducted as follows: in the boys' class, the first term was devoted to individual sports, such as athletics and swimming, as determined by the curriculum. In the girls' class, however, the emphasis in the first term fell on ball games, such as football, handball, and small games with a ball. In the second term, the regimen was turned around. At the beginning of the year, after the first term, and at the end of the second term, both classes completed a questionnaire under the teacher's supervision. In addition, three sociograms and a systematic observation were conducted with both classes.

a) Pupils' socio-cultural background

The composition of both classes has already been outlined above. – Because of the long distances involved, all of the African pupils, and two of the Coloured pupils, were accommodated in the hostel on the school premises. The other ten Coloured pupils commuted between their homes and school by bus, each trip taking them more than an hour. The majority of "mother-tongue" learners traveled between home and school by car; none of them spent more than 15 minutes on the road. The African pupils had attended primary schools in one of Cape Town's townships; their classes had numbered between 42 and 50. Four of the eight African candidates spoke Xhosa as first language, one was Zulu-speaking, and three spoke English at home. The Coloured pupils had attended primary schools in one of the "Coloured" townships, where the size of classes varied between 30 and 35 pupils. Eight of the twelve pupils spoke English at home, the remaining four both English and Afrikaans.

Next, the pupils were asked whether they had any hobbies, and multiple responses were allowed. A total of 13 hobbies were indicated by the eight African pupils, the twelve Coloured pupils gave a total of 25 responses, and the

19 White learners mentioned a total of 34 hobbies. As expected, the advantaged White learners thus recorded both the greatest number, and the broadest variety, of pastimes. It is instructive to break down the pastime behaviour according to population group and gender. Of the total group of 39 pupils, 30 participated in sport. The favourite pastime among the African and Coloured girls was reading; other hobbies included a variety of sports, listening to music, and visiting friends. The hobbies mentioned by White pupils only were playing a musical instrument and looking after pets.

b) What is the pupils' opinion of the German school?

The reasons for attending a German-language private school were essentially the same as those given by respondents quoted in chapters 3.1 and 3.2. Instructive were the pupils' likes and dislikes, as indicated at the beginning of the school year and at the end of the second term.

How do the pupils feel at the DSK?
What impresses them as favourable/unfavourable?

1. African pupils

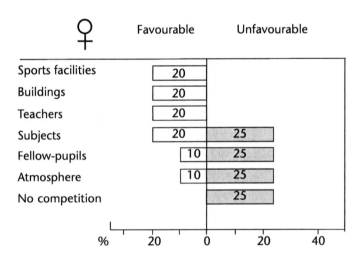

Fig. 17a: Responses (in percentages) given at beginning of school year by female African pupils to the question what had made a favourable or unfavourable impression on them at the German school (N = 5; multiple responses allowed)

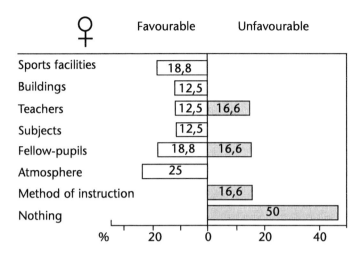

Fig. 17b: Responses (in percentages) given after six months by female African pupils to the question what had made a favourable or unfavourable impression on them at the German school (N = 5; multiple responses allowed)

Male pupils

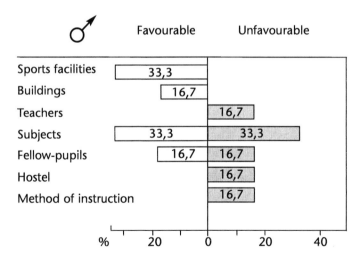

Fig. 17c: Responses (in percentages) given at the beginning of the school year by male African pupils to the question what had made a favourable or unfavourable impression on them at the German school (N = 3; multiple responses allowed)

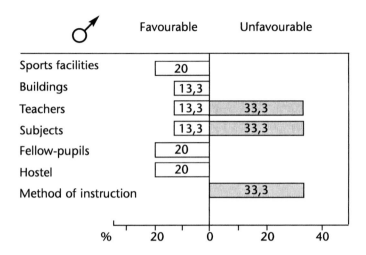

Fig. 17d: Responses (in percentages) given after six months by male African pupils to the question what made a favourable or unfavourable impression on them at the German school (N = 3; multiple responses allowed)

2. Coloured pupils

Female pupils

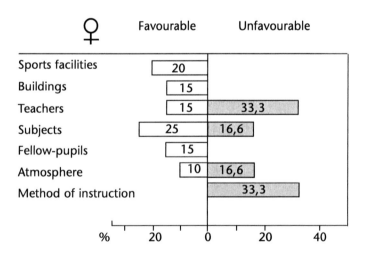

Fig. 18a: Responses (in percentages) given at the beginning of the school year by female Coloured pupils to the question what made a favourable or unfavourable impression on them at the German school (N = 11; multiple responses allowed)

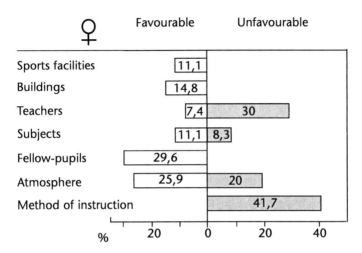

Fig. 18b: Responses (in percentages) given after six months by female Coloured pupils to the question what made a favourable or unfavourable impression on them at the German school (N = 11; multiple responses allowed)

N.B. Since there was only one male Coloured pupil in the research group, I refrained from presenting his responses as percentages in table form.

3. White pupils

Female pupils

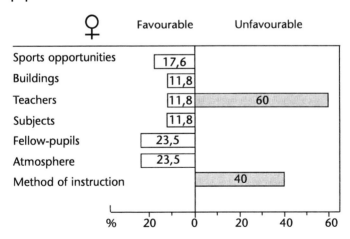

Fig. 19a: Responses (in percentages) given at the beginning of the school year by female White pupils to the question what made a favourable or unfavourable impression on them at the German school (N = 9; multiple responses allowed)

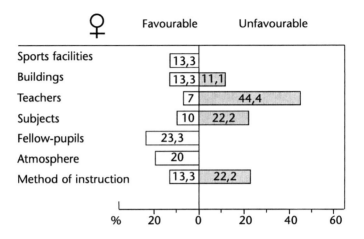

Fig. 19b: *Responses (in percentages) given after six months by female White pupils to the question what had made a favourable or unfavourable impression on them at the German school (N = 9; multiple responses allowed)*

Male pupils

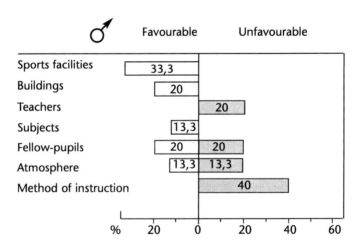

Fig. 19c: *Responses (in percentage) given at the beginning of the school year by male White pupils to the question what had made a favourable or unfavourable impression on them at the German school (N = 10; multiple responses allowed)*

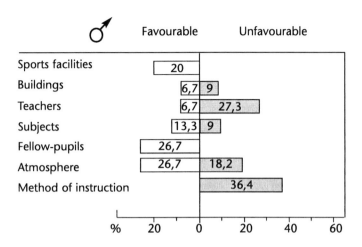

Fig. 19d: *Responses (in percentages) given after six months by male White pupils to the question what had made a favourable or unfavourable impression on them at the German school (N = 10; multiple responses allowed)*

Figures 17a through to 19d indicate that sport is of great importance to respondents of all population groups: Regardless of population group, most learners were very favourably impressed by the sports facilities.

The figures further demonstrate a significant change in attitudes within the first six months, particularly among female pupils. At the beginning of the school year, female pupils (with the exception of White females) were most favourably impressed by sports facilities, teachers and the choice of subjects on offer; by the end of the second term, i.e. within the "foreign-language" pupils' first six months at the DSK, the preference had clearly shifted towards the atmosphere and the fellow-pupils. The same trend applies to the single male Coloured pupil, who has been omitted from the graphic presentation.

At the beginning of the school year, two-thirds of the African pupils indicated that they missed games like softball and hockey, which they had occasionally plaid at primary school; after six months, this had dropped to half. Seven out of nine Coloured pupils continued to miss primary school friends.

c) Social interaction between pupils: The relationship between "foreign-language" and "mother tongue" pupils

This part of the investigation focussed not only on new friendships which the "foreign-language" pupils fostered at the German school, but also on their "old" friends from before this time. For this reason, they were asked how many friends they had in their class at their "old" school, in the preparatory class at the German school, and in their present class. The same choice of possible answers was offered as in chapters 3.1 and 3.2, the categories being adapted to the size of the class involved. Furthermore, it was determined to which population group these friends belonged. By contrast to the previous question, gender was not taken into account. However, it should be remembered that the African students had been admitted to the school at the beginning of the previous school year, whereas the Coloured pupils had only been at the school for a few weeks when the first poll was conducted.

1) "Foreign-language" pupils' social interaction at their "old" schools

Of the five African pupils who answered this question, one answered that she had "very many" friends at her previous school, three indicated "some" friends, and one had "few" friends. All friends at the primary school in the township had been African. Nine of the ten Coloured pupils who responded to this question, had "very many" friends, while one indicated "very few" friends. Once again, all friends belonged to the same population group as the respondents.

2) Foreign-language pupils' social interaction in the preparatory course at the German school

One of the eight African pupils mentioned "very many" friends in the preparatory course, two respondents each opted for the categories "many" and "few" friends, and three opted for "some" friends. The ten Coloured respondents answered as follows: two had found "very many" friends, three claimed "many", and five chose the category "some friends".

3) Social interaction/relations between "mother tongue" and "foreign language" pupils in an integrated class at the DSK at the beginning of the school year and at the end of the second term

From the start of the school year, it was clear that the Coloured pupils found it less difficult to foster friendships than the African students. The results of this first poll resembled those of the research described in chapter 3.2 above. By the end of the second school term, a marked improvement had occurred: the African pupils, particularly the boys, had begun to establish new friendships. The following picture emerged:

Population group profile of pupils' friendship patterns
1. African pupils (Females and Males)

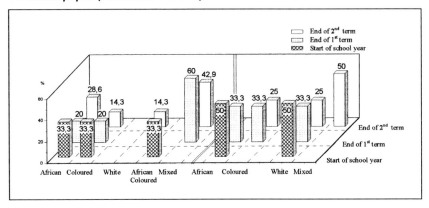

Fig. 20: *Profile of friendship patterns (by population group) of female (N = 5) and male (N = 3) African "foreign language" pupils at DSK (multiple responses allowed)*

2.Coloured pupils

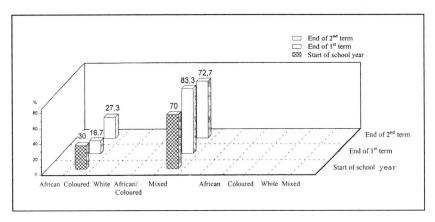

Fig. 21: *Profile of friendship patterns (by population group) of female Coloured pupils at the DSK (N = 11; multiple responses allowed)*

N.B. Since there was only one male Coloured pupil in the survey group, I refrained from presenting his responses in statistical table form.

3.White pupils (Females and Males)

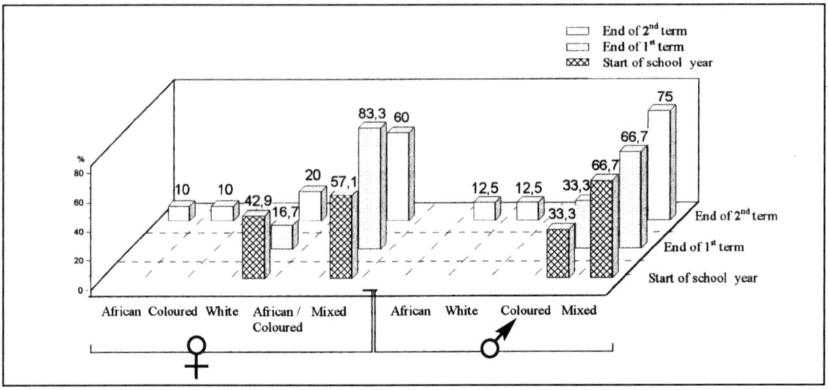

Fig. 22: Profile of friendship pattern (by population group) of female (N = 9) and male (N = 10) White pupils at DSK (multiple responses allowed)

Figures 20 to 22 illustrate changes in friendship patterns within six months of the arrival of "foreign-language" pupils at the DSK, and of their integration into a single class with "mother-tongue" pupils. On the whole, the majority of pupils of all population groups were able to form friendships across the "cultural divide" – if not within the first term, then at least by the end of the second term. Even so, some pupils of all groups – two African girls, one African boy, one Coloured girl, three White girls, and one White boy – had difficulties in this regard, even after six months. The reasons given by these pupils for their own difficulties may be of interest: the two African girls and the African boy had the impression that many of the non-African pupils did not like them; furthermore, the girls experienced anxiety at not knowing how to communicate with the other children. The Coloured girl, on the other hand, found many of the "mother-tongue" pupils very conceited and unfriendly. The White girls blamed their lack of social interaction with the "foreign language" students on the fact that these lived far away, and on the attitude of the "foreign language" pupils themselves; the White boy gave no reasons for not having befriended any of the "foreign language" pupils. Surprisingly, the language factor was not cited as a source of difficulty.

Some pupils are by nature more extrovert than others. Given these differences in temperament, the relatively low number of pupils failing to foster friendships was not regarded as unusual or alarming.

Results of the statistical evaluation

Given the limited sample of pupils, it was impossible to establish any significant differences between different "population groups", let alone to draw any conclusions. However, a significant gender difference emerged from this study: at the end of the first term, the girls had fostered significantly more inter-cultural friendships than the boys ($p < 0.05$), but this difference no longer existed after the second school term. The pupils' own assessment of the difficulty (or otherwise) of fostering inter-cultural friendships may serve to illuminate this phenomenon:

Is it difficult for "foreign language" and "mother tongue" pupils to foster friendships across the cultural divide?

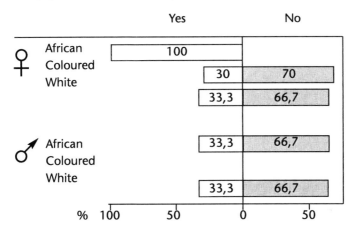

Fig. 23a: Pupils' responses (in percentages) at the beginning of the school year to the question: Do you find it difficult to foster inter-cultural friendships? (N = 36)

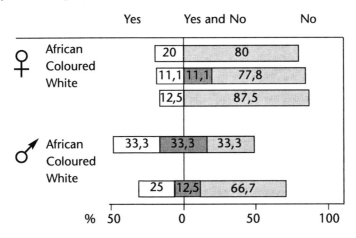

Fig. 23b: Pupils' responses (in percentages) at the end of the first school term to the question: Do you find it difficult to foster inter-cultural friendships? (N = 33)

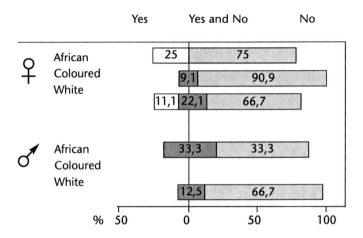

Fig. 23c: Pupils' responses (in percentages) at the end of the second school term to the question: Do you find it difficult to foster inter-cultural friendships? (N = 34)

Results of the statistical evaluation

By the end of the first term, there is a significant increase (p < 0.05) in the number of girls (n=22) who find it easy foster inter-cultural friendships (as compared to the findings at the start of the school year). There is no similarly significant increase in the findings gathered at the end of the second term. The sample of boys (n=13) was too small to allow for findings in statistical terms, and only certain penchants could be discerned: there was a tendency among boys to pronounce inter-cultural friendships "not difficult" at the beginning of the school year, followed by the response "don't know" at the end of the first term, and a return to the judgment "not difficult" at the end of the second term.

The limited scope of the sample obviously makes it risky to generalise on the basis of these findings. However, it should be remembered that the girls' group was instructed in team sports during the first term, while the boys were engaged in individual sports; at the end of the first term, there was a switch-over, with the girls changing to individual sports, and the boys moving on to team sports. By the end of the first term, the majority of girls had no difficulty in fostering inter-cultural friendships, while the majority of boys was undecided; there was a significant divergence between the responses of the two groups (p < 0.01). No such difference was discernible by the end of the second term. On the basis of these results, it seems probable that team sports are better suited than individual sports to promote social interaction between youths from different population groups, particularly during the early stages of the integration of "foreign language" pupils into a former "minority language group" school.

How do the students feel about having PE lessons with pupils from other language or cultural groups?

From the start of the school year, "mother tongue" and "foreign language" learners had joint, integrated PE lessons, though these were split along gender lines. The pupils' own judgment on this practice was generally favourable.

How do the students feel about integrated PE lessons?

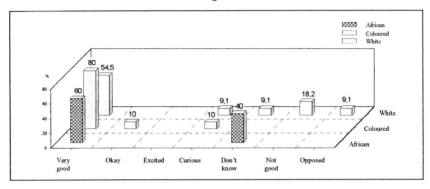

Fig. 24: Girls' feelings at the start of the school year about having integrated PE lessons (N = 26; 5 African, 10 Coloured and 11 White girls)

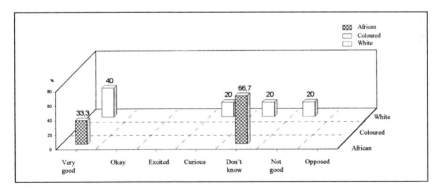

Fig. 25: Boys' feelings at the start of the school year about having integrated PE lessons (N = 13; 3 African, 10 White boys)

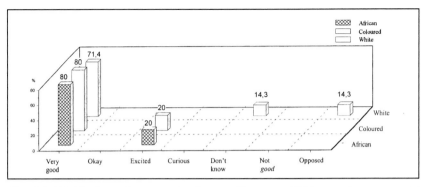

Fig. 26: *Girls' feelings after one school term of integrated PE lessons in team sports (N = 22; 5 African, 10 Coloured and 7 White girls)*

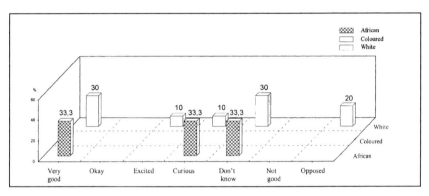

Fig. 27: *Boys' feelings after one school term of integrated PE lessons in individual sports (N = 13; 3 African, 10 White boys)*

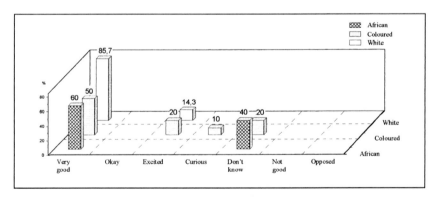

Fig. 28: *Girls' feelings after two school terms of integrated PE lessons in individual sports (N = 24; 5 African, 10 Coloured and 9 White girls)*

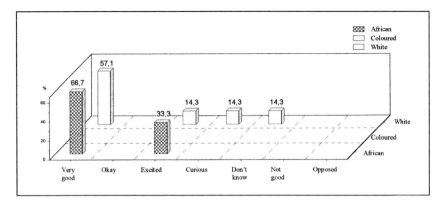

Fig. 29: *Boys' feelings after two school terms of integrated PE lessons in team sports (N = 13; 3 African, 10 White boys; multiple responses allowed)*

The figures above indicate that the overwhelming majority of pupils from all cultural and language groups approach integrated PE lessons with an open mind. Especially the girls seem to enjoy culturally integrated PE lessons. Figure 31 illustrates that the team sports and ball games of the first term made the girls even more favourably disposed towards integrated PE lessons; the same development was observed in the boys' class after this group switched to ball games in the second term. The favourable influence of team sports was confirmed by the following observation:

Results of the statistical evaluation

If one compares the pupils' reactions to integrated sport, it is instructive that only the White students voiced any negative sentiments. No significant difference could be established between "favourable" and "uncertain" reactions after the first and the second term. However, a significant difference occurred between the reactions of girls and boys at the end of the first term: the girls' reaction was predominantly favourable, whereas the boys were still "uncertain" or undecided regarding integrated PE lessons. By the end of the second term, however, this difference had disappeared.

Influence of the sport code or discipline on integration

As noted above, the girls' class practised team sports and ball games (soccer, handball, small games) during the first term, while the boys were instructed in individual sports (swimming, athletics); in the second term, this order was reversed. At the end of each term, all pupils had to indicate how that had found the integrated PE lessons, choosing one of the following answers: "very good", "good", "okay", "not so good", "not good at all. The following table lists the pupils' responses:

GIRLS

Table 11: Comments on the integrated PE lessons in the first term (A) and in the second term (B); girls' class (N = 25)

Comment Term Pupils	Very good		Good		Ok		Not so good		Not good at all	
	A	B	A	B	A	B	A	B	A	B
African Girls	1		4	2		2		1		
Coloured Girls	5	1	2	2	3	5	1	2		1
White Girls	1	4	4	2	4	3				
Overall Reaction	7	5	10	6	7	10	1	3		1

One Coloured girl failed to submit a questionnaire at the end of the first term.

BOYS

Table 12: Comments on the integrated PE lessons in the first term (A) and in the second term (B); boys' class (N = 14)

Comment Term Pupils	Very good		Good		Ok		Not so good		Not good at all	
	A	B	A	B	A	B	A	B	A	B
African Boys	2		1	1	2					
Coloured Boys					1	1				
White Boys	2			4	4	1	1		5	
Overall Reaction	4		1	5	7	2	1		5	

Three White pupils failed to submit questionnaires at the end of the second term.

From the girls' and boys' motivations for their answers, it became equally clear that team sports and ball games were more popular than individual sports. Improvements suggested at the end of each group's term of individual sports called for more ball games, while the answers submitted after each group's term of team sports were full of praise for ball games. This tendency is clear from the following illustration:

Pupils' preferred sports codes in integrated PE classes (by population group)

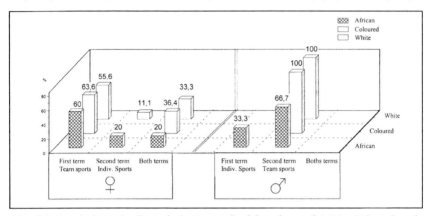

Fig. 30: Break-down by "population group" of female pupils' (N= 25) and male pupils (N= 14) preferences (in percentages) regarding sports codes in integrated PE lessons.

There is a significant difference (p < 0.01) in the girls' and boys' preferences for each of the two terms, which points to a shared preference for team sports and ball games: each group preferred the term in which they were occupied with ball games, the girls' group the first term, and the boys the second. No significant difference was discernible in the preferences of different population groups, except that White pupils showed a slightly greater liking for individual sports than the other pupils. The overwhelming majority of pupils – 94% - agreed that team sports provided better opportunities for getting to know one's fellow pupils than individual sports did.

Summary interpretation of the findings of investigation 3 (reactions of a "multi-cultural" PE class)

On the basis of preceding research (cf. chapters 3.1 and 3.2 above), the present investigation aimed to answer two questions: firstly, if sport could be used as a means of improving relations between "mother tongue" and "foreign language" pupils at a recently integrated school, and secondly, if there was a discernible difference between the efficacy of team sports (ball games) and individual sports for this purpose (hypothesis II).

In order to determine the conditions under which respondents participated in this investigation, socio-cultural parameters such as residential area, school, class size and hobbies were first established. The "foreign language" pupils all came from disadvantaged peri-urban residential areas (i.e. African or Coloured townships on the outskirts of Cape Town). Prior to being admitted to the German school, they had attended primary schools in their residential areas. In some of these schools, especially in the African townships, classes were very big. White pupils indulged in a broader range of hobbies and pastimes, but all pupils – with the exception of African girls – appeared to like sport. There was a tendency among girls to prefer individual sports (such as swimming, dancing and table tennis), while the boys clearly preferred team sports (soccer, basketball, and cricket).

The reasons given by "foreign language" pupils for attending the German school closely matched those of respondents in chapter 3.2, as did their sense of loss and longing: both studies revealed that African and Coloured students were missing their old friends, teachers, and parents.

Prior to their admission to the German school, none of the "foreign language" respondents had any personal interaction, let alone friendship, with any member of any other "population group". The findings reflected in figures 19a to 19c suggest that some of the difficulties experienced in establishing cross-cultural friendships are gender-specific: even after a year in an integrated class, many African girls had not yet established friendships with "mother tongue" pupils, and (like respondents in chapter 3.1 and 3.2) continued to spend play-time with other African girls. African boys, on the other hand, though constituting a small minority within the sample group, appeared to be much more confident and outgoing, and had far less difficulty in establishing social links in their new environment.

Team sports versus individual sports

Responses to questions concerning the suitability of different sports coded for the promotion of social interaction all point in the same direction: the girls' and the boys' class both preferred team sports to individual sports, because the former provided better opportunities for getting to know class mates and establishing social contacts.

The research therefore indicates that team sports can be very effective in easing "foreign-language" pupils into a previously mono-lingual or mono-cultural school, and that such sports can significantly contribute to the social integration of "foreign language" and "mother tongue" pupils. On the other hand, it is equally clear that it cannot be left to sports alone to overcome the old social and psychological barriers of apartheid: school management and teachers have to undertake concerted efforts to create a social atmosphere in which pupils from all cultural groups feel welcome and at home – an atmosphere which encourages all pupils to reach out to school mates from other cultural groups. In this connection, it appears that particular attention needs to be given to the socio-cultural situation of African girls.

These findings appear to confirm hypothesis II, i.e. the assumption that team sports are more likely to promote social interaction than individual sports. On account of the small size of the sample group, it is not claimed that this verification is scientifically conclusive. However, first points of reference have been established, and the verification process is to be continued and complemented by investigation 7, which is totally focussed on the effects of individual vs. team sports on inter-cultural social integration.

To answer this question conclusively, different sports codes need to be investigated; chapter 3.5 therefore seeks to establish the effects of integrated dancing lessons on a group of pupils from different cultural and social backgrounds.

3.5   Sport Beyond the PE Class: The Pinelands Project

The most natural – and probably most effective – way of promoting national unity and nation-building in South Africa, would be to have children from the various "population groups" grow up together. However, because of the following reasons, most South African children continue to grow up in relative isolation from "other" groups:

a) At the time when this study was conducted, South Africa still did not have a single, unitary Education Department for all its children. Although such a Department has in the meantime been established, its effects will only be felt in years to come.

b) Many social barriers, which under apartheid were entrenched in legislation, continue to exist as social conventions, or as a result of socio-economic stratification. Thus, despite the scrapping of the Group Areas Act, most residential areas have retained their pre-liberation demographic character. Since many (perhaps most) children attend the local school in their own residential area (for reasons of convenience, economy, etc.), this widespread persistence of "residential apartheid" often entails "educational apartheid".

c) The persistence of "social apartheid" patterns also means that few possibilities have been developed for children of different groups to meet and interact outside the institutional framework of school.

The project described in this chapter was an attempt to establish just such a field of social interaction beyond the institutional confines of any particular school. Given the popularity of sport in South Africa, the decision to use this area for such an experiment was almost a foregone conclusion. From these considerations arose, in 1994, a multi-cultural, co-educational "integration-through-sport"-programme: teachers and pupils from two African, two Coloured, and two White schools were invited to join in afternoon coaching sessions, under the supervision of professional coaches and instructors. The aim of the exercise was to establish whether such an extra-mural, multi-cultural sports project, operating beyond the institutional confines of any one school, could promote social interaction between children from different cultures or population groups, and whether there was any significant difference between team sports and individual sports in terms of promoting such interaction.

At the start of the project, the participants were divided into two groups, according to their own preferences: group A for athletics, and group B for baseball. The control group consisted of fellow-pupils at the participants' schools who did not take part in the sports project. A breakdown of the participants reads as follows:

Tab.13: Breakdown of participants in the Pinelands project

Group Participants	A Athletics	B Baseball	C Control group	Total
African pupils	27	30	17	**74**
Coloured pupils	13	20	10	**43**
White pupils	6	7	10	**23**
Total	**46**	**57**	**37**	**140**

The duration of the project was one school year. Data were collected at the following stages:

T1: January 1994 (start of project)
T2: June 1994
T3: December 1994 (end of project)

The baseball project was continued on the basis of data collected after six months. For this reason, data at the end of the project (T3) could only be gathered from members of group B and C (N = 87). The following section proposes to evaluate the data gathered from pupils (for an evaluation of the participating teachers' responses see Group 8).

Participants' socio-cultural background

1. Residential area

The project was conducted with children from different population groups. They came from residential areas where apartheid, though no longer enforced by law, continues to exist as a social convention. The African children lived in the townships Langa, Gugulethu and Khayelitsha, the Coloured kids came from Athlone and Bridgetown, and the Whites from the upmarket, reputedly conservative suburb of Pinelands, and some from Cape Town proper.

2. Mother tongue/home language

Most of the African participants spoke Xhosa at home (93%), some spoke English (3%) or Afrikaans (3%) as home language, and some both English and Afrikaans (1%). The Coloured children's home language was either English (43%) or Afrikaans (28%), or both these languages (26%). Of the White pupils, 75% spoke English as home language, and the remaining 25% both English and Afrikaans.

3. Pastimes

Respondents were allowed to give multiple responses to this question. The answers of the African and Coloured children were comparable to those given by the respondents in chapter 3.3 above. Of the African pupils, 30% indicated that they performed household chores such as cooking and cleaning, 24% said they practised sport (running/jogging and soccer), 16% said they read, 13% met with friends, 6% said they did "nothing", and 4% mentioned "drawing" as pastime. The Coloured pupils practised sport, such as cricket, soccer and basketball (28%), a further 28% said they played with friends, 12% each said they did school homework and domestic work, reading and eating were mentioned as pastimes by 7% each, and 5% said they watched television. Of the White participants, 41% said they practised sport, such as swimming, sailing, riding, and soccer; 18% said they played with friends, and 11% each mentioned watching television, reading, and doing school homework; 7% indicated that they practised playing a musical instrument.

4. Participants' social contacts/interaction at school

The African pupils from the primary schools in Langa indicated class sizes of between 30 and 47 pupils. 94% said their classes were not "multi-cultural" or "mixed"; the remaining 6% of African participants attended schools which were not predominantly African. Class sizes in the participating Coloured schools varied between 25 and 45, and no White pupils had at that stage been admitted. However, some African pupils had already enrolled, prompting 86% of the Coloured pupils to respond that their classes were in fact "culturally mixed"; the remaining 14% said their classes were not. The participating White high school, with class sizes of between 30 and 33 pupils, had already admitted some African and Coloured pupils, enabling 91% of the White pupils to describe their classes as "culturally mixed"; the numbers of African class mates cited by the White pupils varied between one and five, and those for Coloured class mates between two and seven.

Although the understanding of the term "friendship" may differ widely from person to person, the participants were asked how many friends they had among their class mates; they were instructed not to include good acquaintances, but to restrict themselves to real friends with whom they enjoyed spending playtime, and with whom they would even share secrets.

At the start of the project, the average number of friends cited by African pupils was eight to ten, the corresponding figure for Coloured pupils was 15 to 17, and for Whites 11 to 14. Of the four African pupils attending a predominantly Coloured school, three claimed one Coloured friend each, and the remaining pupil four. None of the African pupils had any White friends. – Of the 43 participating Coloured pupils, 37 stated that their school classes were "culturally mixed". Of these 37 pupils, a total of 27 said at the start of the project that they had African friends among their class mates, 13 claiming one or two African friends, six indicating three to four, and eight saying they had five African friends in their class. The 95% of the Coloured pupils who attended predominantly Coloured schools, said they had no White school friends; the 5% (two pupils) who attended a formerly White school, each said they had two White friends. Of the 21 White pupils from "culturally mixed" classes, eight lay claim to between two and five African friends, while five said they had between one and three Coloured friends in their classes.

As far as the number of friends and the demographics of friendship was concerned, no significant change was observed by the end of either the first or the second half of the school year, with the exception of Coloured pupils: by the end of the year, 29 pupils (or 78%) said they now had friends among their African classmates, which constituted an increase of 5%.

5. Social interaction between different population groups beyond the school grounds

37% of the African pupils indicated that they had already been in the homes of members of other population groups. 20% said, they had already been to a predominantly White residential area, and 4% had gone to see their mothers at work in a White area; a further 4% said they had been to Cape Town, 1% had been to a formerly White beach, and a further 1% said they had practised sport in a White residential area. 5% of the African pupils had been to a predominantly Coloured residential area.

Of the Coloured pupils, 19% said they had been in the home of a member of a different culture/population group. 9% said this had been in a White residential area, 5% indicated they had been to "Cape Town", among them 2% who said they had paid a visit to their mothers' place of employment; another 2% said they had been to an African township. 35% of the White participants said they had already paid visits to residents of Coloured residential areas, but none had been to an African township.

6. Participants' previous experiences of sport in "culturally mixed" groups

At the start of the project, the pupils were asked whether they had any previous experience of "intercultural" or "multicultural" sport. Eleven (15%) of the African pupils (N = 74) answered in the affirmative: seven had played soccer in a Cape Town stadium, and four had participated in athletics in a Coloured residential area. From among the Coloured pupils (N = 43), 20 (46%) had already had sports contacts with members of other population groups. Eleven of these had competed against African pupils from other predominantly Coloured schools, in the context of an athletics meeting under the auspices of the then Department of Education and Culture; five said they jointly trained with African pupils of their own schools in the afternoons, and three more said they had played with African pupils on the municipal sports grounds of their residential areas; one pupil indicated that he had participated in a sports meeting in a White area.

Of the participating 23 White pupils, ten (43%) said they had already participated in sports with members of other population groups; six of these said they had joint practise sessions at school, two said they joined in ball games with the neighbouring African or Coloured children in their residential areas, and one pupil participated in ball games in a Coloured area; one pupil had spent time in the USA, where she had participated in sports with Black children.

What thus emerged from this investigation, was that only 15% of the African pupils, 9% of the Coloureds, and 13% of the Whites had any previous sports contacts with members of "other" South African population groups.

The Pinelands coaching programme

The attempt to gain an impression of the pupils' attitude to sport in general, and to the Pinelands project in particular, produced the following results:

1. What was the pupils attitude towards sport in general?

All pupils indicated that they like sport. Among the African pupils, the most popular disciplines were baseball (25%), soccer (22%), and athletics (21%). The Coloured pupils liked soccer (21%) most, followed by softball (14%) and hockey (13%). White pupils preferred athletics (19%), hockey (17%) and tennis (12%).

2. The Pinelands coaching programme

2 a)   Pupils' assessment of the programme

After the **first six months**, the members of **Group A (athletics)** assessed the programme as follows (in percentages):

	very good	good	okay
African pupils	87	4	9
Coloured pupils	85	8	8
White pupils	33	17	50

After the same period of time **(six months), Group B (baseball)** players assessed the coaching programme as follows (in percentages):

	very good	good	okay
African pupils	97	–	3
Coloured pupils	74	21	5
White pupils	40	20	40

At the end of the school year, the same **Group B (baseball)** pupils assessed the coaching programme as follows (in percentages):

	very good	good	okay
African pupils	91	6	3
Coloured pupils	85	–	15

Tab. 14: *Pupils' assessment of the Pinelands coaching programme (after 6 month as well as after I year)*

2 b)   Difficulty/ease with which course was accomplished

Neither the athletics nor the baseball coaching and training programme posed any major difficulty to the girls. The majority of the African pupils (56%), and half of the Coloured (50%) and White pupils (50%) found the athletics training "easy" to "fairly easy".

The reaction to the baseball training course was not quite as uniform or unanimous: whereas 69% of the African pupils and 53% of the Coloured pupils found this course "easy" to "fairly easy", only 33% of the White pupils shared this carefree assessment.

2 c)   Assessment of the "culturally mixed" training group

In answering the question how they had liked the multi-cultural training programme, the participants were allowed to submit multiple responses. **After six months,** they responded as follows:

How did the pupils feel about the multi-cultural training programme?

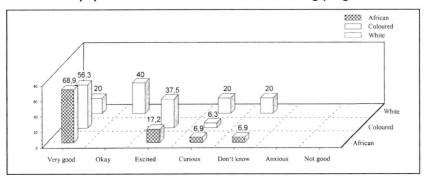

Fig. 31a: Responses (in percentages) by members of group A (athletics) to the question: How do you feel about the multi-cultural training programme? (N = 50, multiple responses)

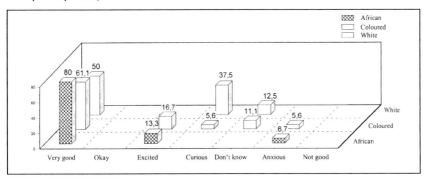

Fig. 31b: Responses (in percentages) by members of group B (baseball) to the question: How do you feel about the multi-cultural training programme? (N = 56, multiple responses)

Results of statistical evaluation

As Figures 31a and 31b indicate, the overwhelming majority of participants felt good about the multi-cultural programme, despite some uncertainty or apprehension among some of the pupils; given South Africa's apartheid past, this (very limited) ambiguity is hardly surprising. **More importantly, there were no significant differences between members of different population groups regarding their feelings about the "mixed" training programme.**

At the end of the school year, the participants' responses to the same question read as follows:

Baseball

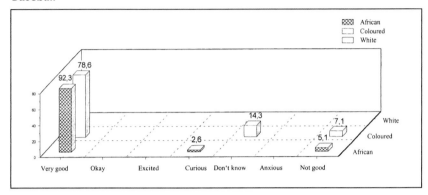

Fig. 31c: *Responses (in percentages) by members of Group B (baseball) to the question: How do you feel about the multi-cultural training programme? (N = 53, multiple responses)*

Results of statistical evaluation

As Figure 31c shows, the overwhelming majority of African and Coloured pupils felt good about the baseball training, with only a small minority being less enthusiastic by the end of the year. **Once again, no significant difference was noticed between the reactions of pupils from different population groups.**

2 d)   Pupils' preferences

The pupils were subsequently asked what aspect of the multi-cultural training programme they had liked best. Their answers are given under the following abbreviations: **Responses, given by Group A (athletics) and Group B 1 (baseball), after the first six months; responses given by Group B 2 (baseball) at the end of the school year.**

Table 15 indicates that, regardless of the sport code or discipline chosen, African and Coloured pupils liked the culturally mixed group very much, whereas the White pupils were rather reserved on this score. No dislikes were articulated, except for one African pupil, who said he did not like the athletics coach.

2 e)   Continuation of the programme

After only six months, surprisingly many participants answered in the affirmative when asked whether they would like to continue with the training programme:

Table 15: Participants' responses (in numbers) to the question: What aspect of the multi-cultural training programme did you like best? Answers given after six months (Group A and B1; N = 27) and at the end of the school year (Group B2; N = 53). Multiple responses were allowed.

Pupils	African pupils (N=27) (N=53) Group			Coloured pupils (N=13) (N= 23) Group			White pupils (N= 6) Group	
Preferences	A	B 1	B 2	A	B 1	B 2	A	B
Multi-cultural group	26	17	27	13	8	13	1	
Coach/trainer	7	5	9	1	5	5	3	2
Style of instruction	6	7	12	9	5	12	2	2
Atmosphere	1		5	1		5	2	2

Group A (athletics): 92% of the African pupils, 69% of the Coloureds, and 50% of the White children indicated that they would like to continue participating in the programme; 8% of the Coloured pupils and 50% of the Whites said they did not wish to continue, and 8% of the African and 23% of the Coloured pupils were undecided/uncertain.

At the end of the school year all participants (100%) indicated that they would like to continue. Asked for suggestions to improve the programme, five African pupils (8.8%) said they would like to have something to eat before each training session, and two pupils indicated that they would also like to be trained in other disciplines, such as swimming and netball.

A total of five participants (8.8%) - two African, two Coloured and one White pupil – wanted longer training sessions, one Coloured pupil (1.8%) wished for more competitions or contests, and another (1.8%) said she wanted better sports fields.

2 f) Changes in social interaction and/or relations between pupils of different groups resulting from the Pinelands project

1. How difficult is it to foster multi-cultural friendships?

At the start of the school year (and of the project) and again after six months, the participants were asked whether they found it difficult to foster friendships with pupils from other groups. This is how each of the two groups responded:

Did the pupils find it difficult to foster friendships with pupils from other cultures/population groups?

Group A (athletics)

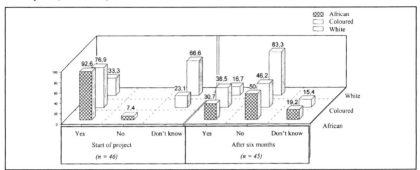

Fig. 32a: Participants' responses (in percentages) to the question: Do you find it difficult to foster friendships with pupils from other cultures/population groups?

As Figure 32a indicates, the majority of African and Coloured pupils, as well as one-third of the White pupils, believed **at the start of the project** that it was difficult to establish multi-cultural friendships; at that stage, two-thirds of the White children were uncertain about this question. Only six months later, half of the African pupils, almost half of the Coloured children, and more than eighty percent of the White participants were no longer apprehensive of obstacles to multi-cultural friendships; in addition, a significant percentage of African and Coloured children had moved from the pessimistic position ("inter-cultural friendships are difficult to establish") to one of uncertainty ("don't know").

Group B (baseball)

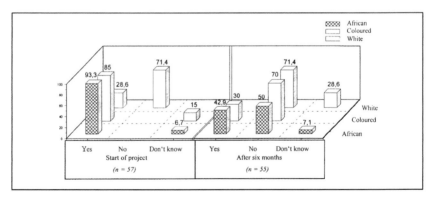

Fig. 32b: Participants' responses (in percentages) the question: Do you find it difficult to foster friendships with pupils from other cultures/population groups?

At the start of the project, the overwhelming majority of African and Coloured baseball players, as well as about one-quarter of the White children in this group, thought that multi-cultural friendships would be hard to foster; six months later, half the African pupils, and more than two-thirds of the Coloured and White participants, had overcome these apprehensions. In addition, the formerly pessimistic White children (28,6%) appear to have moved to the more neutral "don't know" position (cf. Fig. 32b).

Control group C:

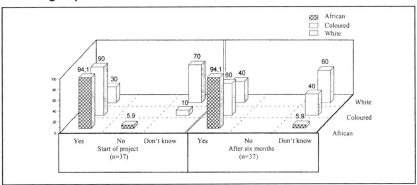

Fig. 32c: Responses (in percentages) by members of Group C (control group) to the question: Do you find it difficult to foster friendships with pupils from other cultures/population groups?

Here again, the overwhelming majority of African and Coloured pupils felt at the start of the school year that it was difficult to foster inter-cultural friendships; almost one-third of the White pupils shared this view.

Six months later, the number of pessimists among the African pupils remained unchanged, while that among Whites even increased; of the Coloured pupils, roughly one-third had moved from the negative to the neutral position.

Here are some of the reasons quoted by members of all groups for the alleged difficulty of inter-cultural friendships:

- the "language barrier", unfamiliarity ("one does not know each other"), geographical distance ("distant living areas"), past separation ("one was separate for so long"), past experience ("negative experience with whites"), the situation at schools ("no integration in schools"), aloofness ("people are not approachable"), and the shyness of African pupils ("feeling shy").

By the end of the school year, the members of Group B (baseball) responded to the same question as follows: almost half of the African pupils (43%), and a quarter of the Coloured pupils (25%) still believed it was difficult to foster intercultural friendships, whereas a majority of African pupils (57%) and half of the Coloureds saw no such difficulty. It must be added, however, that a further quarter of the Coloured pupils chose not to answer the question. – Of the 22 African pupils who gave reasons for their pessimistic assessment, 17 continued to blame the perceived difficulty on language problems, as did three of the ten Coloured pupils who motivated their answer. Two of the Coloured pupils said they regretted their lack of contact with pupils from other groups, while three African pupils said it was a pity that the White pupils would not visit Africans in their township homes. Four African and five Coloured pupils believed that sport made it easier to foster friendships, and felt that the participants of the multicultural training programme had already become quite well-acquainted with one another.

Group C (Control group)

The responses given by the control group at the end of the school year did not differ substantially from those offered after the first six months. The same applies for the reasons given by this group to support their sentiments.

Results of the statistical evaluation:

a) **Both the athletics and the baseball training programme significantly changed participants' perceptions regarding fostering friendships with pupils belonging to other cultures/population groups (p < 0.01). By contrast, attitudes remained virtually unchanged in the control group, both after six months and at the end of the school year. Joint training sessions, be it in athletics or in baseball, therefore appears to have a positive effect on pupils' attitude towards members of other cultures/population groups.**

b) **There was no significant difference between the effects of athletics, as opposed to baseball, on the participants' attitude towards pupils from other cultures/population groups. The nature of the particular sports code practised therefore appears to have little or no bearing on the participants' attitude.**

2. **Friendships between pupils from different population groups outside the institutional school setting**

In order to monitor and evaluate possible changes and developments regarding social relations and interaction within the training groups, participants were asked **at the start of the project** and again **six months later** how many friends from other population groups they had beyond the confines of their own schools, and to what cultures/population groups these belonged. The following is an overview of their responses:

Number of friends from other cultures/population groups

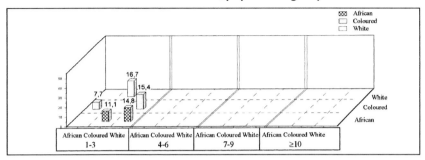

Fig. 33a: Responses (in percentages) by members of Group A (athletics) to the question: How many friends from "other" cultures/population groups do you have outside your own school, and to which culture/population group do they belong? (N = 46; 27 African, 13 Coloured, and 6 White pupils)

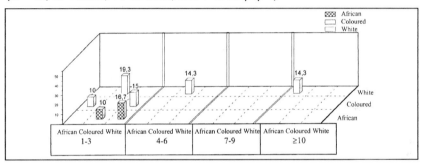

Fig. 33b: Responses (in percentages) by members of Group B (baseball) to the question: How many friends from other cultures/population groups do you have outside your own school, and to which culture/population group do they belong? (N = 57; 30 African, 20 Coloured and 7 White pupils)

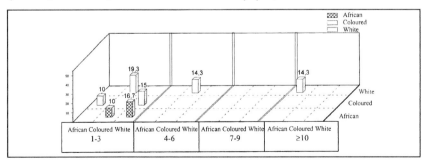

Fig. 33c: Responses (in percentages) by members of Group C (control group) to the question: How many friends from other cultures/population groups do you have outside your own school, and to which culture/population group do they belong? (N = 37; 17 African, 10 Coloured and 10 White pupils)

Figures 33a-c illustrate the situation as it existed at the start of the project: very few pupils had friends from other cultures/population groups. For instance, not a single White member of Group A (athletics) had any African friends, although some of them had "culturally mixed" classes at school. In Group B (baseball), there was a smattering of "intercultural" friendships, but with two exceptions, none of the group members had more than three such friendships. On the other hand, no member of Group C (control group) had more than one friend from a different culture/population group – except one White girl, who boasted six African friends. None of the White respondents had any Coloured friends outside their own schools.

Six months later, the respondents were once again asked how many friends from other cultures/population groups they had outside their own schools. Here is an overview of their answers:

Number of friends from other cultures/population groups

After six months

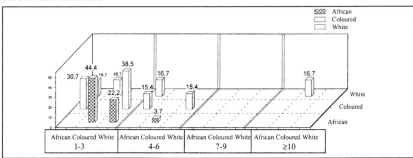

Fig. 34a: Responses (in percentages) by members of Group A (athletics) to the question: How many friends from other cultures/population groups do you have, and to which culture/population group do they belong? (N = 46)

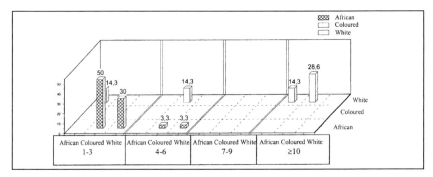

Fig. 34b: Responses (in percentages) by members of Group B (baseball) to the question: How many friends from other cultures/population groups do you have, and to which culture/population group do they belong? (N = 57)

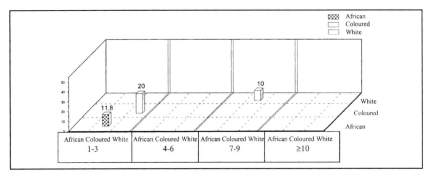

Fig. 34c: Responses (in percentages) by members of Group C (control group) to the question: How many friends from other cultures/population groups do you have, and to which culture/population group do they belong? (N = 37)

Figures 34a – c illustrate the increase in the number of friends from other cultures/population groups among participants of the Pinelands project. Not only was there an increase in the number of multi-cultural friendships per participant – there was also a rise in the total number of participants who recorded such friendships. The change is particularly noticeable if the results are compared with the figures for the control group, and also appears from the statistical evaluation below.

Results of the statistical evaluation:

Within a period of six months, there was a significant increase in the number of members of the athletics training group who had friends among pupils from other cultures/population groups (P < 0.01). The same applied to the baseball training group (p < 0.01). By contrast, no such change occurred in the control group, where the number of multi-cultural friendships remained virtually unchanged. It would therefore appear that participation in a multi-cultural sports group has a direct influence on the number of multi-cultural friendships. No significant difference could be established between the "inter-cultural social" effects of athletics on the one hand, and baseball on the other. It would therefore appear that the nature of the sport code/discipline practised has no significant bearing on the social effect of such an intercultural training programme. What influences this effect, however, is the duration of the programme, as discovered at the end of the school year, when the following data were gathered:

Group B (baseball):

By the end of the school year, 77% of the African pupils said they had between one and nine Coloured friends from other schools, and 30% said they had between one and three White friends from other schools. Of the Coloured pupils, 45% said they had one to seven African friends at other schools, and 15% even claimed more than ten African friends from outside their own schools. 25% of the Coloured pupils said they had between one and six White friends, and 5% reported more than ten White friends who were not school friends.

Control group C:

17.6% of the African pupils in this group reported that they had one Coloured friend, but none had any White friends. Among the Coloured members of this group, 20% had one to three White friends, and 10% they had one African friend outside the school.

The baseball group recorded a significant increase in the number of multicultural friendships from the end of the first semester to the end of the school year (p < 0.01). This was in contrast to the control group, where no such increase was recorded. A longer period of joint training therefore appears to produce a greater amount of social interaction, and hence a greater number of inter-cultural friendships.

3. **Did the training programme give the participants an opportunity to interact socially?**

The following diagram illustrates the situation in the various groups:

Did the training offer an opportunity of inter-cultural social interaction?

Athletics

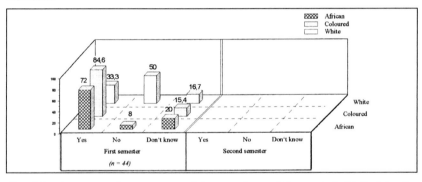

Fig. 35a: Responses (in percentages) by members of Group A (athletics) to the question: Did the training programme give you the opportunity to interact socially with members of other cultures/population groups? (N = 44)

As Figure 35a indicates, the African and Coloured members of **Group A (athletics)** were much more optimistic about the opportunities of inter-cultural social mingling than their White counterparts: while roughly three quarters (72% and 84,6% respectively) of the Africans and Coloureds saw such opportunities, half of the White participants (50%) denied this, and only one third (33,3%) answered in the affirmative. Whereas a small number of Africans were pessimistic (8%), a far greater number of Africans and Coloureds (20% and 15,4% respectively) opted for the more neutral "don't know". – Two African pupils chose not to answer the question. Next, the participants were asked what the intercultural training programme had taught them about children from other cultures/population groups. In Group A (athletics), roughly a third of the pupils from each group said they had found the "other" children very friendly and likeable. About a quarter of the African pupils said they had learnt that everybody likes sport, and had enjoyed practising together – a feeling echoed by one-third of the White respondents, and by one-tenth of the Coloured students. While only 7% of the African children commented on how good the pupils from the other two groups were at athletics, one-third of both the Whites and the Coloureds made similar remarks about the respective "other" groups. 7% of the African pupils had the impression that some of the "other" pupils were watching them with apprehension, with no Coloured or White respondents recording similar sentiments.

A further 7% of the African pupils said their Afrikaans and English skills had benefited from the joint training, while 11% of the Coloured children reported they had learnt a few words of Xhosa; no such inter-cultural linguistic progress was reported by the White participants. However, one-third of the White pupils said they had learnt to look at various issues from a different angle for a change.

Baseball

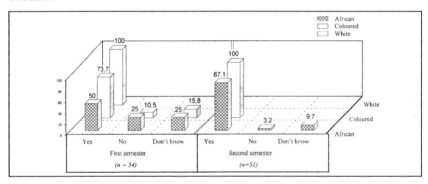

Fig. 35b: *Responses (in percentages) by members of Group B (baseball) to the question: Did the training programme give you the opportunity to interact socially with pupils from other cultures/population groups?*

Figure 35b illustrates the sentiments expressed by members of the baseball training group after the first semester and at the end of the school year. After the first semester, 100% of the White students felt the training gave them the opportunity of "multicultural" social interaction, as did 100% of the Coloured students by the end of the second semester. Surprisingly, less than three-quarters of the Coloured students (73,7%) had felt this confident after the first semester, with 10,5% answering "no", and a further 15,8% recording a sceptical "don't know". However, the most striking increase in multicultural confidence occurred among African pupils: only half of these respondents thought "multi-cultural" social interaction possible by mid-year, with 25% each replying "no" and "don't know". By the end of the year, more than four-fifths

(87,1%) believed the training programme could lead to social interaction, with only 9,7% remaining sceptical, and only 3,2% rejecting the possibility outright.

The members of this group were then also asked what they had learnt, in the joint training programme, about the respective "other" cultures/population groups. Once again, one-third of the Coloured and White pupils reported they had found the "other" participants very friendly and likeable, with more than half of the African pupils (53%) taking such a positive view of their fellow-participants.

A further 18% of the African respondents said the training had taught the participants to respect one another, with 12% reporting they had learnt that the White and Coloured children were good at baseball; 8% of the Coloured children paid the African and White children a similar compliment. 6% of the African children said their English and/or Afrikaans language skills had improved, while 42% of Coloured pupils believed their Xhosa and English skills had benefited. Lastly, one-third of the White pupils noted that relationships within the training group had improved remarkably since the start of the programme, and a further third had noted that many African pupils lacked proper sports gear.

Members of the control group were also asked at the end of each semester whether the past six months had offered them much opportunity for social interaction with members of "other" cultures/population groups. As the accompanying Figure 35c shows, the overwhelming majority of students answered in the negative, with the Coloured students showing the greatest shift towards the negative end of the scale in the course of the year. On the other hand, the "yes" reading showed a slight increase for African and White students by the end of the year. It was interesting to note what pupils from each of the three cultures or population groups believed to have learnt about the respective "other" groups (Table 16).

Control group

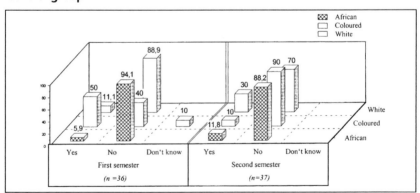

Fig. 35c: Responses (in percentages) by members of Group C (control group), at the end of each semester, to the question: Did you have much opportunity of social interaction with members of other cultures/population groups over the past six months?

Table 16: Breakdown of pupils' responses (in percentages), at the end of the 1st and 2nd semester respectively, to the question: What did you learn from/about pupils from other cultures/population groups?

Group	A	B	C	B2	A	B	C	B2	C2	A	B	C	B2	C2
New Insights														
No apartheid, all nice	33	53		44				50		33	33		33	
Other pupuls taught me a lot				8	8			17					33	
Respect for one another		18		4			30	8						
All like sport	27	6											17	
Join sport is fun	27			12	11					33				
Other pupils also do well at sport	7	12		16	33	8		25	6					
Other pupils lack sport gear							10				33			
Other pupils fear me	7												17	
Improved English/ Afrikaans	7	6	6	16		20								
Improved Xhosa					2	22	11		6		11			6
Discipline		6												
Different angle on many issues										33				
Relationship much improved											33		33	
Other pupils ask many questions													17	
African pupils are different									6					12

The scope and variety of the answers listed in Table 16 were a pleasant surprise. They show that, for many students, the joint training programme was an eye opener, which sensitized them to facets of their fellow-students' existence of which they had not been aware. This newly-won information and insight made for constructive social interaction, as appears from the results of the statistical evaluation:

Results of the statistical evaluation:

Both the athletics and the baseball training programme gave pupils the opportunity to meet fellow-pupils from the respective "other" South African cultures or population groups. Judging by the responses, the African and Coloured students were very well-disposed towards this opportunity. This becomes even more obvious when one compares the two training groups' responses with those of the control group, where no significant change or increase in multi-cultural friendships occurred.

No significant difference was detected between the effects of athletics and baseball on social interaction. Among White pupils, there was a tendency to favour baseball over athletics as an agent for social interaction, but due to the small sample, no statistically valid inferences can be drawn from this. However, a significant increase in the number of pupils reporting social interaction occurred in the second semester as compared to the first ($p < 0.05$), suggesting that longer programmes of this nature are more effective than shorter ones.

4. Did the multi-cultural training programme change pupils' attitudes towards the respective "other" cultures/population groups?

Subsequently, the participants were asked whether the joint training programme had changed their attitudes towards pupils from the respective "other" cultures/population groups. **At the end of the first semester**, the members of Group A (athletics) answered as follows:

Did the joint training programme change pupils' attitudes towards members of "other" cultures/population groups?

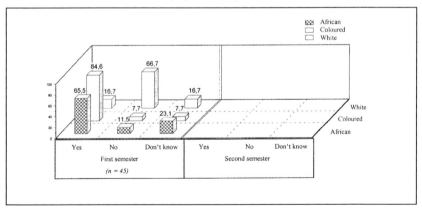

Fig. 36a: "Changes of attitude" (in percentages) by members of Group A (athletics) by the end of the first semester (n = 45).

As Figure 36a indicates, by the end of the first semester, almost two-thirds of the African (65,5%) and more than three-quarters of the Coloured pupils (84,6%) believed that their attitudes towards members of the "other" groups had changed; one African pupil did not reply. - On the other hand, two-thirds of the White pupils (66,7%) had noticed no change in their own attitudes; the remainder of the White students was equally divided between those who had perceived a change, and those who said they didn't know (16,7% each).

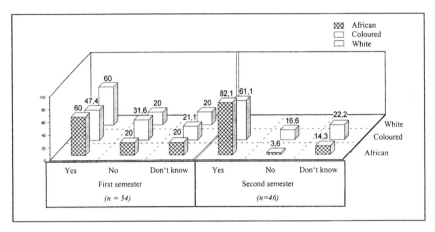

Fig. 36b: *"Changes of attitude" (in percentages) by members of Group B (baseball) by the end of the first semester (n = 54) and by the end of the second semester (n = 46)*

Figure 36 b illustrates that, *by the end of the first semester*, 60% of the African and White pupils and 47,45 of the Coloured children believed that their attitudes towards pupils from "other" cultures/population groups had changed. Almost one-third of the Coloured pupils (31,6%) denied that their attitudes had changed, as did one-fifth of the African and White pupils (20% each). Roughly one-fifth of each of the three groups (between 20 and 21,1%) felt unable to answer this question.

Asked to give reasons for their perceptions, 58% of the African pupils said they simply enjoyed the training, and were happy to be part of a "mixed" training group. 21% explicitly said they liked the "mixed" group, and that they felt accepted and liked by the "other" pupils; 10% said they were glad to be able to learn from "other" students (e.g. some expressions in their languages, etc.), and a further 10% said the atmosphere had improved much since the start of the project, and that they were not anxious or apprehensive anymore. Only one-third of the White pupils gave reasons for their answers, by saying they felt at home in the "mixed" group and liked the "other" pupils.

Six months later, **by the end of the school year**, the number of African and Coloured pupils whose attitude had changed, had risen by roughly 22% and

13% respectively, with a corresponding drop in the number of those who saw no change. The number of "don't knows" among African pupils had also dropped, as against a small increase in this category among the Coloured pupils.

Results of the statistical evaluation:

The effects of the training programme are presented in diagram form below. Participants' responses indicated that both the athletics and the baseball training programme had changed pupils' attitudes, with no significant difference between the effects of the two disciplines. However, by the end of the second semester, there was once again a significant increase in the number of students whose attitudes had changed ($p < 0.05$), suggesting that the duration of such inter-cultural programmes directly influences their effectiveness as tools for change.

At the end of the first semester, a sociogram was drawn up, with the aid of both the training groups and the control group. Pupils were asked whether they would invited children from the "other" population groups to their birthday party.

Table 17: Responses (in numbers) by members of Group A (athletics), B (baseball) and C (control group) to the question: Would you invite pupils from "other" population groups to your birthday party? (multiple responses allowed)

Pupils	African pupils			Coloured pupils			White pupils		
	N=24	N=29	N=17	N=13	N=20	N=10	N=6	N=5	N=10
Invitation	A	B	C	A	B	C	A	B	C
Yes	22	27	7	13	19	1	5	3	6
No	2	2	8		1			1	2
Don´t know			2			9		1	2

The responses set out in Table 17 constituted a pleasant surprise: Virtually all participants in the Pinelands project adopted an open-minded attitude towards members of "other" cultures or population groups, especially when compared to the responses of control group C.

Next, the respondents were asked from which culture or population group they would best like to invite pupils; multiple responses were allowed.

Table 18 once again illustrates that the members of training groups A and B were much more amenable to social interaction with members of "other" cultures/population groups than the pupils in control group C.

Table 18: Responses (in numbers) by members of Group A (athletics), Group B (baseball) and Group C (control group) to the question: Members of which culture/population group would you invite to your birthday party? (5 African, 9 Coloured and 3 White members of control group C made no reply to this question)

Pupils	African pupils			Coloured pupils			White pupils		
	N=24	N=30	N=6	N=13	N=20	N=10	N=4	N=7	N=10
Invitation	A	B	C	A	B	C	A	B	C
wish (es) to invite: African pupils	14	16	1	7	9		1	4	1
Coloured pupils	8	13		6	10	1	1	2	1
White pupils	8	7		6	7		2	3	7

It was quite instructive and revealing to learn the pupils' reasons for wishing to invite pupils from the respective "other" cultures/population groups. The participants in the Pinelands project answered the question as follows: 70% of the African pupils in Group A and Group B (N = 54; 3 pupils did not reply) said they liked the children from "other" population groups, 24% said they wished to invite the children with whom they practised sport, and 5% said they believed in the "new South Africa". Of the Coloured respondents, (N = 33), 21% said they liked the "other" children, and an equal percentage (21%) said they had come to know the "other" pupils very well through joint training sessions; a far greater percentage (57%) pointed out that they had been practising sport together, adding that they found the "mixed" group "great".

The White pupils' responses were divided in equal parts (33.3% each) between the following reasons: they wanted to help the "other" pupils; they thought the "mixed" group was a good idea; and they welcomed the proximity of the schools involved in the project, because this obviated the need for public transport.

Among the members of the control group, 50% of the African pupils motivated their wish to invite "other" pupils by their desire to meet new friends; the majority of the White pupils (70%) said they wanted to invite the "others" because they shared the same school. The African pupils who did not want to invite "other" children, blamed this on the language problem (657%), while 33% said they did not like White children.

10% of the White children also pointed to the language problem in justifying their reluctance to invite "other" pupils, while 20% of the White and 10% of the Coloured pupils said they did not want to invite people whom they hardly knew.

At the end of the school year, the same question was asked once more. This is how the pupils responded the second time around:

Table 19: Responses (in numbers) by members of Group B2 (baseball) and members of Group C2 (control group), at the end of the school year, to the question: Would you invite children from "other" cultures/population groups to your birthday party? (Multiple responses allowed; 2 African, 8 Coloured and 2 White pupils did not reply to this question.)

Pupils	African pupils N=30 N=17		Coloured pupils N=20 N=10		White pupils N=0 N=10	
Invitation	B2	C2	B2	C2	B2	C2
Yes	28	6	20	2		6
No		9				1
Don´t know		2	9			1

Multiple responses were also allowed to the question: From which culture(s)/population group(s) would you like to invite pupils to your birthday party?

*Table 20: Responses (in numbers) by members of Group B2 (baseball) and Group C2 (control group), **at the end of the school year**, to the question: From which culture(s)/population group(s) would you like to invite pupils to your birthday party? (Multiple responses allowed; only 17 members of the control group [N = 37] replied to this question.)*

Pupils	African pupils N=30 N=17		Coloured pupils N=20 N=10		White pupils N=4 N=10	
Invitation	B2	C2	B2	C2	B2	C2
To be invited African pupils	13	1	11			1
Coloured pupils	14	1	8	5		1
White pupils	9		4			8

Table 20 indicates that after the second semester of multi-cultural sports training, the members of the baseball group were even more keen than after the first to invite pupils from other cultures/population groups. There was no such shift in the control group. This seems to indicate that, left to their own devices and without initiative from the educators' side, children prefer to interact with fellow-pupils from their own culture/population group. – The reasons pupils indicated for wishing to invite, or not to invite, pupils from "other" cultures/population groups roughly echoed those given in the first questionnaire (at the end of the first semester).

4. In the pupils' view, what contribution can sport make to social integration?

At the start of the project, at the end of the first semester, and again at the end of the school year, pupils were asked from which population group(s) they would choose fellow-participants for sports activities. This is how they responded:

Pupils' preferences for fellow participants in sports activities

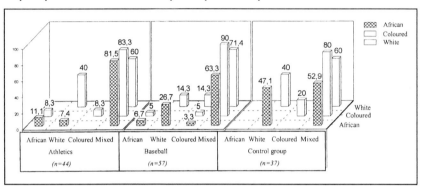

*Fig. 37a: Responses (in percentages) by members of Group A (athletics), B (baseball) and C (control group) **at the start of the project,** to the question: With fellow-participants from which culture(s)/population group(s) would you best like to practise sport?*

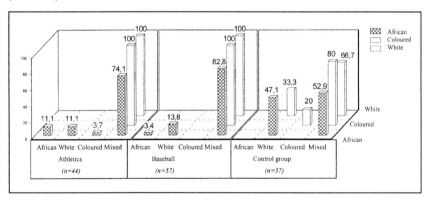

*Fig. 37b: Responses (in percentages) by members of Group A (athletics), B (baseball) and C (control group), **at the end of the first semester,** to the question: With fellow-participants from which culture(s)/population group(s) would you best like to practise sport?*

Figure 37a shows that the majority of pupils preferred to practise sport with fellow-participants from all population groups: in all three groups, there was a clear preference for the "mixed" option, though this was less pronounced in the control group than in the two multi-cultural training groups. Surprisingly, a varying percentage of African pupils in each of the three groups (7,4% in Group A, 26,7% in Group B, and a substantial 47,1% in Group C) said they wanted to practise sport within an all-White group.

The following diagram shows to what extent the situation had changed by the end of the first semester:

Figure 37b shows that, with the exception of the African pupils in Group A, there was a general increase in support for "mixed" sport among the participants of the Pinelands project in the course of the first semester. The control group, on the other hand, showed very little change. – An even more pronounced improvement among members of Groups B and C was recorded at the end of the school year:

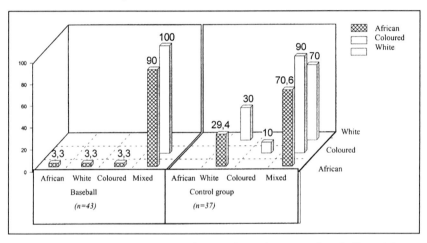

Fig. 37c: *Responses (in percentages) by members of Group B (baseball) and Group C (control group),* ***at the end of the school year,*** *to the question: With fellow-participants from which culture(s)/population group(s) would you best like to practise sport?*

All Coloured members of Group B (100%), and 90% of the African members, chose a "mixed" sport group, i.e. one in which all South African population groups were represented; only small minorities of African students favoured an exclusively African, Coloured and White sport group respectively. Even within the control group there was a noticeable shift in favour of a "mixed" group.

The reasons given for the general preference for a "mixed" group, was that children would get to know and help one another in this way. Many African pupils added that they liked White children who had "everything" (47%), were "better at sport" (12%), or could help African pupils to improve their English (12%); a further 12% said that inter-cultural friendships would promote peace in South Africa. A smaller percentage of African children (6%) said they would like to see how good the White children really were at sport – a sentiment echoed by 14% of the Coloured pupils, who said they loved to compete. A similar competitive attitude, coupled with the wish to see which population group performed best, motivated more than half of the White children (57%) in their wish to participate in "mixed" sport. The overwhelming majority of Coloured children, on the other hand, showed a friendlier frame of mind, saying they would like to meet pupils from "other" groups and foster friendships with them. 14% of the White children echoed this sentiment, adding that children from different groups should help one another; an equal percentage said they supported the "new South Africa", or simply enjoyed being part of a multi-cultural group.

Results of the statistical evaluation:

Members of all three groups (athletics, baseball, control group) were in favour of a culturally "mixed" sport group. In this regard, no significant difference in attitude could be established between the groups either before, during, or after the project.

The following diagram convey the pupils' views on the possible role of sport in facilitating friendships between members of different cultures/population groups. The same question was put to the pupils at the start of the project, and again at the end of the first semester:

Does sport make it easier to get to know persons of "other" cultures/ population groups?

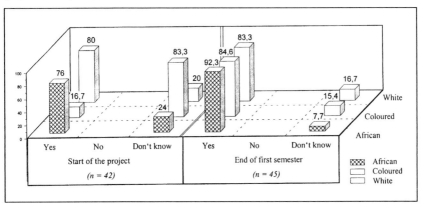

*Fig. 38a: Responses (in percentages) by members of Group A (athletics) **at the start of the project** and **at the end of the first semester** to the question: Does sport make it easier to get to know members of other cultures/population groups?*

139

Figure 38a illustrates the increase in the number of participants in Group A of the Pinelands project, and the increase in the number of participants who believed that sport provided good opportunities for getting to know pupils from "other" cultures/population groups. **At the start of the project**, roughly three-quarters of the African and White respondents (76% and 80% respectively) believed that joint sports training could facilitate social interaction. Only 16,7% of the Coloured participants at that stage shared this optimistic view, with over four-fifths (83,3%) opting for the cautious "don't know" stance; roughly one-fifth of the African and White pupils (24% and 20% respectively) were equally sceptical. However, **by the end of the first semester**, this scepticism had been overturned, with more than four-fifths of the Coloured and White students (84,6% and 83,3% respectively) avowing the social virtues of inter-cultural sports; among African students, the percentage supporting this view now stood at 92,3%. Remarkably, not a single students claimed that sport did not provide opportunities for multi-cultural friendships; however, a handful of students (7,7% of the Africans, 15,4% of the Coloureds, and 16,7% of the Whites) remained unconvinced that sport could make a positive difference, and stuck to the neutral "don't know" answer. Within one semester, the number of students who believed that sport could be a tool for integration rose from 25 to 40, which constituted an increase of 60%.

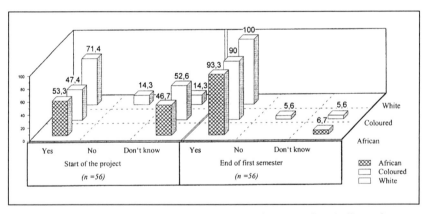

Fig. 38b: Responses (in percentages) by members of Group B (baseball), at the start of the project and at the end of the first semester, to the question: Does sport make it easier to get to know members of other cultures/population groups?

As Figure 38b indicates, there was an even more dramatic shift in favour of sport in Group B (baseball). **At the start of the project**, only about half of the African and Coloured students (53,3% and 47,4% respectively) believed that sport could promote social interaction between pupils of different cultures/ population groups. By the end of the first term, a minimum of 90% of all participants shared this view (93,3% of the Africans, 90% of the Coloureds, and a full 100% of the Whites). There was a corresponding drop in the number of "don't know" sceptics, who had at first constituted about half of the African and Coloured contingent of the baseball group (46.7% and 52,6% respectively). Overall, across all "cultures" or "population groups", the number of believers in the social virtues of sport in this group rose by a whopping 73%.

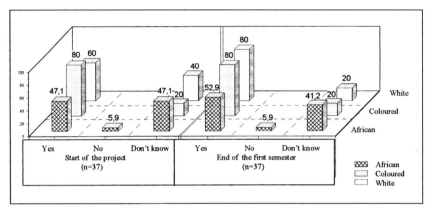

*Fig. 38c: Responses (in percentages) by members of Group C (control group) **at the start of the project** and **at the end of the first semester** to the question: Does sport make it easier to get to know pupils of other cultures/population groups?*

At the diagram indicates, even among the control group there was a swing of 14% in favour of the view that sport could facilitate and promote social action between members of different cultures/population groups. – At the start of the project, respondents who were of this view were asked to motivate it. Multiple responses were allowed, and there was no significant difference between the reasons given by members of the three groups (athletics, baseball, control group). 30% of all respondents said sport brought people together and got them to talk to one another; 20% said sport did not distinguish between Black and White, and 16% were convinced that everybody liked sport, regardless of race. Among the African respondents, 40% were motivated by the fact that a joint training programme would give them access to the superior sports facilities in predominantly White areas, while 60% of the Coloured pupils hoped pupils from all cultures/population groups would get to know one another. 76% of the White and 28% of African pupils said joint training would promote social interaction, because it would make competitions between the various schools a distinct possibility.

Six months later, respondents motivated their optimism by pointing to their personal experience of multi-cultural sport; many (53%) said this had taught them that joint sport could foster multi-cultural friendships; 7% believed sport could help them in future. – The control group's reasoning did not differ much from that at the start of the programme.

Another six months later, *at the end of the school year*, all baseball players (members of Group B2) said they now believed that sport could promote inter-cultural friendships. The control group remained more cautious or sceptical: 59% of the African pupils, and 80% of the Coloureds and Whites believed sport could help bridges and friendships, but 41% of the Africans, and 20% of the Coloureds and Whites chose the "don't know" option. Remarkably, not a single pupil in any of the three groups claimed that sport could not promote inter-cultural social interaction.

By the end of the project, three-quarters of the participants (76%) believed that sport made people forget whatever differences might exist between them, and thus helped them to get to know one another. 24% said they liked the "mixed" training group, and believed that they would jointly achieve the best results possible. The control group, on the other hand, repeated more or less the same views as six months earlier.

Results of the statistical analysis:

A significant number of the pupils participating in either the athletics or the baseball training programme changed their views on sport as a possible tool for social integration from an undecided "don't know" to an affirmative, supportive position (p < 0.01). By contrast, the control group failed to produce a similar change of views. It would therefore appear that pupils' views were influenced by their participation (or non-participation) in the training programme. No such significant difference, however, occurred between the "athletes'" views on the one hand, and those of the "baseball players" on the other. Neither was any significant difference recorded between the views professed by the baseball players after a whole year's programme, and those put forward at the end of the first semester. This circumstance suggests that the pupils' positive opinion of sport as a tool for integration had already been formed within the first six months, i.e. by the end of the first semester.

The salutary influence of sport on the integration of pupils from different cultural and social backgrounds is also demonstrated by the following: with the exception of two White pupils, all participants subscribed to the view that sport could promote social interaction and integration. Most pupils held this view even before the project began. Among the reasons cited for this confidence in the integrative function of sport were the following:
- sport makes people stand together, they need one another and help one another (70%);
- sport promotes peace (20%);
- everybody in the "new South Africa" can participate (8%);
- joint participation in sport improves one's knowledge of languages spoken by fellow-South Africans (3%).

The control group expressed the following opinions:
- sport can promote peace, especially since people in the past did not have

the opportunity of becoming acquainted, and the consequences of apartheid are still being felt (50%);
- through joint sport for everybody, people get to know one another and meet new friends (48%).

Summary interpretation of research into Group 7 (Pinelands project)

Research connected to the Pinelands project served the purpose of verifying hypotheses I, II and III, as formulated in the introduction. Preparatory research into the socio-economic and cultural conditions of the respondents showed that these were comparable to those of the subjects of research projects 2, 5 and 6 (see above). Once again, the long-term effects of the "Group Areas Act", as well as the effects of gender-specific differences and/or gender discrimination on patterns of leisure behaviour, commanded attention.

Since the aim of the research project was to get pupils directly and actively involved in sport, the project participants were asked to name their favourite sport codes/disciplines. Like other research projects within the overall ambit of this study, the responses by participants in the Pinelands project confirmed once again the overwhelming enthusiasm for soccer among African and Coloured boys, and the almost corresponding position of netball among African and Coloured girls. For reasons of traditional values, culture, and gender roles, active participation in sport is much more widespread among African and Coloured boys, than among the girls. African girls in particular appear to be subjected to severe restrictions by the traditional values of their society. Coloured and African girls usually devote a far greater part of their spare time to domestic chores, reading, and watching television, than to active participation in sport. Among White pupils, on the other hand, no gender-specific patterns of leisure behaviour were observed. Surprisingly, African girls cited netball as their favourite sports code, even if they had never played before. This can probably be partly attributed to the way in which netball is presented in the media, e.g. on television, and partly to the excitement and anticipation with which the participants approached the project.

At the start of the project, very few of the participants had any personal experience of social interaction with members of other cultures/population groups. The exception to this rule was the small percentage of pupils whose schools had begun admitting pupils from different population groups. Beyond the classroom and school playground, however, there was hardly any contact, let alone interaction. What little knowledge Coloured and African pupils had of the living conditions of White youths, was gleaned form occasional visits to shopping malls, or to their parents' places of employment in White residential areas. The White respondents, on the other hand, had never been to any Coloured or African township. Furthermore, very few pupils had any prior experience of multi-cultural sport; where such experience existed, it came from school, or from competitions (mostly in athletics) organised by the WPPSSU (Western Province Primary School Sport Union), in which (formerly) White schools were not represented.

As the evaluations by pupils and coaches/instructors indicate, the overwhelming majority of participants thoroughly enjoyed the Pinelands training project. Analysis reveals that both athletics and baseball were popular, though baseball slightly more so, especially among African and White pupils.

Figures 31 a) to c) indicate that many African and Coloured pupils were at first rather nervous about participating in either the athletics or baseball group. This may have been because for most pupils, this was the first time that they participated in sport outside their own residential areas, and jointly with pupils from other cultures/population groups. The White pupils, who also had little or no prior experience of multi-cultural sport, reacted with curiosity, rather than with nervous tension.

Pupils generally felt quite at home in the "mixed" group, and there was no significant difference between the athletics and the baseball group in this regard. Asked what aspect of the training programme they had enjoyed most, the majority of participants from both groups chose one of four given possibilities, viz. the fact that the training had taken place within a "mixed" group. The few suggestions put forward to improve the programme, included wishes for a meal before training sessions, improved sports facilities, and the inclusion of more sport codes/disciplines. Especially the first of these requests was a timely reminder of the constant presence of the socio-economic inequalities and problems, which many people from disadvantaged communities continue to face.

The results of the Pinelands Training Programme

The Pinelands project brought about a remarkable change in the relationships and patterns of social interaction between its participants. Figures 32 a) – c) indicate the general lack of social interaction between pupils from different groups prior to the start of the project. At that stage, the majority of African and Coloured pupils admitted that they thought it difficult to foster friendships with youths from other cultures/population groups.

The reasons offered for this perceived difficulty, especially by members of the control group, were revealing: after the language problem, cited by 50% of respondents, the most frequently quoted causes were the lack of contact between different groups, the physical or geographical distance between the residential "group areas", and the resulting isolation and mutual alienation, which most rightly linked to apartheid. The results of the statistical evaluation in Figures 36 a) to 36 b) and 38 a) to 38 c) illustrate that the project not only prompted pupils from different cultures/population groups to become acquainted with one another, but also improved their general attitude towards members of "other" groups. As Figures 37a to 37c show, this especially applied to White pupils.

Figures 33 a) to 34 c) show a remarkable increase in the number of friends from "other" cultures/population groups among participants of the Pinelands project, especially when compared to the control group. The decisive factor here appears to be the duration of the mutual exposure, rather than the sports code or discipline chosen.

These findings are corroborated by responses to the control questions, viz. a) whether the training itself offered much opportunity for social interaction, and b) whether the training project changed participants' attitude towards pupils from other cultures/population groups. It is true that attitudes within the control group also changed somewhat over time, but change here was rather negligible when compared to the significant shifts in the training groups.

Furthermore, the findings based on questionnaires were also supported by socio-metric research and analysis of video recordings. The training sessions were regularly recorded on video tape, and the frequency and duration of instances of social interaction were noted and compared. The measurements showed a steady progression: brief and furtive at first, the "instances of interaction" soon expanded into long conversations and games.

As noted above, the wish to practise "mixed" sport was present not only among members of the training groups, but also within the control group. This means that the wish for mutual contact existed before, and was not dependent on, any intervention by educators. It can therefore safely be assumed that many young South Africans from all population groups would gladly meet and mingle on the sports field or elsewhere, if only the political, social and economic legacy of apartheid did not put practical obstacles in the way. Initiatives like the Pinelands project can therefore help young South Africans to achieve the more relaxed and unrestrained social interaction which they already wish for.

The findings set out above confirm hypothesis I, i.e. that sport can help to build bridges and overcome divisions between young South Africans of different cultures/population groups, and thus contribute towards overcoming the legacy of apartheid. Furthermore, the Pinelands project also proved that planned, organised sport projects at grass roots level contribute towards social interaction and integration, thus confirming hypothesis III. By contrast, no evidence was found to support hypothesis II, i.e. that team sports are more effective than individual sports disciplines in promoting social interaction. It would therefore appear that decades of apartheid have generated such a lack of, and need for, social interaction between South Africans from different cultural and social backgrounds, that virtually any kind of joint activity must be regarded as an improvement on the status quo.

Empirical research findings: Group 8
Teachers and trainers participating in the Pinelands project and/or dance workshop

Not only the pupils, but also the teachers, trainers and instructors participating in the projects studied here were asked to fill in questionnaires. The aim was to find out how effective these educators found sport as a tool for social integration, and to trace the participants' history of experiences with multi-cultural or "mixed" sport.

a) Socio-cultural background

The sample consisted of one dancer from an African township, one dancer who specialised in "street dance" and lived in a Coloured residential area, two South African Indian dancers, one White, Afrikaans-speaking dance instructor, and two Coloured and two White sports coaches. In addition, a number of teachers from participating schools acted as coaches in the Pinelands project (one White, three African and three Coloured teachers). Overall, the group consisted of five women (one PE teacher and four dancing instructors) and eleven men. The average age was 28.6 years (the oldest trainer was 65), and all the instructors lived in residential areas traditionally reserved for their "population group". The dancing instructors had undergone training for periods varying from two to ten years, the coaches were university- or college-qualified PE teachers with three to four years' formal training. Only one teacher had no such qualification, but he was a practising high-performance sportsman. Two of the teachers participating in the Pinelands project were formally qualified as PE teachers (with three years' training), while the rest were experienced PE instructors without formal training.

b) Sport at school

None of the participating African schools had either a sports field or a gymnasium at its disposal, and the teachers described the schools' sports equipment as "insufficient". None of them followed any sports curriculum, for the simple reason that none existed for their schools; had there been one, it would in any event have been a mockery, given the lack of facilities. Neither did the participating Coloured schools enjoy the "luxury" of sufficient equipment, though teacher confirmed that a curriculum was actually being followed.

The White school hosting the project had a gymnasium and several sports grounds, as well as equipment in sufficient variety and quantity. PE was taught at the White and Coloured schools, but not at the African township schools. All schools did, however, offer sport as an extra-mural activity and/or coaching for the members of the schools' sports teams.

The following table highlights the discrepancies in the provision of school sports facilities, and the corresponding variation in the numbers of pupils participating:

Numbers of participants in various extra-mural sport disciplines

Table 21: Numbers of participants in extra-mural sport disciplines at schools

Number of participants / Sport code/Discipline	African schools	Coloured schools	White schools
Netball	20	36	120
Athletics	50	unknown	70
Soccer	21	35	
Cricket	14		170
Hockey		20	350
Cross-country/jogging		12	
Volleyball		20	
Table tennis		12	
Chess		10	
Rugby			80
Basketball			160
Swimming			60
Water polo			200

PE teachers are assisted by other teachers with coaching and/or extra-mural sports activities in the afternoons. At the White schools, parents also lend a hand.

Teachers at each of the (traditionally) segregated schools to a large degree agreed among themselves regarding the major problems facing PE instructors and coaches, notwithstanding differences among teachers from different schools. To most teachers at African schools, their own lack of training presented a "major problem", as did the shortage of sports facilities and equipment; this was complemented by the learners' lack of motivation, which was considered "quite serious". On the other hand, African teachers had "no problem" with the large classes, or with their own motivation. All Coloured teachers were likewise aggrieved by the "major problem" of a lack of equipment, but only half regarded their own deficient training in the same serious light. Half of the Coloured teachers saw large classes, their own lack of motivation, and their students' disinterest as "rather serious" problems, while their colleagues were quite comfortable with these aspects. To the White teacher, his own lack of training and his learners' motivation levels were "minor problems", but he was content with class sizes, the provision of facilities and equipment, and with his own motivation.

c) Previous multi-cultural sports experience

By their own admission, none of the African teachers had ever instructed a multi-cultural group in PE. The same applied to three of the Coloured teachers. One Coloured teacher and his White colleague had instructed culturally mixed groups before, with the difference that the previously White school was now being attended by pupils from all population groups, whereas the predominantly Coloured school had been joined by some African pupils, but not by Whites. Six of the coaches/dance instructors had previously worked with culturally mixed groups, but a further two had no such previous experience. 62% of the teachers and coaches/dance instructors with previous multi-cultural experience saw no difference between the physical skills of pupils from different population groups. One White teacher believed African pupils were better at long-distance running than Whites, and one Coloured teacher thought African children were weaker gymnasts than Coloureds. Another Coloured teacher believed that, on account of socio-economic and cultural reasons, African pupils were physically not as strong as their White counterparts.

Asked to name difficulties experienced in multi-cultural coaching, teachers mostly referred to language problems, inappropriate use of unfamiliar sports equipment, and an insufficient knowledge of sports rules. Two teachers confessed to their own nervousness when dealing with multi-cultural classes.

d) Experiences in the multi-cultural sports projects

Table 22 reflects the predominantly positive impressions and opinions with which instructors (coaches and dance instructors) and participating teachers looked back upon the Pinelands project.

The teachers were also asked to name the greatest difference between pupils from their own school and those from other participating schools. Only five teachers replied to this question. One African teacher emphasized the difference in physical size (occasioned by dietary differences), as well as a difference in linguistic competence. The Coloured teachers found the African children less disciplined than Coloured pupils, and the White children more assertive and perseverant than their own charges. The White teacher mainly saw differences in socio-economic background, and mentioned the fact that only the White pupils had any previous experience of being coached. Asked for their impressions of their pupils' feelings during the last session of the programme, the African and Coloured teachers replied unanimously that their students had looked forward to the session, and the White teacher reported that his students had shown great interest. Seven dance instructors reported a similar reaction

Table 22: Rating of the Pinelands project by coaches/dance instructors (N = 9) and by participating teachers (N = 7).

Research groups/samples Questions	Dancing instructors/coaches (N=9)	Participating teachers (N=7)
Describe your feelings when approaching your first training session	I looking forward to session 8 curious	I looking forward to session 1 nervous 5 curious
How did you like the coaching/training	6 very much 3 much	4 very much 2 much 1 ok
How competent did you find the trainers?		5 very competent 1 competent 1 partly competent
How qualified did you find the teachers?	6 partly qualified 2 not qualified 1 gave no reply	
In your opinion, to what extent did the teachers benefit from the coaching programme?	3 to a very large extent 1 to a large extent 5 gave no reply.	
To what extent did you yourselves benefit from the coaching programme		3 to a very large extent 3 to a large extent 1 partly
In your opinion, did the pupils like the coaching programme	4 very much 4 much 1 rather well	2 very much 4 much 1 rather well
How do you rate the pupils chances of getting to know one another?	2 very good 5 good 1 average 1 gave no reply	1 very good 4 good 2 average
What amount of tensions did you note among the pupils?	5 none 4 little	3 none 2 little 2 some
To what extend did language affect the training programme?	3 to a very large extend 1 to a large extent 1 partly 1 hardly 1 insignificantly	3 to a very large extend 2 to a large extent 2 hardly

from their charges, five believed the pupils had looked forward to the session, three teachers had found the children "enthusiastic", and one said the pupils had been "sad" that the end of the course had arrived. – Multiple answers to this question were allowed.

e) Sport as a tool for social integration

Teachers, trainers and dance instructors were subsequently asked to assess the project as a tool for generating mutual understanding between children from different population groups. This is how they responded:

To what extent did the project promote mutual understanding between pupils from different cultures?

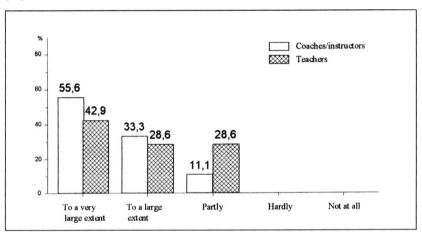

Fig. 39: Answers (in percentages) by coaches, instructors and teachers to the question: To what extent did the Pinelands project promote mutual understanding between pupils from different cultures?

As Figure 39 indicates, the majority of coaches/instructors believed that the multicultural sports project promoted mutual understanding "to a very large extent".

A third of the coaches/instructors, and more than a quarter of the teachers were a bit more cautious, and said mutual understanding had benefited "to a large extent". Some coaches and teachers, however, believed the programme's success in building bridges had been "limited".

Asked whether they personally had found any opportunity of fostering cross-cultural acquaintances or friendships as a result of their participation in the project, the coaches/instructors and teachers answered as follows:

Did the Pinelands project offer you personally any opportunity of fostering acquaintances or friendships with members of other population groups?

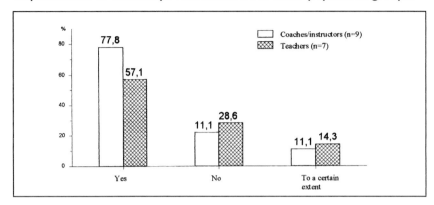

Fig. 40: Answers (in percentages) by coaches/instructors to the question: Did the Pinelands project offer you personally any opportunity of fostering acquaintances or friendships with persons from other cultural groups?

Figure 40 indicates that three-quarters of the coaches/dance instructors had experienced the training project as an opportunity of getting to know someone from another population group. Other respondents disagreed with this view, while yet others felt that only superficial contact had been achieved. Subsequently, the coaches/dance instructors and teachers were asked whether the Pinelands project had changed their attitudes towards members of other population groups. They responded as follows:

Did the Pinelands project change your attitude towards members of other population groups?

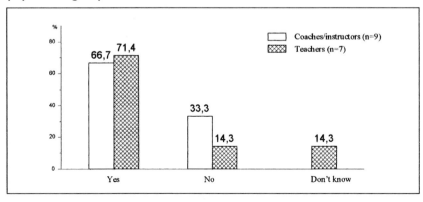

Fig. 41: Answers by coaches/dance instructors and teachers to the question: Did the Pinelands project change your attitude towards members of other population groups?

Two-thirds of the coaches/dance instructors, and almost three-quarters of the teachers confirmed that their attitude towards teachers and pupils from other population groups had changed as a result of the training project. Three coaches/dance instructors and one teacher believed their attitude had remained unchanged, and one teacher was uncertain.

The question whether anything had been learnt about other population groups as a result of the project, elicited a similar response pattern as the previous question. One African teacher said all participants had seemed to enjoy the training, and had reached out to their fellow-participants; another African teacher observed that the atmosphere had been pleasant and warm, while a third had realised that pupils from different population groups had much in common. Two Coloured teachers believed there were no differences between the participants, and a third was convinced that sport could bring people together. The White teacher did not believe that he had learnt anything new about members of other population groups.

Two coaches/dance instructors had the impression that the participating pupils were very keen to acquire new skills, and two others believed that the pupils had learnt something about their fellow-participants' languages and customs. Another two coaches/instructors had found the pupils very gifted, while two others had been surprised by the teachers' high level of motivation. Finally, the course had led one teacher to realise that patience and empathy help to achieve better results.

The respondents were then asked whether initiatives like the Pinelands project could contribute towards building a new South Africa. They answered as follows:

To what extent can initiatives like the Pinelands project contribute towards building a new South Africa?

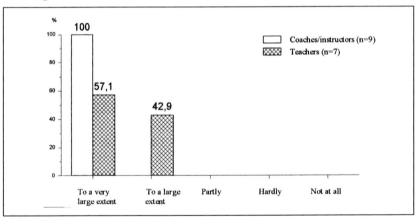

Fig. 42: Answers (in percentages) by coaches/instructors to the question: To what extent can initiatives like the Pinelands project contribute towards building a new South Africa?

Figure 42 shows that all coaches/dancing instructors believed that such projects were an extremely important contribution towards the new South Africa. This opinion was shared by a majority of the seven teachers, namely four. The remaining three were only slightly less enthusiastic, believing that such initiatives could contribute "to a large extent".

All coaches/instructors and participating teachers were of the opinion that sport could indeed help to foster friendships between various population groups. Multiple responses to this question were allowed.

Is sport capable of fostering friendships between members of different population groups? (in the opinion of coaches/instructors and teachers)

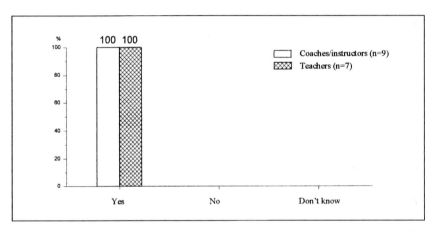

Fig. 43: Answers (in percentages) by coaches/instructors and teachers to the question: Can sport foster friendships between members of different population groups?

Figure 43 indicates that after witnessing the interaction on the sports field between pupils from different population groups, all participating instructors/coaches and teachers agreed that sport can make a considerable contribution towards a better mutual understanding between peoples from different races and classes, as well as improve gender relations.

Asked to advance reasons for this conviction, respondents said that sport caused the animosity engendered by socialisation to wane; children want to get to know one another, friendships are formed, and communication, mutual respect and understanding are strengthened. Some respondents were of the opinion that sport makes people forget such factors as origin and skin colour, that sport can even build bridges without the support of language ("sport is like a language"), that children reach out to one another, and that sport promotes a neutral kind of competition.

More specifically, most respondents also believed that sport could unite people from various suburbs and townships in and around Cape Town. According to them, sport was capable of overcoming the apartheid ideology and of healing the wounds inflicted by that system. The African teachers pointed out unanimously that sport had also divided people on the sports field, that each population group had participated in sport within the limits of the group's economic possibilities, and that the Pinelands project had been a first in terms of overcoming an antiquated system. All the Coloured teachers involved in the project agreed with this; what the Pinelands project had achieved on a small scale, could be repeated at a higher level by selecting national teams from all population groups, with the result that the whole population would unite in its support of such a team. One coach related this vision to the Olympic Games to be held in 2004, for which Cape Town had submitted an application. The White teacher endorsed this view, but believed that such unity would only be brought about by major sporting events, and would thus not occur very often. The coaches and dance instructors believed that sport could bring South Africans closer to one another, provided that the educational system was first improved. A further prerequisite was the improvement of social structures, since children continued to live in different residential areas and to attend different schools.

Summary interpretation of the findings on Group 8

The opinion poll of teachers and coaches/dance instructors was conducted in order to complement the research findings on Groups 4, 5 and 6. Although focussing on a small group of individuals who to a large extent voiced personal and subjective views, the interviews nevertheless produced significant background information and socio-cultural perspectives which supplement and support the information and findings based on observing and interviewing the other groups.

The poll confirmed the disadvantages of the traditionally African and Coloured schools in terms of facilities and equipment, range of subjects offered, and even curricula, and thereby highlighted the discrepancies in the education provided for different population groups. In addition, it reflected the virtual non-existence of multicultural contact and engagement on the sports fields.

The sample group's assessment of the Pinelands project was overwhelmingly positive. Quite apart from its positive effects on the pupils, the teachers and coaches/instructors felt they had also personally benefited from the programme. One difference was that the teachers tended to regard language and linguistic difference as an important factor of communication, even on the sports field, whereas the trainers and coaches seemed to feel that sport generated its own means of communication. Figures 39 and 40 unequivocally demonstrate the multicultural sports project's positive influence on social interaction between members of different population groups. Especially the African and Coloured respondents emphasized how mutual understanding had grown and attitudes had changed for the better as a result of shared experiences on the sports field (cf. Fig. 41). This supports hypothesis III.

All the teachers, trainers and coaches involved in the Pinelands project shared the opinion that sport could help to build friendships between members of different population groups, and consequently saw the Pinelands project as an important contribution towards the "new South Africa."

3.6 Dancing Across the Barriers: An Extra-mural Dance Project

The dance project had several, simultaneous aims. Firstly, I wanted to establish to what extent extra-mural, non-curricular activities could promote the social integration of "mother tongue" and "foreign language" pupils, especially in the initial phase. Secondly, I believed that if the students' interest in South Africa's diverse and rich cultural heritage could be wakened, a personal interest in fellow-pupils - as bearers of these cultural traditions - might be a welcome spin-off. To achieve this, it was vital to involve indigenous dancers in the project.

The first dancing workshop, conducted during the first school term of 1992, was advertised as "African Dance Workshop", and focussed on "African Dance and Street Dance". A fairly large number of pupils enrolled, by entering their names in the list of participants. However, some of the "mother tongue" pupils later withdrew their registration, on the grounds that their parents did not approve of the project. The second dance workshop was held two years later, in 1994, and covered Street dance, Indian dance, and Afrikaans folk dancing. For the purposes of evaluation, the responses to both projects were examined jointly, except for a few cases of clear divergences, which are indicated below. In both cases, the participants were asked to complete two questionnaires each – one at the first workshop session, and one at the last. The participant responded as follows:

a) Participants' socio-cultural background

1. Age and "cultural" or "population" group
In 1992, four pupils from each of the three "cultural" or "population" groups – Africans, Coloureds and Whites – participated; they were 12 to 14 years old. In 1994, there were 23 participants ranging from 8 to 15 years of age – ten African girls, six African boys, four Coloured girls, and three White girls.

2. Pastimes
At the beginning of the project, the participants indicated a total of 71 pastimes of hobbies. The most popular among these were reading (21%) and sport

(59%), dancing (15%) and swimming (13%) being the most-mentioned codes or disciplines. Other pastimes were singing, listening to music, playing with friends, watching TV, drawing, pets, and going to the beach (4% each). By the end of the project, there had been a 10% swing towards dancing: sports continued to be the favourite pastime (at 72%), with dancing and swimming increasing their ratings to 25% and 18% respectively. Reading (17%) and spending time with friends (7%) were also mentioned.

b) What were the participants' views on sport in general, and on PE at the German school in particular?

At the beginning of the project, 25 out of the 35 participants said they liked sport, as opposed to six who disliked it, and four who "sometimes" liked sport. By the end of the project, all 35 said they liked sport. The reaction to PE classes was almost as positive: In the first pole, 18 respondents said they liked the PE lessons, 14 found it okay, and only two disliked these classes; by the time of the second pole, the number of those who "liked" sport had risen to 25, the "okays" had dropped to eight, but the two who "disliked" sport remained adamant. The respondents could give multiple reasons for their attitude towards PE lessons; the greatest number (36%) simply said they enjoyed sport, but a significant 12% believed that PE lessons, and in particular the instruction in team sports, could promote social integration. Asked what sport codes and disciplines they practised during PE lessons, the pupils' responses indicated the prevalence of individual sports – athletics (31%) and swimming (23%) – over team sports and ball games such as soccer (10%), handball (9%) and basketball (8%). In 1994, a staggering 72% of responses named individual sports. By contrast, the students own preferences favoured team sports: 17 pupils said they preferred team sports, with eleven respondents giving the "thumbs up" to individual sports; four pupils indicated an equal liking for individual and team sports.

c) Reasons for participating and first reactions to the dance workshop

Asked for their reasons for joining the workshop, 21 of the respondents said they liked dancing, and eight wanted to try "something completely different"; significantly, four girls, all of them African, hoped to find new friends among their fellow-participants.

None of the participants had any previous experience of inter-cultural dancing lessons or workshops, though about two-thirds had attended some dancing lessons (e.g. ballet, contemporary, etc.). It is therefore not surprising that they entered this project with mixed feelings: 20 were excited, 10 curious, and five (most of them White) were nervous; one African pupil indicated a certain anxiety. Despite these apprehensions, 19 of the participants like the first lesson "very much", eleven "liked" it, and only one participant was not satisfied.

The respondents were then allowed to give multiple responses to the question: What did you like best/least about the dance workshop. The following figure indicates the responses:

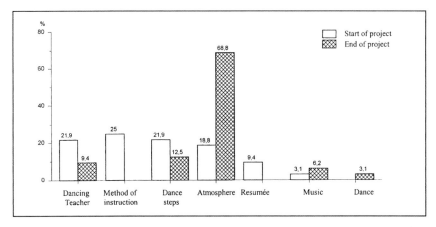

Fig. 44: Participants' responses (in percentages) concerning "likes and dislikes" regarding the multi-cultural dance workshop; polls taken at start and end of workshop course (N = 32)

Figure 44 indicates a shift in participants' preferences from aspects such as the method of instruction, the instructor, dance steps etc., which were particularly valued at the start of the course, towards "atmosphere" (i.e. aspects such as "group feeling", "fun", and meeting with new friends), which gained importance in the course of the workshop. This trend was perceived in both the 1992 and 1994 intakes. None of the 1992 participants indicated any "dislikes" pertaining to the workshop. Of the 1994 group, one member each indicated a dislike for one of the following elements: the dance steps, the grade 5 pupils, the résumé, and the demonstration of the dance steps; the rest of the group indicated that there was nothing they disliked about the workshop.

d) Relationship between foreign-language and mother-tongue pupils

At the start and the end of the two courses, the participants were asked how they felt about the inter-cultural dance workshop. A break-down of their responses reads as follows:

Start of 1992 workshop (N = 12):
- 5 pupils were thrilled at the thought of participating in an inter-cultural dance workshop
- 3 pupils were apprehensive
- 3 pupils were undecided
- 1 pupil did not like the idea

End of 1992 workshop (N = 12):
- 7 pupils liked the workshop very much
- 5 pupils rated the workshop "okay"

Start of 1994 workshop (N = 22):
- 14 pupils were thrilled at the thought of participating in an inter-cultural dance workshop
- 3 pupils found the idea "okay"
- 3 pupils found it exciting
- 2 pupils were uncertain (did not know what to think)

End of 1994 workshop (N = 22):
- 16 pupils liked the workshop very much
- 4 pupils rated the workshop "okay"
- 2 pupils found it exciting

According to the Mc Nemar-Chi square test, which was used to calculate the significance of the two inter-dependent samples, a significant number of pupils displayed a change of attitude between the start and the end of the workshop: seven pupils who had been uncertain at the start of the course, showed a favourable attitude by the end of the course. This indicates that the inter-cultural workshop influenced their attitude towards inter-cultural projects, and towards members of other "culture" or "population" groups. At the end of each of the two courses, participants were asked whether the workshop had given them the opportunity of getting to know a fellow-pupil belonging to a different "culture" or "population" group. In 1992, all the African and White participants answered this question in the affirmative, as did three-quarters of the Coloured pupils. In 1994, all the Coloured and White participants answered in the affirmative, as did 15 of the African pupils; only two African pupils were uncertain about this question, and one answered in the negative. These responses are reflected in the following graph:

Did the dance workshop give pupils the opportunity of inter-cultural social interaction

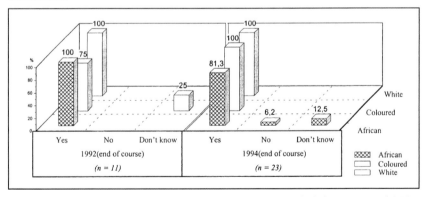

Fig. 45: *Participants' responses (in percentages) at the end of the 1992 and 1994 courses to the question: Did the dance workshop give you the opportunity of inter-cultural social interaction?*

Neither in 1992 nor in 1994 was there any significant difference ($p < 0.05$) between the responses of participants from different population groups. In other words, both workshops offered participants of all groups the opportunity to get to know members of other groups.

At the end of each course, the participants were asked what this experience had taught them about members of other population groups. The question elicited a wide spectrum of responses:

- Seven pupils had learnt that there were no differences between children from different groups, and that skin colour was irrelevant;

- Seven pupils had learnt that children from the "other" group were very good dancers;

- Four pupils had learnt to speak a few sentences in the "other" participants' mother tongue;

- Four pupils had learnt that children from different groups could help one another and co-operate with one another;

- Four pupils were of the opinion that the initial stages of working together on such a project were difficult, but that social or cultural differences became irrelevant in the course co-operation;

- Three pupils had learnt that everybody is "special" in respect of some activity, even though this might strike one as unusual at first;

- Three pupils had learnt how pupils from other groups "feel about things";

- Two pupils had discovered that children from "other" groups could be quite "likeable";

- One pupil said she had learnt to be more self-confident when meeting children from "other" groups.

Asked whether their attitude towards children from "other" groups had changed in the course of the first school term, 14 respondents said this had been the case, eight others had observed no change in their own attitude, and 13 replied that they did not know. – A break-down of these responses by "population group" presents the following picture:

Did the dance workshop change participants' attitude towards "other" population/culture groups?

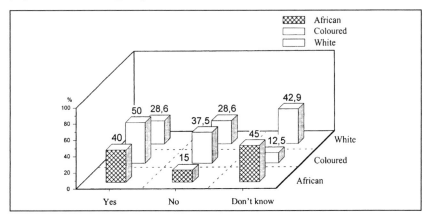

Fig. 46: Participants' answers (in percentages) at the end of the 1992 and 1994 workshops (N = 35) to the question: Did your attitude towards pupils from other population/culture groups change as a result of your participation in the multicultural dance workshop?

There is no significant difference ($p < 0.05$) between respondents from the three groups as regards changes in their attitude towards members of "other" groups as a result of the multicultural dance workshop. Any differences which may have been recorded should be regarded as purely incidental.

Asked to explain how and why their attitudes had changed in the course of the project, twelve respondents said they had joined the workshop with "mixed feelings", and they had not expected the participants from "other" groups either to be so "likeable", or to be such "accomplished dancers". Eight respondents believed that the workshop had taught them to accept pupils from "other" groups as they were, because they had learnt that all human beings are equal. A further eight participants believed that, given time, participants from different groups should (and would) get used to one another. Seven participants conceded that they had been "nervously excited" about the workshop, but the reason for this had not been any belief that children from "other" groups were in any significant way "different" from themselves.

In order to establish to what extent participants from different population/culture groups had got to know one another in the course of the workshop, sociometric tests were conducted. The participants were asked to identify the following persons: the best dancer, and the jolliest, the most serious, the liveliest and the quietest persons among the workshop participants. The results were as follows:

In 1992, as in 1994, pupils' perceptions of fellow-participants were quite objective, i.e. independent of such variables as age, school grade, or skin colour. For instance, the majority of participants in the 1992 workshop (two-thirds of the African pupils, half of the Coloureds, and one-third of the Whites) voted a Coloured girl the best dancer of the workshop. In 1994 (N = 23), an African boy was voted best dancer by 16 of the 23 participants. Of the 1992 intake (N = 11), ten voted an African girl jolliest member of the workshop. In most other categories, both workshops showed similarly high levels of consensus.

Participants' comments on the dance workshop

At the end of both the first and the last meeting of each workshop, the participants were asked how they felt about the project. The following graph gives an overview of both the 1992 and 1994 responses:

How did the pupils find the dance workshop?

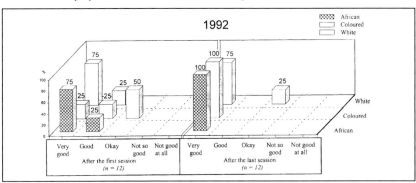

Fig. 47a: Answers (in percentages) by participants of the 1992 workshop (n = 12) to the question: How did/do you like the intercultural dance workshop?

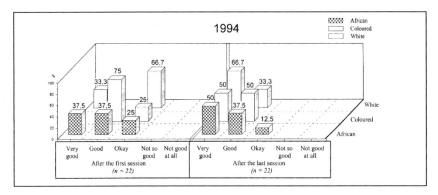

Fig. 47b: Answers (in percentages) by participants of the 1994 workshop (n = 22) to the question: How did/do you like the intercultural dance workshop?

The significance of the two interrelated samples presented here was established with the aid of the Mc Nemar-Chi square test. According to my findings, a significant number of participants ($p < 0.01$) were undecided at the start of the course and rated it only "okay", but more enthusiastic by the end of the course. It would therefore seem that the dance workshop succeeded in giving participants a more favourable impression of such intercultural activities.

Both in 1992 and in 1994, all participants indicated that they had enjoyed the workshop. Similarly, the pupils had liked all the dances practised during the course, with the Indian dance (15 responses) proving the most popular, with the Street Dance/African Dance combination and the folk dance sharing the second place (10 responses each).

A combined number of 31 participants in either of the two workshops would have liked to continue with the course, with 23 of these respondents giving reasons for this wish. Significantly, three African pupils gave the reason that it was good to discover one's own abilities, and to become part of a group. Two participants were of the opinion that the workshop had been a good opportunity for "getting to know one another". Only four participants were undecided as to whether, given the opportunity, they would have continued to attend the workshop. Of these, one White pupil said his/her parents were opposed to the workshop, two Coloured girls were planning to attend a Xhosa workshop instead, while the remaining (African) respondent gave no reason for not wishing to continue.

Ten respondents of either of the workshops responded to the call to submit proposals for improvement. Half of these – all of them Africans – suggested that the workshop organise a public performance, while two participants wanted the workshop to continue for the whole school year.

Finally, the participants were asked to react to two statements, by choosing any one of the following replies: I agree strongly, I agree, I don't know, I disagree, I disagree strongly. The two statements – and the participants' choices – read as follows:

a) Statement 1: "Dancing makes it easier to meet pupils from other population/culture groups" (in this case: "mother tongue" and "foreign language" pupils respectively):
- Four respondents agreed strongly, 19 agreed, and twelve said they did not know;

b) Statement 2: "A dance workshop is better suited than any other extra-curricular activity to introducing people to different cultures":
- Eleven respondents agreed strongly, 18 agreed, and six said they did not know.

Summary interpretation of findings relating to research sample 4

The study indicated that sport is a favourite pastime among pupils of all population groups. Even the curricular PE classes, especially the training sessions devoted to team sports, were regarded as possible tools for social integration by two-thirds of the African respondents, and by one-third of the Whites. Furthermore, it became clear that Coloured and African pupils greatly appreciated PE instruction and extra-curricular sports activities at the DSK. For many of these pupils, this was their first experience of sports codes and disciplines of which apartheid had deprived them in the past (e.g. swimming and basketball). The majority of Coloured and African pupils preferred team sports, whereas White pupils showed a preference for individual sports.

None of the African participants in the 1992 dance workshop participated in any of the other workshops on offer at the DSK, whereas Coloured and White pupils generally enrolled for more than one workshop. A possible reason for this difference may have been the reticence and shyness shown by many African pupils when they first attended the DSK. In turn, this shyness most probably results from the sharp difference in equipment and funding between the DSK on the one hand, and African (and, to a lesser extent, Coloured) township schools on the other. To many African pupils, the DSK with its ample sports facilities, generous equipment, and hostel regime of warm meals, TV and videos, must at first have seemed like paradise – at least in material terms. In addition, before being admitted to the DSK, many of the "foreign-language" students were subjected to a very authoritarian regime at some township primary school.

At many township schools, corporal punishment was the rule, rather than the exception, and directly addressing one's elders, or expressing a personal opinion (especially if it happened to differ from the 'official truth') was considered a breach of protocol, if not a form of misbehaviour. For this reason, many African pupils, and especially the girls, are at first rather intimidated by the more individualistic and easy-going routine at a German-language private school, were much store is set by developing pupils' individual personalities. Many African pupils take some time to become accustomed to this unfamiliar regime.

As the findings indicate, the number of female African pupils participating in the DSK' workshops had risen by 1994. Most pupils, of all population groups, tend to enjoy dancing. Most participants in either of the two dance workshops agreed that the workshop
a) had a significant and beneficial effect on pupils' attitude towards multi- or intercultural activities;
b) led pupils from different population/culture groups to get to know one another, to learn more about (and from) one another, and to co-operate with one another;
c) made it much easier for pupils from different population/culture groups to interact with one another on a social level (cf. Figure 45);

163

d) generated and/or enhanced mutual respect among pupils from different population/culture groups, and enhanced pupils' willingness to re-examine their own opinions about "other" pupils and, where necessary, to change them. – Fig. 46 shows how much progress was made, within only three months, in improving pupils' mutual attitudes.

Undoubtedly, the choice of dances practised in the workshop, and the selection of the dancers who presented these dances, contributed greatly to the success of the project. Each dance was presented by an "authentic" member of the relevant cultural group, and the culture concerned was not only reflected in the dance itself, but also in the dancers' clothing and language. This greatly impressed the participants in the workshop, who showed great motivation right from the start. The motivation to learn more about the particular cultures was further enhanced by background information on the dances, as well as by visual aids, such as maps, illustrations of traditional costumes, etc. (cf. Fig. 47a/47b).

Dance was very important to the workshop members, especially to the African pupils, whom it helped to overcome their shyness, and the limitations which language and social barriers often imposed on their possibilities of self-expression. In this way, the dance workshop raised the African pupils' self-confidence and improved their self-image. - When I returned to the DSK in 1996, I was happy to find that the African pupils who had participated in either the 1992 or the 1994 workshop, had formed a dance group, which not only rehearsed regularly on school premises, but also often performed at functions, both within the school and beyond.

As video recordings of the workshops show, dance releases emotions, and the African and Coloured children took great pleasure in teaching dance steps to their White fellow-pupils. For once, they enjoyed an advantage which, on account of their often deficient prior education at township schools, they seldom experienced in class time, or at any of the other workshops, such as those devoted to swimming or computers. Especially with the African dances, the workshop used to break up into smaller groups, each of which practised particular steps and movements, which were then demonstrated to other groups, and eventually to the plenary. This structure and method of instruction proved very popular, since it helped to reduce the levels of nervousness and apprehension which had been noticeable at the start of both workshop courses.

By way of summary, it can be stated that the present study very clearly demonstrated the suitability of sport in general, and of dance in particular, as a mechanism for promoting intercultural social integration. This finding is not only borne out by the participants' responses, but also by personal observation, and by the analysis of video footage.

Dance as a multicultural activity is particularly suited to promoting not only the visible interaction between members of socially and/or culturally diverse groups, but also to exert a positive influence on the attitude and emotions of pupils. In this way, it can generate feelings of togetherness and social cohesion among participants, which can – temporarily, at least – override cultural and social divisions.

Organised in the form of an extra-curricular, voluntary workshop, dancing can be more effective in promoting intercultural social integration than, for instance, any of the compulsory academic subjects taught at schools. In this way, it can be used to help pupils "settle in" in new and unfamiliar school surroundings, especially in the difficult initial phases of interaction and integration. Dancing can thus be used as a preventative strategy of social intervention, to help pupils overcome initial discomforts and difficulties, such as social isolation and culture shock. No gender-specific differences were observed in relation to these effects.

The findings of this study confirmed hypotheses I and III, as developed in chapter 1. Hypothesis I: By promoting social interaction, sport can be used to bridge the gap between population groups previously separated and mutually antagonised by apartheid. Hypothesis III: Consciously conceived and planned multi-cultural sports projects at grass-roots level can draw together members of socially or culturally diverse groups.

3.7 Selected Interviews with Stakeholders and Roleplayers in Politics, Education and Society

Between 1993 and 1997 I conducted a substantial number of interviews with stakeholders and roleplayers in politics, the church, education and sport. The aim was to get a more comprehensive view of the transformation processes under way in South Africa, and to gain additional insights into multilingual cultural politics, the South African educational system, and of sport structures in South Africa.

The following umbrella summary of conversations with various partners is an attempt to reflect the broad spectrum of opinions voiced. I believe this aim is best served by grouping divergent views under appropriate topic headings, rather than by reproducing entire interviews, one after the other. This latter method has only been adopted in the case of Archbishop Desmond Tutu and Dr. Neville Alexander.

The topic "schools as multicultural meeting places" elicited opinions from pupils, teachers, school principals and others involved with education, and from representatives of the German Federal Government.

"Schools as multicultural meeting places"

It was interesting to note that there appears to be no uniform understanding of this concept. The principal of the Foreign Language stream at the *Deutsche Schule Kapstadt (DSK) (German-language School, Cape Town)* believes it refers to

> *... a school at which pupils of different cultures and languages are taught together. The language in which they are taught, is of secondary importance, the important thing is that they are being taught together. All German schools (abroad) are such multicultural meeting places. However, the system has not yet been fully developed – we are still experimenting with standard 3 (form 5), and only once these kids reach high school will we know whether it has been successful.*

This differs considerably from the concept of intercultural "meeting" or convergence advanced by the German subject adviser for German-language schools in Southern Africa:

> *The concept of convergence refers exclusively to the final examination and qualification: the German Abitur and the South African Matric: their convergence would be such an 'intercultural meeting'. In terms of this pre-established definition, none of the German-language schools (in South Africa) is a 'multicultural meeting place', because no cultural treaty exists on the mutual recognition of qualifications.*

Yet another view is held by the principal of the DSK, who sees such a "multicultural meeting place" as a "school where kids from different cultural backgrounds get together to be taught together." According to him, "all German-language schools (in South Africa) are such multicultural meeting places", although he, too, understands "integration" to mean the "integration of qualifications".

The South African subject advisor for German as a foreign language at South African schools, for his part, believes that the "*DSK* is in the process of becoming an 'intercultural meeting place'". All stakeholders agree that the German-language schools in South Africa have made good progress. The German Consul-General at the time believed that German-language schools in South Africa were "leading by example", but conceded that there had been problems initially, and that such developments needed time. The *DSK* principal was of the opinion that the school parents should, and could, "make a greater effort at integration", and that there was "hardly any contact at that level".

Asked about problems of integration at German-language schools, the respondents tended to describe these as "minor", and advanced following explanations:

Factors hindering integration

Principal of the foreign-language stream at the DSK

> *Problems occur wherever people lived in separation. Pupils of the same culture and language tend to flock together wherever possible. The*

foreign-language pupils isolate themselves from the others, not because they feel rejected, but because they prefer it this way. Our job is to counteract this tendency. That is why we have changed the seating arrangements. ... Adapting to new conditions is a (long) process. It is difficult for the foreign-language kids, especially if one thinks of the 'virtues' we expect from our (German) children, such as always having the relevant school books and material with you, doing homework regularly, appropriate dress and hygiene, punctuality, reliability, keeping promises – apparently the Black children don't attach so much importance to these matters.

Principal of the DSK:

The conservative attitude of parents continues to obstruct integration:

The German-speaking middle class suffered a decline (economic situation), and this dismantled the privileged position which people occupied under the pretext of having an (exclusively) German-language school. All that has come to an end. By taking in foreign-language pupils, we embarked on a system of open competition.

In the case of the African children, too little educational work has been done at home and at (the pupils' previous) school. There is a kind of 'speechlessness among Africans' which obstructs education, for instance, African families do not have enough discussions at home.

The German subject advisor for German as a foreign language:

Material conditions differ. There are tensions and psychological obstacles on both sides. For this reason, for instance, invitations do not lead to counter-invitations.

Teachers and pupils regarded the following factors as obstacles to integration: differences of language, religion and culture, and transport problems. The Consul-General and the South African subject advisor felt that contradictory (and possibly mutually exclusive) aims were being pursued with relation to culture: on the one hand, foreign language students were expected to "fit in" and "feel at home" at the German-language school; on the other hand, they were to retain their cultural identity, and not be alienated from their cultural roots.

Boarding home educators (tutors)

According to the boarding home tutors, the *DSK* could not be regarded as a "multicultural or intercultural meeting place", because White pupils moved out of the boarding home as soon as African children moved in. African pupils were expected to adopt White (or even European) customs and submit to White (or

European) rules. Noise levels, language problems, and confrontations between White and Coloured children on the one hand and African children on the other, were quoted as examples. Another factor was the different prior education, particularly in the case of African girls; according to the tutors, the African boys were more easily accepted by their peers than the girls. The tutors felt that the boarding home needed more Coloured and White children in order to fulfil its "meeting place" function.

Asked to name **factors promoting integration**, stakeholders unanimously named the following: workshops, the school bazaar, extra-curricular cultural events, theatre visits, and class excursions. According to the school principal, there was "no longer any open rejection, colleagues and parents have adapted to the situation and become used to it". Surprisingly, some stakeholders also claimed that the boarding home promoted integration, despite testimony to the contrary by boarding home tutors, and also despite the fact that White children left as soon as "foreign language" pupils moved in.

Stakeholders were then asked why the foreign-language stream at the DSK continued to exist even after government schools had been opened to all population groups. The reply was that this was a **"political decision"**, and that all German-language schools outside Germany had to be "multicultural". "The German school abroad has to be modelled on the 'intercultural meeting-place' concept", said the principal of the DSK. The Consul-General, on the other hand, still believed that the German-language schools were "leading by example". He regarded it as "desirable that the country's elite send their children to the German-language school, so that political and economic contacts may be forged later on."

For the principal of the foreign-language stream, on the other hand, the continued admission of learners from the foreign-language to the mother-tongue stream constituted a major problem, mainly because the school's new language policy required at least 50% German-medium tuition:

> *(This) 50% - 50% (regulation) has nothing to do with education, but is rather a political decision. Because we were running out of money and there was a new self-confidence after the reunification of Germany, people started to say: 'How can one attend a German-language school, without having German-medium instruction? However, from an educational point of view, the question should rather be: 'What helps the apartheid victim most?' And the answer can hardly be German-medium instruction, but rather a proper education, which was not accessible to Black South Africans under apartheid. This new development means that a foreign-stream pupil must have an enormous linguistic competence in order to achieve what the politicians demand. And we do not find this linguistically highly competent learner among the African population, and I daresay we hardly find this type of learner among the Coloured population, who have easier access to German (than the African children) because of their English or Afrikaans mother tongue.*

I subsequently enquired from the DSK management what happened to learners who dropped out of the German-language school after one or two years because they found it impossible to catch up. My question remained unanswered.

To be fair, the Federal German government finds itself in a difficult situation. On the one hand, the German-language schools are supposed to build bridges and foster contacts in the host country. On the other hand, the academic and social integration of foreign-language speakers into the German-language school community clearly poses problems. Statements by the school management suggest a lack of knowledge of the foreign-language learners' cultures, and a tendency to unquestioningly regard the "Western" education system as the norm to which everyone should aspire.

Serious consideration should be given to opinions such as that voiced by the principal of one of the *DSK's* partner schools in the African township of Khayelitsha. According to him, the *DSK's* recruitment drive in the townships and its preparatory programmes for foreign-language pupils generated great expectations among students and parents alike; however, the ensuing culture shock was often simply too great for township children once they were admitted to the German-language school.

Let us now turn to statements by South African representatives from the spheres of politics, education and society. As above, these contributions are recorded under particular topic headings.

Integration

The interview partners with sociological training and the representative of the church shared the same understanding of the term **integration: integration was not seen as the assimilation** of African children to White standards, but rather as **the acceptance of difference and a holistic understanding of people's cultural background.** The term **rainbow nation** was often quoted in this context, evoking not the blending of colours (and their subsequent disappearance) in one common hue, but rather their continued and complementary co-existence. Both Archbishop Desmond Tutu and Dr. Neville Alexander regarded this as a prerequisite for successful integration.

> Tutu: *"True integration is when the norms of all those who want to become a unity are taken very seriously into account and you then do not try to produce a mish-mash but rather a recognition and celebration of diversity where everyone is made to feel proud of whom they are."*

Separate residential areas, the language problem, socio-economic imbalances and persisting racial prejudices were cited as obstacles to integration. Respondents unanimously agreed that **"positive intervention" on the part of** the government and of non-governmental organisations was necessary to change people's ideologies, and to contribute towards the creation of a national identity. **The foundation to this common identity had to be laid at school,** since school was "the main instrument of socialisation in a modern society" (Dr. Neville Alexander). Even at pre-school level, instruction needed to be **"multi-lingual and multi-racial"**, which presupposed a multicultural teaching staff. In addition, respondents unanimously called for **changes to curricula, teaching methodology, and teacher training.**

Curricular changes

Changes to the school system, e.g. by opening formerly White schools to children from all population groups, appointing African teachers to these schools, and the introduction of new curricula were designed to change the perceptions and consciousness of the younger generation. New curricula should focus on changes in the subjects history, politics, art and literature, with the aim of providing the youth with an appropriate knowledge of **South African history and culture.** This would enable learners to find **role models** from within their own population groups with whom they could identify without reservations.

Improved teacher training

Pupils, school principals and educationists are unanimous in demanding measures to improve teacher training programmes. **Basic and further training in terms of a "model for integration"** is seen as important; this would entail a change of methodology, and particularly of the teaching style. To achieve these changes is considered extremely difficult, since until recently, teachers used to be trained in terms of a "segregation model", as the chairperson of the "Principals' Organisation" put it. He deplores the **shortage of qualified teachers, the total absence of PE teachers at African primary and high schools, and levels of demotivation among teachers.** Courses such as those introduced by the "Principals' Organisation" and others, e.g. in "conflict management for principals" and in "staff motivation", are seen as a step in the right direction.

For the head of the ANC's Education Department, the main aim is to provide **schooling for all children in South Africa.** On the other hand, he does not regard integration as an overall answer to the country's problems:

Integration plays some role, but not a major one ...
like non-racial cities. Education for all our children is most important.

In this respect, he differs from Dr. Neville Alexander, for whom the **integration of the towns and cities** constitutes a major prerequisite for the gradual unification of South African society. Dr. Alexander, like others in education, and like Archbishop Tutu, believes that multicultural schools will continue to grapple with problems as long as the socio-economic conditions of formerly disadvantaged children do not change, especially since these children return to the townships at the end of the school day. Tutu calls them **"commuters between two worlds"**. For the late Minister of Security, Steve Tshwethe, formerly Minister of Sport, the main obstacle to social interaction between different population groups are not differences in the cultural and socio-economic environment, but rather **language and communication.**

Various interview partners repeatedly refer to the **lost generation,** i.e. that part of South African youth that committed itself to the struggle against apartheid, and is now aimless. Many educationists see the reintegration of these youngsters into society as one of the major problems facing South Africa.

The role of sport

Most of the respondents believe that **sport can influence the transformation process in a very positive way and contribute to the creation of a national identity.**

The former Minister of Sport (and late Minister of Community Security) Steve Tshwete and representatives of the press believe sport exerts an immeasurable influence as a **unifying force for reconciliation and for the process of nation-building.** The president of the NSC and the chairperson of USSASA regard sport, and particularly team sport, as the **chief catalyst for change:**

> *I think firstly sport to me, and many South Africans is the chief catalyst for change and it is the one area which enables people to come together and work together. To a certain extent, we have been successful even though it has been difficult. Take for example, when SA won the (Rugby) World Cup in 1995, everyone for that moment forgot their differences and were one. That is one example of how sport has managed to bring people together and break down barriers. In a team sport, the one depends on the other and (they) have to work together and people see what a role they play in this country and can see that they are equal. So sport plays an important role in reconciliation.*
> *(The President of the NSC)*
>
> *Sport is the biggest catalyst to bring people together,*
> *especially team sports.*
> *(Chairperson of USSASA)*

Other respondents see the advantages of sport in the fact that it **"speaks a simple language" and is able to change attitudes and create role models.** In this way, it can increase people's self-esteem and help the disadvantaged to discover and experience their own strengths. The role of **soccer** is repeatedly mentioned, particularly the support of all population and culture groups for the national team **(national pride).**

Teachers and pupils emphasise the spirit of fellowship which sport promotes between them, as well as its positive influence on the atmosphere prevailing at a school.

However, there are also **critical voices**, like those of the sociologists Denver Hendricks and Neville Alexander. Hendricks points out that sport can raise expectations, but hardly improve people's economic situation. **"Do not overestimate sport"**, he therefore cautions. Apart from economics, the educational system needs to be changed ("education is the key"), but that takes time. Hendricks takes a positive view of sports projects, but notes that they **can make people aware of inequalities, and thus contribute to a feeling of frustration.**

The chairperson of the "Principals' Organisation" summarises this aspect as follows:

In the 1950s we came from a missionary education where our school system was dominated by Whites with certain values. We were playing rugby and cricket. When 1976 came, all those values were destroyed and interest in sport disappeared. We come from that culture where our people do not attach any meaningful value to sport. With us sport does not have the same kind of benefits. There are no role models. We have no professionals who have made a living from sport so they do not attach any material value to it. With us you just have enough to eat and then you relax.

In the opinion of representatives from the University of the Western Cape, sport can play a certain role in nation-building. It could perform this function more easily if **the teams were more culturally mixed.** However, the exclusively White composition of most national teams means that they do not meet this requirement. The situation is hardly improved by the **awareness among the disadvantaged population groups that sport used to be reserved for Whites,** and that their participation gave many Whites access to privileges, such as overseas trips and exemption form military service. There is also some apprehension that sport may give rise to a kind of **nationalism and patriotism** that could become dangerous.

The specific role of sport in South African society ("no normal sport in an abnormal society") was recalled by all respondents from the fields of politics, sport and education, especially by the former SACOS members among them, but also by representatives from the press. The consequences of the abuse of sport by the apartheid government (through lack of facilities and equipment) were also stressed. The fact that virtually all sports venues are situated in White residential areas is generally regarded as an obstacle to social integration. **The persisting "artificial walls" between communities** can only be overcome if, as former Sports Minister Steve Tshwete points out, sport in the formerly disadvantaged areas is no longer treated as a stepchild, **but receives its rightful support and promotion in order to overcome the old inequalities. Sport for recreation, sport for the handicapped, and sport for senior citizens, especially in the rural areas and in the townships, need to be promoted, and the provision of sports facilities and the institution of PE instruction at all schools ought to be prioritised by the government.**

According to the President of the NSC, the government has the intention of meeting all these needs, but the practical implementation of such improvements is a time-consuming process:

There is a definite move, positively of sport into the townships. Facilities is still a big inhibiting factor. The government is supposed to build these facilities, but are (sic) doing it very slowly.

It is hoped that **the Department of Education, teachers, parents and communities** will lend support to such a development programme.

The **South African club system** is seen as an **obstacle** to the desired development. According to Libby Burrell, former Head of the Department of Human Movement Studies and triathlon coach at the University of the Western Cape, meaningful sports development can only occur at club level. The **club system** is being described as **highly competitive and performance oriented**, and a system such as the German one is therefore seen as very desirable. Club membership in South Africa in many cases continues to reflect apartheid divisions. Although there are some clubs in the townships, they mostly lack facilities and equipment. Most of the White clubs are reluctant to open up their membership to other population groups, and their structures are described as very conservative. Libby Burrell:

Sport broke many barriers but it must also break the political ones. If a sports person wins, and proves himself it should not matter where he comes from!

In addition, Libby Burrell also feels that **women's sport** should be promoted to a greater extent. Another proposal concerns the idea of "partnerships between clubs", which could promote the search for new talent, especially in the formerly disadvantaged communities. This idea is of great importance to the Department of Sport ("Sports Academy"). Representatives of the press widely criticise the **attitude of sponsors**, who are reputedly more interested in publicity than in development. Their **generous financial support for the spectator sports, i.e. rugby, cricket and soccer,** is being criticised, particularly since **no development plans for disadvantaged sports persons** are being put into place. The **multitude of sports organisations** is also seen as a problem, because these are reluctant to co-operate, or to sacrifice their position in favour of a strong umbrella organisation such as the NSC.

By way of summary, the views of Neville Alexander and Denver Hendricks are to be endorsed. Alexander believes that South African society can only be changed through *"struggle on all fronts"*. Sport, like education or like the integration of towns and cities, is merely one aspect of a broader problem. The more sport can contribute towards overcoming the effects of apartheid, the better, Hendricks feels. – The important thing, however, is to achieve a change of consciousness among the South African population. All respondents share Archbishop Tutu's hope of gradually changing the attitudes of people formerly mutually alienated by apartheid, so that all South Africans can meet the future with optimism. The overwhelming majority of respondents felt that sport can contribute towards this aim.

SUMMARY –
AND A LOOK AT THE WAY FORWARD

CHAPTER 4

4.1   Revisiting the Initial Hypotheses

*T*he present study sought to establish to what extent sport could promote social integration in the multicultural society of the "New South Africa". Initially, it was planned as an investigation into the situation at the five German-language schools in Southern Africa regarding the "integration of Non-White pupils", with particular reference to the role sport could play in this process. However, as a result of the rapidly changing political situation in South Africa, especially after the first free and democratic elections, the frame of reference broadened: instead of early and isolated instances of integration, its backdrop now became an entire society in transformation.

The research and study projects conducted point to political and socio-economic problems inherited from the apartheid past. They also identify problems on the path of the "New South Africa", and the possible role of sport in solving these.

South Africa's situation at the start of this study presented itself as follows:

4.1.1   Point of Departure

Politically, the integration of South Africa has become a reality as a result of the scrapping of apartheid (1991), the introduction of universal suffrage (1994), and the adoption of the new constitution (1997). However, society is still marked by inequalities along racial lines, and the legally enforced separation of the apartheid society persists in the legacy of social segregation. The studies and research projects reveal that the divisions and fragmentation of the apartheid order continue to be felt seven years after the first democratic elections. The socio-economic differences between the population groups are clearly visible on the surface. The different population groups continue to inhabit different residential areas; the majority of Africans still live in the same townships as under apartheid, often under equally difficult conditions. The same applies, *mutatis mutandis*, to the majority of Coloureds and Indians, while the majority of Whites continue to live in the formerly exclusively White areas (cf. Bydekarken, 1992).

In the field of education, the apartheid legacy is particularly evident. The research conducted as part of the present investigation clearly indicates the inequalities and disparities in the provision of educational facilities, in the quality of instruction provided, and in the educational levels of teachers and pupils. Equally clear is the lack of social interaction between teachers and pupils belonging to different population groups. These findings are supported by research done by NGOs such as IDASA, and by the statements and views expressed by interview partners from the fields of politics, society, and the church, such as Archbishop Desmond Tutu, the former Minister of Sport, Steve Tshwete, and the sociologist Dr. Neville Alexander.

The depth of the problem can be gathered from a spate of racial incidents at universities and colleges about two years after the first democratic elections (cf. Sunday Independent of 19th May 1996). Similar problems occurred at formerly White schools in the Northern Province when these admitted African pupils (cf. the news on TV 1 on 16.01.1996 regarding Petrusville High School; SABC radio news on 31.8.1996 and in February 1997 concerning N. Marais Primary School); cases of discrimination reportedly also occurred at restaurants (Weekend Argus of 24th May 1997). Even the cities still experience many problems as a result of the continuing divisions between population groups, as city manager of Cape Town, Andrew Boraine, reported:

> *A grim picture of a divided city fraught with problems has been sketched by Cape Town's city manager Andrew Boraine, after his first 100 days in office. He says its people are divided by location, economic access, race, language, party politics, culture and religion... (Cape Argus of 30th May 1997, p.1)*

Without targeted suitable measures, this situation is unlikely to change within the foreseeable future.

With its Reconstruction and Development Programme (RDP), the new government under President Nelson Mandela planned far-reaching measures for the improvement of the living conditions of all South Africans. The programme was aimed at improving the most vital elements of infrastructure, i.e. health services, housing, education, water services and land ownership. Further objectives were to comprehensively democratrise society, and to initiate economic, educational and cultural programmes along non-racial lines. Specific steps to overcome the apartheid legacy and to promote the growth and development of a "New South Africa" are being taken by the government, NGOs, and organisations and institutions such as PRAESA, IDASA, universities, and private schools. Such steps and programmes include "affirmative action" measures and the opening up of all schools to members of all population groups. A great deal is expected of sport when it comes to generating a general atmosphere and spirit conducive to such reforms. Sport is often regarded as a tool for nation-building, or as an equaliser in an unequal society, as the following two quotes from a weekend newspaper illustrate: "ANC looks to sport as an equaliser", and: "The ANC has recognised sport as the single biggest 'healer' in a country torn by race and cultural differences." (Weekend Argus, 5 and 6th March 1994, p. 16).

To the best of my knowledge, the present thesis is the first scientific study of attempts at opening private schools to all South Africans. It is also the first investigation of the use of sport as a tool for social integration at school level.

4.1.2   The Research Programme

Prior to the present study, sport as a potential tool for social integration in South Africa had received no attention from either sports science or from sociology. To establish the framework of the study, South Africa's situation under apartheid first had to be outlined, followed by a description of developments towards the "New South Africa". Based on certain assumptions, which were adapted and refined as additional data became available, certain hypotheses were formulated regarding relations between the various population groups, and regarding the potential use of sport; these were then tested by way of empirical research. The result was an exploratory, empirical study, which is both descriptive and analytical in nature, in the way that any pilot study would be. Far from claiming to formulate a comprehensive theory on the integration of the various population groups in South Africa, or on the use of sport as a tool for social integration, the present study merely intends to stimulate further research in this field.

In order to verify the initial hypotheses, nine research projects were conducted with a multicultural sample, consisting of African, Coloured and White pupils at the five German-language private schools in Southern Africa; twenty government schools; teachers, parents, coaches and dance instructors, as well as representatives from politics, society, and the church. Below follows a summary of the research findings.

4.1.3   The Findings

Realistically speaking, it has to be admitted that, as a "tool for nation-building" and as a factor contributing to social integration, sport has not quite lived up to the high expectations held by pre-scientific "common sense", or even to the hypotheses formulated in the initial stages of this study, at least not in the quantitative sense. This must be attributed to the complex situation in the country. In a qualitative sense, the projects produced many valuable indicators and insights for a user-centred and practice-oriented approach to sport-related projects for the promotion of social integration between members of different population groups.

The following hypothesis was formulated as a departure point for the subsequent empirical research:

Most South Africans continue to interact with members of their own population group, and there is little social contact between members of different population groups. All individual research projects comprising the overall study confirmed this hypothesis.

Respondents' replies to questionnaires and in interviews indicated that the racial barriers which were formerly enforced by law, continue to exist as social conventions and that they have created chasms between the population groups. These chasms are evident in day-to-day life, e.g. in the educational institutions visited in the course of this study, and they are obstacles to social integration.

Interview partners from politics, society and the church confirmed this observation. Steve Tshwete, the former Minister of Sport, puts it this way:

> Africans and coloureds are enemies. The loss of the Western Cape to the National Party can be attributed to the coloureds' vote... It is difficult because of the apartheid segmentation of the country. Take Mitchell's Plain which is exclusively a coloured residential area where no blacks really go. There is an artificial wall which says this is a coloured residential area and that is a black residential area. This makes it difficult for people to get together.

Asked to give reasons for the lack of social interaction, the sociologist Neville Alexander replies:

> Well, I think there are three things: The one is the spatial aspect, the other is the language barrier and the third is a socio-economic class barrier. Over all that is the colour racial prejudice issue...

Replies by pupils and teachers from all population groups indicate that the situation has as yet not changed much for the "new generation". Research at both private and state schools, regardless of the population group for whom these were reserved under apartheid, showed that pupils hardly interact at all with fellow-pupils from other population groups. Even at culturally mixed schools, interaction between members of different population groups is very rare, and is usually confined to the pupils' own class, or even to the classroom. Multicultural friendships hardly occur.

The same finding applies to the German-language schools in Southern Africa. These schools have been accessible to pupils from all population groups since the late 1980s; since the early 1990s, they have attempted to become "multicultural meeting places", by instituting "foreign language streams" from which learners could progress to the (German-language) "mother tongue stream". The practical implementation of this model is problematic, as became apparent in research at each of the five German-language schools supported with staff from the Federal Republic of Germany.

4.1.4 Measures for Promoting Mutual Contact and Social Interaction

a) "Foreign-language stream" at German-language schools – a model fit for promoting integration?

Since the early 1990s, the German-language school in Southern Africa recruit Coloured and African children for their "foreign-language streams".

To the Coloured parents, and even more so to their African counterparts, this signifies the opportunity of giving their children a high-quality education, and a way out of the often unsatisfactory situation at township schools. However, research has shown that the Coloured and African children attending German-language schools have to grapple with many problems; in the case of culturally mixed classes, the same applies to their White, German-speaking class mates. These problems relate to the socio-economic disadvantages to which especially the African pupils are subject, as well as to the discrepancies between the different (still widely apartheid-influenced) schools where these children received their prior learning. – The inequalities between children from different population groups manifested themselves in the following areas:

a) Socio-economic situation

Whereas the majority of "mother-tongue" pupils at the German-language schools belong to the middle or upper classes, the "foreign-language" pupils in the research sample came from the lower classes.

The African pupils are the most disadvantaged. The majority live in townships on the periphery of the cities, many under inadequate living conditions, e.g. in shacks, informal settlements, etc. Many come from big families, where regular meals, healthy nutrition, and appropriate leisure activities are unknown luxuries. The long distances which many parents have to travel to and from work deprive many children of a healthy family life.

b) Educational situation

The inequalities in the provision of education is clearly visible in most primary schools in African residential areas: overcrowded and poorly furnished classrooms, inadequate equipment, under-qualified and under-motivated teachers (partly as a result of inadequate payment), limited choice of subjects (e.g. absence of PE classes), corporal punishment. Many pupils are over age when they are sent to school, and many repeat several classes.

The situation at schools in Coloured areas is not quite as bad, although there are also shortages and inadequacies. These manifest themselves in an inadequate infrastructure, under-qualified teachers, and in a lack of proper equipment.

c) Leisure

Among the disadvantaged section of the population, healthy and appropriate leisure activities do virtually not exist. There is an enormous lack of facilities for leisure activities in the townships, and many children have to perform household chores. Traditional culture assigns rights and duties to women and girls, which determine the pattern of their spare time activities.

The findings presented in the body of this thesis attest to the pre-eminence of sport among pupils' leisure activities. Generally speaking, the interest in sport is strong, although active participation varies greatly in accordance with personal and social conditions. Important factors determining personal behaviour are gender and previous experience. Whereas traditional norms of behaviour and household duties prevent many girls from actively participating in sport, it plays an important role in the spare time activities of boys. The investigation also revealed the overwhelming importance of soccer, which was the sporting activity most frequently mentioned by boys (This finding correlates with research conducted on the spare time activities of immigrants in Germany. Cf. Abel, 1984, p. 118).

d) Social interaction

Social contacts between members of different population groups hardly exist, even less so beyond the school premises, as the findings indicate. Consequently, pupils have hardly any personal experience or first-hand knowledge of the socio-cultural conditions under which the "other" population groups live. In the case of African pupils, such first-hand knowledge is often confined to visits or shopping excursions to the (formerly) "White" city centres, or to occasional visits to their parents' place of employment. By contrast, many White pupils have never been to an African township (Some of the White pupils have been on an 'official visit' to an African township, on the occasion of some 'inauguration ceremony'; but even in these cases, there was palpable opposition to an 'excursion into such a dangerous area' on the part of some parents.).

Research at open schools, such as the German-language schools, point to cultural and gender-specific differences which govern social conduct. While the girls among the "foreign-language" pupils were very shy during the introductory phase, the boys – though a minority – were much more self-assured and amenable to social interaction, and hence found it easier to come to terms with the unfamiliar environment.

African pupils clearly found it much more difficult to settle down and to feel at home in the German-language schools than Coloured children did. This is partly due to the language difference, and partly to the socio-economic background of the African pupils. Once again, the apartheid legacy persists.

Social interaction between children from different population groups in the culturally mixed classes was a greater problem to the "mother-tonguers" than to the "foreign-language" pupils, who were much more amenable to cross-cultural contacts and friendships (research project 2). Additional research and conversations with African and Coloured pupils who had "dropped out" of the "foreign-language" stream and left the DSK, revealed why they had done so: discrimination and the separation into "mother-tongue" and "foreign-language" streams were the reasons most frequently given.

As the research indicates, mutual acceptance of pupils of different population is much higher in fully or partly integrated classes than in totally segregated classes, or in classes where "mother tongue" and "foreign language" pupils have joint tuition in only one or two subjects. At schools where the pupils were not combined in a common class, at least for the non-verbal subjects, hostile feelings are generated, or at least existing prejudices on the part of the "mother tongue" pupils persist.

It is evident that the problem mainly lies with the "mother tongue" pupils and their rejection of the "foreign language" children. Discriminatory behaviour among the "mother tongue" pupils was noted at all five German-language schools, and was even criticised by fellow-members of the "mother tongue" classes (research sample 2). Even where "mother tongue" pupils had personal experience of joint instruction with the "foreign language" pupils, like at the DSK, the majority among them rejected the idea of a combined class. Reasons given included a possible drop in standards in certain subjects, as well as what were called "great cultural differences".

This attitude displays certain prejudices, which may originate in the pupils' homes and possibly reflect parents' opinions. The DSK subjects foreign-language pupils to an entry examination (consisting of an IQ test and an examination in English and Mathematics), to ensure that only pupils are accepted who are on a par with the school's standards (The parents of the mother-tongue pupils are aware of this entry examination.).

The research conducted among "mother tongue" and "foreign language" pupils at all five German-language schools in Southern Africa indicates that many obstacles and problems still stand in the way of integration, or of any meaningful "meeting of cultures". These obstacles contribute to the fact that children prefer to interact within their own population groups, and that the Coloured children, and in particular the African pupils, do not feel fully integrated into the school community.

Archbishop Desmond Tutu clearly identified a major obstacle to integration at schools which have opened their doors to pupils from all population groups:

We must also remember that they (the black children) still have to go back to their ghetto after school. They are commuting between two worlds, and so they are suffering from schizophrenia which has been typical of South Africa.

By way of summary, the problems experienced by various stakeholders and role-players in the attempt to overcome the apartheid legacy at educational institutions, can be presented as follows:

Problems and obstacles experienced by various stakeholders and role-players in the attempt to integrate South African schools

Mother tongue and foreign language learners	separate classes
	different mother tongues/home languages different living conditions at home differences of culture and education lack of common school spirit and atmosphere
Foreign language learners	rejection and discrimination at the hand of mother tongue pupils not feeling welcome at school social deprivation (missing old friends, teachers, and family/relatives) identity problems (culture shock, alienation) psychological stress gender differentiation of traditional culture difficulty of adapting to unfamiliar teaching style and class atmosphere pressure of unfamiliar demands (standards, amount of work required, etc.) problems relating to German as "third language", especially for Xhosa speakers who learn English and Afrikaans as official languages practical problems relating to transport, physical distance between township and school
Teachers of foreign language stream	pupils' different mentality
	pupils' different cultural background pupils' different work ethic, resulting from an authoritarian school system English as medium of instruction insufficient knowledge of pupils' cultural background and socio-economic situation
Parents of mother-tongue pupils	apprehensions about drop in standards of children's education as a result of the admission of foreign-language pupils conservative attitude
German-language schools	drop in student numbers, especially since government schools have been opened to pupils from all population groups
	expectations and demands from German Federal Government, which finances the schools (and the integration programme)

The research findings show that the German-language schools in Southern Africa cannot yet be described as "meeting places of different cultures" – at least not in terms of the official umbrella plan for German cultural policy abroad. According to this plan, such an "intercultural meeting place" ought to be the scene of a "genuine coming together of South Africans from all population groups, based on social openness and on the prohibition of all forms of discrimination on the basis of race, religion, or ideology..." (Auswärtiges Amt, 1980, p. 21 ff). As the research projects indicate, such a "getting together" has not yet occurred. Admittedly, this is hard to achieve, especially if the German-language school simultaneously wishes to fulfil the commitment embodied in the statutes of its governing body, i.e. to maintain and nurture the German culture and language (cf. statutes of the governing body of the *Deutsche Schule Kapstadt* of 23.4.1975).

Addendum:

A study conducted at seven South African schools (government schools and private schools) indicates that, with the exception of difficulties relating to German as a "third language" for foreign-language pupils, similar problems beset the attempts at integration. The rejection of African and Coloured children by White pupils was particularly noticeable at elitist private schools. However, at church schools and at government schools, which were only opened to all population groups in 1992/3, social interaction between pupils from different population groups was much healthier than at the German-language schools. Social interaction was particularly advanced at (formerly White) schools situated on the borders of African and Coloured townships, and at schools which offered extensive bridging programmes and extra-mural sports and culture workshops in the afternoons.

4.1.5   Sport as a Tool for Integration

Many people regard sport as a means of promoting nation-building in South Africa.

Neville Alexander:

I think that sport, music and art are inherently capable of playing the integrative role where they can teach one another about their cultural background. Through sport we bring people together.

Archbishop Tutu:

It (i.e. sport) is probably breaking down barriers, but more importantly perhaps, just the image which you can get through a soccer match. Watching black and white players as a team makes integration normal... when Chester Williams excelled on the rugby field many prejudices whites had against blacks were broken down.

183

Former Minister of Sport, Steve Tshwete:

Sport has the capacity to address the whole issue of reconciliation. It can do it because it speaks with a simple language. It brings people together and they forget about their background. On the issue of nation building, it is a force because it brings people together.

In the course of attempts to integrate ethnic minorities, e.g. in the case of migrants in Germany, it is often assumed that sport can contribute towards social integration. This assumption is then applied to the target group in question, without any prior assessment of the preconditions and nature of such integration processes.

In its support programme for sports development in South Africa, the *DSB (Deutscher Sportbund – German Sports Association)* calls sport a "very important factor of foreign policy", and emphasises its "task to contribute towards the integration of different sectors and marginalised groups", without having done any research or initiated any projects for this purpose (cf. DSB 10/94).

To my knowledge, the present thesis constitutes the first scientific attempt to assess whether sport can in fact perform the functions of social integration often ascribed to it.

Summary of the findings:

a) The popularity of sport

Sport is an important and popular field of interest among South Africans of all population groups. For pupils of German-language schools in South Africa, sport ranks among the three most frequently mentioned likeable and constructive factors of schooling experience, the other two being excursions and cultural events. African and Coloured pupils at these schools specifically mention sport as a means of reducing or counteracting the "feeling of not being welcome". Even among the "drop-outs", more than three-quarters of all respondents said they enjoyed participating in sport, especially team sports. Among the foreign-language pupils, gender-specific differences relating to sport were noted: for reasons of culture and tradition (the position of women in society, etc.), sport tended to be a rather negligible spare-time activity for Coloured girls, and even more so for African girls, whereas the boys were quite actively involved in the pursuit of sport. Among White pupils, no such gender-specific differences emerged.

b) Multicultural PE classes

For nearly all pupils, multicultural sports events and PE classes constituted a new experience. However, the majority of both mother tongue and foreign-language pupils at the German-language private schools thought such classes were a good thing. This even applied to pupils who had not yet experienced such instruction themselves, and to pupils at schools in African and Coloured townships.

c) Individual sports vs. team sports

Team sports are especially popular among Coloured and African pupils. By far the most popular sport among the boys was soccer, while the girls preferred netball. The White pupils, on the other hand, preferred individual sports (research project 4).

Hypothesis 2 – **Team sport codes are more effective than individual sport codes in promoting the integration of the various population and culture groups.** This could only be verified in part.

Research project 3 showed that intercultural friendships at school develop more easily with the help of team sports. Especially **during the pupils' introductory phase** at their new school, team sports have a significant positive effect on the integration process of pupils from different population groups.

Provided that an **established organisational framework exists** (e.g. school, PE lessons, etc.), it is quite possible to directly influence social interaction between pupils, and hence the classroom atmosphere, by having the pupils engage in team sports.

Research project 7, i.e. the Pinelands project, revealed that pupils felt equally at home in the athletics group as in the baseball group, both of which were culturally mixed. In this case, no significant difference relating to social interaction emerged between team sports and individual sports.
If sport is presented as an **extramural multicultural activity** (workshop, volunteer group) or in the pupils' **spare time,** it demonstrably promotes social interaction between pupils of different population groups. In this way, it helps to counteract prejudices and promotes the generation of mutual tolerance and respect. The choice of sports code is of secondary importance in this regard.

On the basis of the research findings, it appears that any kind of joint sports or research programme can contribute towards improving the present situation, by creating opportunities for contacts which were suppressed for a long time. It must be remembered that African and Coloured sportsmen and –women have been severely disadvantaged for decades.

The research projects conducted revealed a preference for multicultural sports groups among virtually all pupils, including those who had no previous experience of multicultural sport. **It was clear that the pupils wanted to** participate in joint (multicultural) sporting activities, but that political, economic and social conditions often made it difficult to act in accordance with this wish. Projects like those presented in this study could help to overcome these difficulties.

d) Organised extracurricular and extramural multicultural projects (Pinelands project and dancing workshop)

Organised multicultural sports projects can be regarded as highly successful in bringing members of different cultures and population groups closer to one another. The positive impact of such projects can be demonstrated in various ways. The project findings (cf. Fig. 38 a to c and 32 a to c illustrate the great impact of the Pinelands project and of the dancing workshop. Both projects were highly rated by the participating pupils and teachers, and both had a salutary influence on the attitudes of participants, as demonstrated by significant increases in the numbers of friends from other population groups (Keim, 1996, p. 26).

It is therefore clear that organised multicultural sports programmes promote social contact between pupils from different groups. The sports code chosen is of little significance; of far greater importance is the fact that such programmes must be available, and that they are accessible to interested pupils from the different groups. In this regard, factors like infrastructure (sports facilities and transport), the selection of teachers/coaches, and good planning and organisation (e.g. the time and venue of events, the composition of training groups or teams) are of crucial importance.

The fact that the Pinelands sports grounds are situated in a kind of a "grey area", and that for geographical reasons they are easily accessible to White, Coloured and African participants alike, contributed as much to the success of the programme as the selection of coaches and teachers from all population groups. Equally important was the involvement of the class teachers from the participating schools. It was also of crucial importance to divide the participating school classes from the very start into culturally mixed groups, with both genders represented in each group.

It is true that such multicultural projects are at first met with mixed feelings, especially by pupils without prior experience of multicultural contact. But such apprehensions are easily overcome. In the case of the Pinelands project, the African pupils were at first somewhat apprehensive, while the White children were simply curious. With the dancing workshop, it was just the other way round. It therefore appears that the African and Coloured girls are more self-confident in relation to dancing than to sports. But in both programmes, participants overcame their initial shyness within the very first practice session, proving that the overwhelming majority of pupils felt quite at home among the fellow-participants from "other" population groups.

The multicultural dancing workshop was a great success. All the participating pupils agreed that this workshop had promoted and facilitated the social interaction among members of different population groups. It had enabled the participants to get to know one another, to work together, and to learn from one another, and had instilled in them mutual respect for one another's culture. The workshop had a significant positive effect on the pupils' attitude towards multicultural activities and prompted them to reassess their own opinions and, if necessary, to alter them. **Dancing, particularly in the form of an organised multicultural sports project, clearly promotes social interaction and hence helps the different population groups to move closer together.**

Addendum: Dancing as cultural heritage in South Africa

Dance plays an important role in many African cultures. Some depictions of ritual dances in South African caves are 3 500 to 6 000 years old (information obtained from Kagga Kamma). Some ritual dances related to hunting, others to magic incantations, prayers for rain, and fertility rites. For the African population, dancing has always been closely associated with festivities and rituals, and till today, weddings, initiation festivities and funerals are marked by particular dances. Even at political rallies or at sports events, feelings are expressed by way of dancing. For children from African families, and to some extent also for Coloured children, dancing is an integral part of social and religious life.

Hypothesis 3 – Organised sports projects at grass root level facilitate social interaction between different cultures and population groups – This hypothesis was verified by the research findings.

Despite the great popularity of sport, and the success of integrated PE classes and extra-mural sports projects in promoting social interaction, the verification of hypothesis 1 hinged on certain reservations. This hypothesis was formulated as follows: **By virtue of its suitability to promote social integration, sport can contribute towards the rapprochement between population groups formerly alienated by apartheid.** It was found that sport can only perform this function if certain preconditions are met. The research projects showed that there are still certain factors in South African society which obstruct social interaction between different population groups, even in a sport environment, and that these factors are hard to overcome.

Factors obstructing social integration through sport

1. Unsatisfactory contextual factors (infrastructure, etc.)
2. A lack of organised multicultural leisure programmes.
3. Deficiencies regarding the multicultural composition of sports groups.
4. Racism and ethnic prejudices.
5. Fear of rejection and isolation when members of different groups jointly participate in sport.

6. Lack of knowledge regarding the possibilities of sport,
7. Insufficient training relating to motor nerves among pupils from previously disadvantaged communities.
8. Insufficient awareness and understanding of the value of sport as a leisure activity.
9. The position of women.
10. Lack of co-ordinated development measures; problems of educational and sport policy.

The access of township dwellers to sport is still being restricted and handicapped by obstacles which can only be removed by fundamental changes in their living conditions (e.g. infrastructure, language, residential area). At school level, it becomes noticeable that by contrast to their White and Coloured classmates, African children are subject to disadvantages and obstacles which can only be removed with the concerted assistance of the Department of Education and the sports organisations and bodies, i.e. by a focussed extension of sports facilities and opportunities.

Even today, hardly any predominantly African primary or high school offers PE as a subject. There is also a great shortage of trained PE instructors and sports coaches at African and Coloured schools in South Africa. Further obstacles to integration are ethnical prejudices and racism – attitudes which were ingrained by apartheid, but which continue to exist even after the transition to democracy, because they are impervious to change:

> When black and white athletes meet in sport, they often carry a great deal of racial baggage... (and) prejudices are unlikely to evaporate with the sweat as they play together ... Any display of negative behavior is likely to reinforce existing biases... (cf. Lapchick, 1984).

The problem is compounded by the fact that success in team sports does not depend on personal contacts or friendships between team members. Matches between teams or players do not necessarily improve attitudes. Coakley and Lewis believe that normal contests quite frequently reinforce prejudices held by players and/or spectators (ibid., 1990, p. 220). Bröskamp is of the opinion that a meeting of cultures on the sports field can lead to the hardening of persistent prejudices (Bröskamp, 1993, p. 185).

Overall, the research projects show that the possibilities for isolated or individual attempts to change attitudes are extremely limited, on account of existing problems relating to the administration and politics of sport, education and society. Only joint efforts from all stakeholders and co-ordinated measures can lead to lasting changes, and thus improve the situation. A circumstance favouring such a development is the great popularity of sport among all South Africans, regardless of population group. On the other hand, Merkel reminds us that an interest in sport is only generated when *the legal, economic and social problems of the disadvantaged population group (in Merkel's case foreign migrants and immigrants in Germany) are solved, so that sporting activities are no longer overshadowed by life-restricting existential problems" (Merkel as quoted by Fes, 1985, p. 64).*

Many observers would like to believe that sport in South Africa contributes to integration, particularly in relation to a bid for hosting the Olympic Games. However, culturally mixed sports teams are still the exception, rather than the rule, in South Africa. For financial reasons, only the spectator sports (rugby, cricket, golf) have so far instituted development programmes for the benefit of the disadvantaged population groups. But at grass root level, the above-mentioned factors (differences of socio-cultural background, different education, different ways of dealing with the apartheid past) make changes of attitude and practice a long and arduous undertaking. A further obstacle is the total absence of PE instruction at African schools, and its patchy and inconsistent nature at Coloured schools. It is questionable whether, under these circumstances, it makes sense for South Africa to host the Olympic Games.

4.2   Practical Consequences

4.2.1   Considerations for the German-language Schools

By way of summary, it can be stated that the transformation of German-language schools in Southern Africa into "intercultural meeting places", is by no means an easy process. Focussed measures are needed to promote the social integration of pupils from different population groups. Experience has shown that academic successes achieved by African and Coloured pupils at these schools do not necessarily make them feel at home at these institutions, nor do they alone suffice to ensure their continued attendance. The stringent selection process ensures that only gifted and motivated students are admitted; even so, their subsequent integration into the school community has not always been smooth, and at times has failed altogether. The research project has shown that, for many African and Coloured students, a feeling of belonging and of togetherness, of being accepted as a classmate and friend, and of sharing in a common school spirit and atmosphere, is of overriding importance, especially after the decades of alienation through apartheid. In many cases, such positive feelings of belonging were awakened by joint activities such as sport, excursions, or cultural events. The importance of such experiences and events should not be underestimated, especially since the German-language schools have the means of organising such events.

First of all, it is important to create conditions conducive to an **informal atmosphere,** where the pupils feel uninhibited and at ease, and where they find it easy to approach one another and make friends. The fears and problems of children from disadvantaged population groups, i.e. the foreign-language pupils, need to be taken seriously, and qualified teachers and/or counsellors should be at hand to help them solve these. This will often include measures to overcome feelings of inferiority or inadequacy, and to enhance self-confidence. The parents of the foreign-language pupils and the teachers at their previous schools should be actively involved in their process of acquainting themselves with the new surroundings, and of settling down at their new school ("Drop-outs" who discontinue their school careers should be supplied with information on practice-oriented vocational training opportunities).

Specific measures which could help to improve the situation

a) The formulation of a consistent integration concept.

b) Training courses/orientation programmes for teachers of multicultural classes.

c) Introductory courses for the foreign-language pupils, with presentations alternating between the German-language school and partner schools from which the foreign-language pupils are drawn.

d) Consideration and sensibility for the socio-cultural situation of foreign-language pupils, especially the girls.

e) Measures to overcome the disapproving attitude of the mother tongue pupils:
  • the integration of foreign-language and mother-tongue pupils into a joint class at the earliest possible stage;
  • joint instruction of foreign-language and mother-tongue pupils in all non-verbal subjects right from the start;

f) The use of sport, in voluntary extra-mural programmes or in workshops, in addition to the curricular PE instruction, and the use of team sports, especially during the introductory phase of foreign-language pupils.

g) The use of dance workshops as a means of "preventive intervention".

h) Cultural events and excursions with multicultural groups.

i) Appointment of a guidance teacher/counsellor with proficiency in the home language(s) of the foreign-language pupils.

j) Continuous evaluation of the situation, and proper research to assess why foreign-language pupils "drop out" and leave the school.

Ad a)   Formulation of a consistent integration concept

A consistent programme of integration needs to be formulated in consultation with all German-language schools in Southern Africa, with due consideration of the specific circumstances of each of these schools. This programme needs to determine when and how each stage of the integration programme is to take place (i.e. admission to the school, the orientation programme during the introductory phase, the incorporation of foreign-language and mother-tongue pupils into a combined class, etc.). Clarification of these aspects is necessary, because there has been a fair amount of "experimentation" in the past, sometimes at the expense of the pupils. The selection process of foreign-language pupils ought to be conducted with the utmost care and attention. Selectors should also consider the situation of foreign-language pupils, particularly African girls, who may fail to catch up with their classmates after a few years, and consequently have to leave the German-language school. The emotional stress experienced under such conditions (identity crisis, return to township life, former township classmates who mock the returnees as "little Germans", alienation from the parents' traditional lifestyle, etc.) should not be underestimated.

A process of continuous evaluation of the foreign-language stream by pupils, teachers and parents (e.g. in the form of an assessment sheet) could prove just as helpful as frank discussions of suggestions by pupils, teachers and parents on ways to improve the educational programme. Suggestions submitted in the past, some of them by parents of "drop-outs", included the following: integrated classes, an improved attitude on the part of the school and the boarding home towards "other" population groups, and the appointment of multilingual or English-speaking teachers to teach multicultural classes.

Ad b) *Training courses/orientation programmes for teachers of multicultural classes*

Many local White teachers, and even more so the teachers seconded from Germany, are not familiar with the living conditions of disadvantaged Coloured and African communities. Furthermore, the seconded teachers return to Germany after a while, taking all their experience with them, and their positions are then taken up by inexperienced new arrivals. If the returning "veterans" committed their experiences to writing, this might be of great assistance to the newcomers. In addition, an orientation programme for new teachers should be considered, both for local staff members and those seconded from Germany, to familiarise them more thoroughly with the socio-cultural situation of pupils from the disadvantaged communities. Such a programme should include information on family structures, traditions, taboos, social conventions, the situation of women, etc., as well as basic communication skills in the home languages of the South African pupils. This would enable new teachers to conduct themselves with confidence and understanding in unfamiliar surroundings and circumstances. One possibility would be to involve the teachers in the introductory programme of the DSE (especially in the course on "intercultural communication"), and to lay on an additional orientation programme for them at the school where they will be teaching.

Ad c) *Introductory courses for foreign-language pupils, to be offered at the German-language school and one of its partner schools*

The German-language schools should consider offering the introductory courses for their foreign-language pupils, either on an alternating basis or at least in part (e.g. the first and the last month of the course), at one of the schools in the townships where the foreign-language pupils live. (The DSK followed such a system from 1990 to 1992). Apart from sparing the foreign-language pupils the trouble of travelling to and from the German-language school (usually a considerable distance), this would have the advantage of demonstrating a preparedness to "go into the townships" and to meet the foreign-language pupils "on their own turf". The personal contact established in this way would make it easier to build a relationship based on mutual trust. In addition, the teachers at the German-language school would gain a first-hand impression, and possibly a better understanding, of the socio-economic and educational conditions under which their foreign-language pupils live.

Ad d)   Consideration and sensibility for the socio-cultural situation of foreign-language pupils, especially the girls

Thanks to the cultural divergence and variety of the population groups to which the foreign-language pupils belong (e.g. various African peoples with their own languages and traditions, Muslims, Indians, Malay descendants, etc.), great sensibility needs to be shown for the pupils' cultural background, especially in the case of girls/young women. Gender-specific differences came to the fore during the foreign-language pupils' introductory phase at the German-language school, as well as at sporting events. The cultural traditions in which foreign-language pupils are being raised at home, determines to what extent they participate in the activities of the wider society, and hence also their behaviour and conduct at the German-language school (cf. King, 1990, p. 281f; Moyo, 1994, p. 4 and Cace, 1995).

Ad e)   Measures to overcome the disapproving attitude of mother tongue pupils

The research conducted indicated clearly that the disapproving attitude of mother-tongue pupils was the main source of problems relating to social integration. As a matter of urgency, the schools should therefore take any steps necessary to improve the situation. One of the most important measures to be taken is the integration of the mother-tongue and foreign-language streams into a single class, which should be effected at the earliest possible point in time. Joint instruction in all non-verbal subjects should be a matter of course. On the whole, more comprehensive efforts should be undertaken to counteract prejudices and to facilitate a real "coming together" of pupils, so that a true "meeting and cultures" can ensue (cf. research project 4).

Ad f)   The use of sport, in voluntary extra-mural programmes or in workshops, in addition to curricular PE instruction, and the use of team sports during the introductory phase of foreign-language pupils

More attention should be given to the possibility of using sport as a tool for social integration, since sport is of great importance to most pupils. If well organised and used in a proper way, both as a school subject and as voluntary workshop activity, sport can serve an important function, especially during the initial phases, when the foreign-language pupils are settling in at their new school. Under favourable conditions, sport can demonstrably improve the classroom atmosphere and mutual relations between mother-tongue and foreign-language pupils (cf. research project 3), and can even promote "intercultural friendships".

Ad g)   The use of dance workshops as a means of "preventive intervention"

Dance as a "multicultural activity" is particularly suited to promote not only the outer, but also the "inner" (i.e. attitudinal) integration of multicultural groups. Despite the different and diverse cultural backgrounds of the participants, dance can help to generate true feelings of togetherness and belonging (Mc Cloy, 1997, p. 32). Organised in the form of a workshop, i.e. with voluntary participation and without examinations or tests, dancing can be emotionally more effective than academic subjects, and can promote social interaction between pupils from different population groups, especially during the foreign-language pupils' introductory phase at their new school. In this way, dancing can be used as a "preventive form of intervention", in order to help new pupils to overcome the emotional stress of feelings of isolation and culture shock. Gender-specific differences were not noted in this regard.

Ad h)   Cultural events and excursions with multicultural groups

At the German-language schools, conditions need to be created which will make it easier for foreign-language pupils to feel at home here, and which will make their stay at a centre of foreign language and culture a positive and memorable experience. Multicultural events, theatre, dance, debating evenings, sports meetings etc., with the participation of the foreign-language parents (transport is to be provided), as well as excursions with multicultural groups (class excursions and camps) all help to generate a feeling of togetherness and "us-ness", and thus contribute towards building a "school spirit".

Ad i)   Appointment of a guidance teacher/counsellor with proficiency
in the home languages of the foreign-language pupils

The appointment of a guidance counsellor, who can act as a confidant when pupils experience problems, is desirable. Such a position does already exist at some American and South African schools. Such a counsellor should not only be proficient in the home languages of the foreign-language pupils (i.e. English, Afrikaans and Xhosa), but should also have a sound knowledge of the culture and economic situation of each of these population groups. A counsellor fitting this description could be very effective as link and mediator between the foreign-language pupils, their parents, and the rest of the school community (linking Third and First World communities).

Ad j) Continuous evaluation of the situation, and proper research to assess why foreign-language pupils "drop out" and leave the school.

A continuous evaluation of the situation is equally important as regular research to find out why foreign-language pupils decide to leave a German-language school. A regular exchange of views between all German-language schools in Southern Africa, and the institution of suitable measures (cf. a) to i) above) could help to keep the "drop-out" numbers at a minimum.

Efforts like those instituted by the DSK, i.e. to maintain contact with the partner schools by means of mutual visits by teachers and principals, are a step in the right direction. A real meeting or exchange of views can only be achieved through regular contact, not between school principals, but between **pupils** and **parents** from the **different population groups**. Mutual respect and tolerance are the most important prerequisites for such contacts.

In the light of these research findings, it may be necessary to reassess, and perhaps even to redefine, the concept of schools as "multicultural meeting places", and to reach clarity on the motives for establishing "foreign language streams" and "integration programmes" at the German-language private schools, especially since the government schools have been opened to all population groups. Under apartheid, the German-language schools, just like other private schools and some church schools, were at the cutting edge of educational development, because they allowed "non-White" pupils to acquire proper schooling. Today, ever since the opening of government schools to all population groups, the situation is different. Under these circumstances, and in the light of the mission of German-language schools, i.e. to preserve and maintain German language and culture, the "intercultural meeting" between mother-tongue and foreign-language pupils is likely to be little more than superficial contact. Integration for the purposes of "nation building", the goal which the government envisages for both private and government schools, cannot be achieved at the German-language schools. According to Neville Alexander, South African schools with pupils from different population groups have neither the intention nor the capacity to become "intercultural meeting places", in the sense in which the German-language schools use this term:

> South African schools can never be 'Begegnungsschulen', as we do not want to have a racial encounter, but we want to have an integration and convergence. 'Begegnung' means that you can also go away again.

Alexander perceives certain dangers if such an "intercultural meeting" or "encounter" is not conducted properly:

> It is very likely that the 'Begegnung' (= encounter), if not handled properly, can become a 'Vergegnung' (controversy). One has to be quite careful about it as it is a very sensitive issue.

Undoubtedly, there exists a danger that the "school-as-intercultural-meeting-place" ("Begegnungsschule") may deteriorate into a "school-as-place-for-mutual-avoidance" ("Aus-dem-Weg-geh-Schule"), especially if the emphasis is on the number of "foreign-language" pupils admitted to German-language schools, or on the financial support of the German Federal Government for the "foreign-language streams" at these schools. In order to create a real "intercultural meeting place", it is necessary to pay more attention to the social situation, and to undertake even greater efforts to make the foreign-language pupils feel at home in a German-speaking environment (cf. Keim, 1992, p. 23ff). One such effort would be the regular investigation of foreign-language pupils' reasons for "dropping out" of German-language schools, since these reasons may be regarded as reliable indicators for the level of "internal integration". If the German-language schools fail to initiate appropriate measures, they may easily be accused of "window dressing", especially by the African and Coloured partner schools where foreign-language pupils are recruited. South African teachers have on occasion criticised the "foreign-language stream" programme of the German-language schools. In an article on the co- operation between her own school and the DSK, a teacher at a Coloured school couched her criticism in the following terms:

> The German-language school is expected to admit a number of non-white kids, lest it be called a purely white school. The problems which these children experience, and which lead them to leave the school again, are hardly being addressed. My impression is that these problems are being taken too lightly by the DSK. When I come to think of the number of kids who drop out, and that little or nothing is being done about it, I have the impression that 'our' kids are being abused for the purposes of 'window dressing'. This kind of exploitation cannot be allowed to continue. We've had enough of it (Jansen, 1991, p. 30).

If one leaves aside the financial aspect for a moment, i.e. the financial support of the German Federal Government for the "foreign-language stream" at German-language schools, and if one concentrates solely on the pupils' welfare and on the future of the country, surely one has to ask: at what kind of a school should South African children spend their school career? What identity do children have when they have attended a German-language school in South Africa for five or seven years? South African? Germans? German South Africans?

With the exception of children who spend only a short time in South Africa before leaving again with their parents, all children who grow up in South Africa, and who complete their schooling here, ought to leave school as South Africans. Neville Alexander has no doubt in this regard:

> ...children who come out of these schools here in South Africa should be South Africans, not German. I can understand that people such as diplomats and businessmen who are here for short periods of time and have their children with them, want to send their children to these schools when they are here in South Africa. If, however, they were here for longer periods, then they must be South African children, when they come out of these schools.

This concept is hard to reconcile with the German-language schools' aim to preserve and maintain German culture and language.

A viable alternative might be the suggestion put forward by a South African teacher working at the *DSK*. Asked to outline her personal experience of the "school as an intercultural meeting place", and of the foreign-language stream at the *DSK*, this teacher started off by criticising the enormous income difference between teachers seconded from Germany and their locally employed colleagues: despite having to teach a greater number of class periods, the South African teachers earn only about one-seventh of what their German colleagues are being paid. Not surprisingly, this discrepancy does not make for a cordial "intercultural" meeting of the minds. Secondly, the teacher questioned the effectiveness of the "foreign-language stream" concept and practice. To her mind, the German Federal Government could do more for the education of the underprivileged by supporting further and ongoing training measures for underqualified township teachers, e.g. by enabling them to attend evening classes or to enrol at one of numerous teacher training colleges. Not only would the teachers themselves benefit by such a scheme, but also their underprivileged pupils. The effects of such support would therefore be relatively widespread, whereas the benefits of the "foreign-language stream" are confined to a small number of African and Coloured pupils, whose ultimate success is not at all certain.

> *The support of the German government for the F-Zweig (foreign-language stream) should rather be used to support the education of the teachers from the disadvantaged communities. This could be done in the form of In-Service Training or (by) providing the opportunity for them to go to teacher training colleges. This would be more useful for the teachers themselves and for the children at their schools, in comparison to the few black and coloured children at the German school whose chance of success is not good (Interview with a locally employed South African teacher at the DSK).*

If the promotion of the German language and culture in South Africa is the main purpose of intervention, German language courses could be offered to pupils and teachers at government schools. Another meaningful form of assistance could be the establishment of relationships with German enterprises, in order to provide school leavers with "bridging" programmes between school on the one hand and the world of labour on the other. In this way, German institutions and enterprises could help to develop a vocational training system, which has been lacking in South Africa. This could be a valuable contribution, not only to education in South Africa, but also to the economy.

If, however, the present practice of selecting promising candidates from Coloured and African schools for admission to the German-language schools is to be continued, the underlying concept of a "foreign language stream" should be reassessed, and steps be taken to speed up the development of a true "meeting place of cultures". One of these steps could (and should) be intercultural sports programmes and events, because sport has been shown to be an important factor in promoting social integration between pupils of different population groups.

4.3   Thoughts on the Concept of "Integration"

After studying social relations in South Africa and speaking to a number of South African sociologists, ethnologists and anthropologists, I became acutely aware of the fact that the concept of "integration", as it is normally understood in Europe, needs to be redefined if it is to be applied in any meaningful way to the South African situation.

For decades, South African society was subjected to the very opposite of integration, i.e. to the apartheid policy, and the majority of the population lived under conditions of "exclusion" (cf. Luhmann, 1995, p. 250).

The transition to democracy in the early nineties occurred without a revolution. If the divided South African society is to embark on the road to integration, with the ideal of a "rainbow nation" as its guiding aim, the underlying concept of integration must be based on respect for the cultural identity of fellow-partners in this endeavour, however these choose to define their identity. Thanks to the cultural plurality and the history of the country, it must be accepted that the cultural convergence of different population groups can only be achieved up to a certain degree.

To the ethnologist Bettina Schmidt, a democratic form of integration in South Africa means

> the possibility for each South African to choose freely, for instance where one wishes to live or what education or training one chooses to follow, but at the same time the possibility to choose to remain where one is. Important is also the preparedness of all groups to accept one another, and especially one another's differences, as well as a holistic understanding of other people's cultural background, and it is also important that social borders be permeable. In other words, if another culture has something interesting to offer, you have the opportunity of integrating this element with your own culture (Interview with B. Schmidt, 09.11.1996).

European experiences do not necessarily apply to the South African situation, which is particularly difficult to understand from a European point of view. The tendency in Europe is to strive for conformity and to level out differences, and cultural group identity or sub-identity is hardly tolerated (The problems experienced in the former Yugoslavia are only one example of this.). Europeans often have great difficulty in "taking over" or accepting elements of other cultures. In South Africa, however, observing and maintaining delimitations while respecting one another may be the most important conditions for successful integration. As John Sharp, an anthropologist at the University of Cape Town, puts it:

> *If we wish to celebrate our diversity, to have many 'cultures' making up one 'rainbow' nation, we have to ensure that our society offers all its members the opportunity to participate in, and draw benefit from, mainstream political and economical activity, as well as the opportunity to proclaim their difference (Sharp, 1994).*

The ethnologist Paul Drechsel regards the "South African concept of integration" as the solution to problems relating to the country's multicultural society:

> *If a Coloured enters into contact with Indians, he is in the Indian community while he is with them, but he does not become part of that community. He remains Coloured, and the Indians make him understand as much. He does not become a member of this community, but neither does he feel excluded from it. In Germany we have the problem that we want to "flatten" everything, homogenise it. We do not want to do what people do here (in South Africa), i.e. to respect and maintain borders, and still be 'inside'. If people in Europe want to be a multicultural society, that presupposes something quite important: differences. And these differences ought not to be "flattened", but must be stabilised. In other words, the more multicultural a society becomes, the greater the need to stabilise limits and borders. But this also entails that it is possible to jump over the borders to join the others, but without integrating them or destroying their 'otherness'. Meanwhile, people in South Africa have progressed far beyond this point: Here we now have 'the right to root and the right to option' in a multicultural society. If I want to be a Xhosa, that means integration, acceptance of Xhosaness. Here I can do what cannot be done in Europe, namely within the framework of a multicultural society, as the bearer of one culture I can enter into another culture, without having my 'otherness' de-stroyed from the outset. This permeability is a precondition (for this kind of society). And nobody takes away anything from anybody else (Interview with P. Drechsel on 09.11.1996; cf. also Drechsel; Schmidt 1995).*

Integration in South Africa must therefore be regarded as an ongoing process. It should be equated neither with assimilation (as, for instance, in Brazil; cf. Ribeiro, 1995, p. 1ff), nor with the melting-pot model, as in the United States (cf. Roosevelt, 1990, p. 112).

It is possible that South Africa offers the solution which Europe needs, especially with regard to the ongoing unification of Europe, and which cannot easily be reconciled with the notion of a homogenous nation state. For want of a better term, this solution may be described as **UNITY IN DIVERSITY.**

The sociologist Neville Alexander also sees "South African integration" as a confluence of African, Asiatic and European elements, with respect for the cultural diversity of each of the groups:

> In my own opinion integration cannot and should not mean a uniformation of population. It would lead to resistance and would basically be an assimilation policy which could be devastating in (its) consequences. Integration in our present circumstances must mean a convergence, a flowing together of African, European and Asian elements in our society and what I call streams. Including a universalist modern American stream which every nation is today subject to. Now those four elements have to flow together, and they are (doing just that). The important thing is to capture that dynamic in the curriculum and somehow instituting mechanisms and practices to both promote unity and accommodate diversity because diversity would and should continue. I like to use the metaphor of the stream with its tributaries flowing to it and we see this as a convergence and it becomes the mainstream in South African culture, but it should not be seen as an assimilation as in Europe. This mainstream does not overflow the tributaries so that you can't see it, but (the tributaries are) constantly feeding into this mainstream and constantly changing it. That metaphor demonstrates very clearly what I understand by integration. It is also a metaphor of global significance because it is what is happening around the world.

By way of summary, the following factors may be regarded as prerequisites for successful integration within the multicultural South African society:

a) Freedom of choice / decision
b) The preparedness of all groups to mutually accept one another (as a people driven process)
c) A holistic understanding of the cultural background of people and their acts
d) The permeability of social borders
e) The ability to understand integration as an ongoing process, and not to equate it with assimilation

Only if these preconditions are met, can integration in South Africa contribute towards the nation-building process.

Mutual respect and tolerance are vital to peaceful co-existence, and must be regarded as prerequisites for any harmonious multicultural society. Under certain conditions, sport can help to generate the atmosphere, or create the circumstances, under which population groups can begin to move in this direction.

All that we can do is to create an atmosphere, conditions and circumstances that will make it possible for people to develop in that direction. (N. Alexander).

Participants usually do not realise the long-term effects of multicultural interventions (e.g. multicultural sports projects) at the time they occur, especially if the participants are children. It should also be clear that it takes some time before the educational impulses and attitudes motivating such projects bear fruit. Day-to-day life in South Africa is still marked by a great lack of togetherness, because tolerance, mutual respect and understanding, and a co-operative attitude of "give-and-take" could hardly develop under apartheid conditions, and this mindset now has to be established by practice. The survival of democracy depends on these values.

If these considerations and thoughts are valid, no "quick fix" solution exists for the problem of "inner" (i.e. attitudinal) "integration" in South Africa. However, the aim of this study was merely to promote greater awareness of and sensitivity for the situation of this multicultural society.

All stakeholders and role players (governments and non-governmental organisations, both in South Africa and abroad, including sports bodies and organisations) are called upon to strive for a common consistent policy in dealing with the problems described above.

A united, non-racial, non-sexist and democratic South Africa is the best hope for handing over such a society to our children. It is a vision which we promote vigorously. It is a vision which we invite you to examine, to refine, and to enrich. It is, if necessary, a vision which we invite you all to surpass (Mandela, 1991b, p. 13).

4.4 Thoughts on the Use of Sport as a Tool for Social Integration in South Africa

As the search for tools to advance the process of social integration progresses, the importance of sport is widely emphasised, not only by politicians and by various organisations (cf. GTZ 1986, 6), but also by people within sports administrations and sport officialdom themselves. As for the scientific literature on the subject, the social functions of sport are quite controversial, especially its alleged contribution to social integration (cf. in his regard Heinemann, 1979, p. 198ff).

In South Africa, sport is generally seen as a "tool for nation-building" (cf. Weekend Argus 5/6 March 1994, 16 and interviews with the President of the NSC, pupils and teachers).

As far as I am aware, the present study was the first scientific attempt to investigate whether sport could act as a tool for social integration in the South

African context. The research findings indicate that certain preconditions must be met, if sport is to advance the process of nation building, and if it is to fulfil the hopes and expectations held in many quarters.

Four aspects of sport are often emphasised as favouring its use as a tool for the social integration of marginalised minorities (cf. Harms, 1982, p. 6f). If applied to the South African context, these need to be modified or supplemented:

1) Sport as so-called non-verbal means of communication

There is a widespread notion that linguistic and cultural barriers are more easily overcome in sport than in other areas of social life. For this reason, sport is often referred to as the "conveyor of culture of the most accessible symbolism". (cf. Giebenhain, 1995, p. 167 and Harms in Adolph & Böck, 1985, p. 63).

This point was also made by the 6th conference of the sports ministers of German Federal States, when they discussed the "integration of foreign migrants (literally: 'fellow-citizens') through sport" on 24.10.1983. The ministers noted that, thanks to its non-verbal character, sport was "especially suited to the integration of different population groups":

> Since the 'togetherness' engendered by sport ("sport-specific communication") is largely independent of language, it is of particular importance for the integration of foreign migrants (lit.: 'foreign fellow-citizens') (ibid., 1985, p. 66).

Stüwe, who has studied the life situation of Turkish youths in Germany, shares this view:

> Furthermore, sport is marked by a simple and easily comprehensible form of symbolism, which makes it possible to eliminate linguistic barriers and other obstacles to interaction... Sport, with its primarily non verbal and immediately comprehensible interactions, is therefore particularly suited as a medium for overcoming feelings of socio-cultural unfamiliarity and 'otherness' (Stüwe, 1984, p. 303).

However, in South Africa it is not all that easy to "eliminate linguistic barriers and other obstacles to interaction". Language plays a major role here, in the sense that, as an unintentional "sub-text", it indicates that the speaker belongs to a particular (social) class. In addition, it must be kept in mind that, in the past, especially the African population group was also linguistically disadvantaged by the apartheid regime, a fact which played a role in the 1976 Soweto youth uprising against the use of Afrikaans as medium of instruction (Lapping, 1986, p. 212).

For participants of the dance workshop (research project 4) and the integration project (research project 3) at the DSK in Cape Town, language constituted no significant obstacle. On the other hand, language was

repeatedly described as a social barrier within the framework of the Pinelands project, particularly by teachers. Language competence is a prerequisite for fostering social relations. It became apparent that, due to their limited command of the English language, African pupils had greater difficulty than other children in establishing social contacts. For finding one's way and getting along beyond the confines of family and township, one needs to understand and speak the language spoken "out there". If such competence does not exist, children tend to stay among classmates of their own language group, where no problems of articulation or comprehension arise.

Trainers or teachers running programmes for multicultural groups should be able to use all the relevant languages in teaching, because this will make it easier for them to generate tolerance and respect towards all language groups involved. (In addition, it is suggested that additional [voluntary] tuition in English be offered to speakers of African languages at multicultural schools, since English functions as 'lingua franca' among the eleven official languages of South Africa.)

2) Sports programmes as occasions of collective experience and direct physical contact

Sport is also regarded as a possible tool of social integration because it occasions collective experiences, as well as direct physical contact, between the participants.

According to Harms, people jointly participating in active sport, especially in team sports, enter into "direct physical contact" with one another, which practically provokes "the emergence of intensive interpersonal relationships" (Harms, 1982, p. 7).

Some sports sociologists are sceptical about this alleged advantage, and rather emphasise the effect other factors may have on the "pro-integration" potential of sport, such as the general social context (cf. Rigauer, 1982, p. 240 and Wohl, 1981, p. 150). Others point to the feeling of physical 'otherness' (Bröskamp, 1994). The present study was not able to confirm the greater effectiveness of team sports, as opposed to individual sports codes, in promoting social integration. In fact, more "direct physical contact" and "intensive interpersonal relations" were generated by dancing, an individual sports code, than by any of the team sports investigated within the framework of this study.

The present project established how important it is that multicultural sports projects (training programmes, voluntary extra-curricular workshops, PE instruction etc.) be offered at all, the specific code being of secondary importance. Training or coaching events for multicultural groups, whether for team sports or for individual sports, are registered by the participants as noteworthy "collective experience", mainly because sport was not practised jointly under apartheid. A certain respect or even shyness regarding physical or bodily 'otherness' was at first noted in the multicultural groups, but only at the start of the programme. The logistic framework of the undertaking (selection of venue, coaches, regular attendance) was aimed at ensuring a kind of interaction and exchange which would enable the participants to generate mutual acceptance and tolerance, and to reduce the feeling of "bodily otherness". Dance was found to be a most effective medium for overcoming initial obstacles or barriers to interaction.

Sport can only be realised as a collective experience if certain societal, institutional and epistemological conditions are met. Public support and active co-operation between various institutions (e.g. schools, sports clubs, etc.), are just as important in this regard, as is due consideration of cultural factors.

3) Sport as a medium which transcends divisions of class

Sport is often described as a medium which transcends class divisions, especially in childhood an youth. According to Heinemann, class-specific differences in sport behaviour only emerge around the age of 20 (cf. Heinemann, 1979, p. 163). **However, in South Africa, sport accentuates class differences. Apart from the poor socio-economic conditions of the disadvantaged population groups and the deficiencies, if not the total absence of sports facilities in the African townships, class differences are also apparent where sport is being practised: Certain sport codes have for a long time been withheld from Coloureds and (especially) from Africans, and in many of these codes, facilities, equipment and trained instructors are in short supply to this day.**

Sport does not enjoy the same status among Africans as among the Whites (Interview with South Africa's former Minister of Sport, Steve Tshwete). One reason for this state of affairs was the apartheid system and the concomitant lack of facilities in African townships, which in turn spawned deficient notions of leisure-time activity. Another factor are the traditions of the disadvantaged communities themselves, especially as these relate to the position of women. Active participation in sport presupposes a high level of commitment to activities outside the home, and in many cases, this simply does not exist. As a consequence of apartheid, the ability to forge social contacts and to act with self-confidence is often poorly developed among Africans, and particularly among women and girls, which is why many women and girls tend to restrict themselves to tasks within the household and family (Keim & Qhuma, 1996, p. 81ff. It would be interesting to compare this with Abel's findings regarding foreign women migrants in Germany; Abel, 1984, p. 71).

It is therefore necessary to sensitise the disadvantaged population groups for mass-based pastime sport for both men and women, and to generate sport-related self-confidence among these groups. It is also necessary to create facilities and opportunities for mass-based sport, for all population

groups, in such areas and disciplines that allow for interaction between the different groups, such as fun runs/walks and tournaments of matches. Special attention needs to be paid to the logistic elements which determine access to such events, such as transport, the selection of venues, trainers/teachers and participating schools, and to co-operation with public institutions and with providers or presenters of leisure activities and social services.

A further focus of intervention should be the introduction of PE instruction at all primary and secondary schools, and the basic and further training of teachers, coaches and trainers. Only in this way can sport become a medium which transcends class divisions and differences (cf. Keim, 1994, p. 2f).

4) Sport as an instrument of culture

Thanks to the benefit of a prescribed set of norms and rules governing all established codes, sport "displays the greatest number of common features, which transcend specific cultures". As Harms points out, this commonality qualifies sport as a pre-eminent area for intercultural exchange and communication (Harms, 1982, p. 6).

Stüwe describes sport as an "instrument of culture of international character", because of its world-wide presence, which ensures that its rules are known to members of practically all cultures (Stüwe, 1984, p. 303).

The present study showed that, in South Africa, the significance of various leisure activities varies according to people's origin and/or residential area – in short, it varies along race lines. As a long-term effect of apartheid, the different population groups tend to practise different sport codes (with Africans favouring soccer, and Whites indulging in rugby, cricket, swimming, tennis, etc.). In addition, the African cultural heritage (e.g. dances) was in the past neither included in the curriculum, nor regarded as worthy of conservation or further distribution. Joint programmes of mass-based sport for all population groups, as suggested under 2) above, should therefore be established, and the cultural heritage of the various population groups should be included. In doing so, consideration should be given to socio-anthropological factors, (such as age, group membership, language, religion), as well as to the perception of any particular sport in a particular community (past experience, level of competence, significance of sport in the particular community, etc.).

5) A further approach to sport's potential for promoting social integration can be found in Chu's "contact hypothesis". According to Chu et al, contact between members of different groups can under certain circumstances change mutual attitudes and conduct in a positive way. Among these conditions are the following:

Participants
a) enjoy equal status;
b) strive for a common group goal;
c) co-operate with one another in order to achieve this aim (co-operative interaction)
d) are supported by the community in their efforts to foster contacts (environmental support).

"Given these conditions, interracial contacts should lead to amelioration of previously held prejudices and the promotion of positive inter-group attitudes and behaviors" (Braddock, 1980 as quoted by Chu & Griffey, 1985, p. 323).

The present study illustrates the complexity of the South African situation, and the difficulty of applying Chu's hypothesis. It will still take some time before equal status is established between members of different population groups, and before the social environment supports and encourages efforts to bridge the gap. On account of the inadequate provision of facilities and services to black South Africans in sport and education, both these areas help to maintain and reproduce cultural inequality. It is essential to provide facilities and services for the joint use by different population groups, or the principle of equality will never be established, let alone attained.

The following graphic representation illustrates, by way of summary, the possible aims and functions of sport in the multicultural South African society. With due consideration of the socio-anthropological conditions of the target group, attention is also given to the prerequisites of achieving the guiding aim, and to the practical implementation of such a programme for equality.

Determining conditions (I) for multicultural sport in South Africa	
Socio-anthropological conditions	**Aims and functions of sport**

Personal characteristics:
- age, gender
- marital/family status
- language
- religion
	Sport as a medium of/ tool for:
	- equal opportunities
	- health
	- strengthening
	  personal identity
	
	- integration
	- alternative to
	  potential risks or
	  dangers (boredom,
	  drugs, crime)

primary, high school - status, profession - socio-economic conditions sport-related prior knowledge - attitude towards sport - experience of sport - status of sport within community - opportunities of active partici- - pation in sport - commitment of spare time/club - structures	

Determining conditions (II) for multicultural sport in South Africa	
Preconditions for achieving aims of multicultural sport	**Characteristics of opportunities offered**

Societal preconditions
- public support
 	
- political acceptability
  and viability
 	
- co-operation between various
  organisations
	Contents of programmes offered
	- more provision for 'sport for
	  leisure' and recreational sport
	
	- culture-transcending[1]
	  programmes to be offered
	  in all communities (fun runs,
	  dancing, sports festivals)

Preconditions for achieving aims of multicultural sport	Characteristics of opportunities offered
- exchange instead of isolation - mutual tolerance and acceptance	
Institutional/structural preconditions - introduction of PE in- struction to all schools	Organisational framework multicultural sports projects with the participation of all stakeholders and role players (community structures, govern-mental, educational and sport structures)
- facilities for basic and further training (teachers, coaches, instructors, i.a. marginalised and disadvan-taged groups, e.g. women, the handicapped, street children)	special attention to choice of venue, time, transport, coaches, etc.
- Co-operation: school-sports club	club membership
- convenient conditions for participation/access	co-ordinating measures
- creation of prerequisites of participation (trans-port, equipment, infra-structure of amenities) - multicultural sports programmes	- co-ordination with public institutions and structures of government, organised sport, provi-ders of social services and leisure activities

---

[1]   The term "culture-transcending" is used in the sense of "transcending the traditions, codes and practises of any specific culture. It goes without saying that the multicultural sports practice envisaged in this study is seen as an intrinsic and important aspect of a future, democratic "South African culture" which, I believe, is already in the making, but which will take some time to emerge more clearly.

Preconditions for achieving aims of multicultural sport	Characteristics of opportunities offered
Epistemological prerequisites - development stage of scientific research - experience of functions and presentation of sport - experience of cultural background of participants Personal/individual prerequisites - tolerance, open-mindedness - personal situation - involvement in sport beyond the strictly private/personal sphere (in clubs, organisations, etc.)	awareness campaigns - responsibility of media - marketing, sponsors - role models - upgrading of sport for women, senior citizens, the handicapped

(List based, with modifications, on Heinemann,1985, p. 88f; cf. Abel, 1984, p. 154ff.)

Many obstacles remain to be overcome, many problems remain to be solved in order to speed up the process of nation-building, with the stated aim of becoming a "rainbow nation". By way of summary, it can be stated that sport has a meaningful function of socialisation in South African society. Whether sport can, in fact, fulfil this function and play this "socialising" role, depends to a large extent on the specific way in which sport is organised and presented (cf. Heinemann, 1974, p. 71). The present study confirms the Kothy's view that, through its "socially integrative function", sport can contribute towards the dismantling of social barriers and help to overcome social fragmentation and isolation, provided "it grants access to the young" (cf. Kothy, 1982, as quoted in Adolph & Böck,1985, p. 63).

Both the multicultural dance project and the Pinelands project prove that organised sports projects are, under certain conditions, capable of dismantling barriers to integration.

4.5 Follow-up Projects

At present, the author is co-ordinating four projects which emanated from the findings of the present study.

As follow-up projects relating to the topic of "integration through sport", the following initiatives were set up:

!

a) Integration project: School
1. Joint basic and further training for teachers from different disadvantaged communities/population groups: In-Service Teachers' Training Programme (INSET) which developed to a FDE (Further Diploma of Physical and Health Education) at the University of the Western Cape.
2. Integration of teachers and pupils from different population groups at neighbouring schools into joint PE classes.

b) Integration project: street children
Support for the integration (or reintegration) of street children into the community through the medium of sport.

c) Integration project: Women and handicapped persons
Support for the integration of women and handicapped persons into the community by means of sport.

d) Integration programme: Recreational programme:
Sport for everyone Organisation of various sports events for all population groups in disadvantaged residential areas.

(Details about the various projects can be obtained from the author)

4.6 Conclusions – and the Way Forward

4.6.1 The Multicultural Society in the New South Africa

On a reduced scale, educational institutions in South Africa reflect the same problems that beset the society as a whole. As a consequence of apartheid, the country and its society are "more fragmented than other conflict-ridden societies: in categories of skin colour, ideologies, classes, languages, religions, history, values..." (von Lucius, 1994). The divisions between different population groups should not be underestimated in manifest themselves in day-to-day life. It will take a long time, and require concerted efforts, before the injustices and inequalities of apartheid have been redressed, if only in approximation, especially in the social and economic spheres. Due to their generally low level of education, and the high level of unemployment, many Africans have little prospect of improving their situation in the short term. The combination of poor prospects and persisting social injustice generates tensions, frustrations and frictions, which manifest themselves in rising crime levels. Crime in turn bedevils the nation-building process in the new South Africa, thereby giving rise to further frustrations.

The research projects, questionnaires and interviews conducted in the course of the present study revealed many factors which influence the interaction between the various population groups. By way of summary, these factors have been listed in the following diagram. Apart from factors impeding or complicating the integration or convergence between the population groups, the diagram also records supportive influences, which may suggest possible solutions.

Factors that influence the social interaction and integration of the various cultural groups/population groups in South Africa

Factors that hinder integration	Factors that facilitate integration
- segregated areas	- opening of schools, multilingual and multi-racial schools
- artificial walls between black (African) and Coloured residential areas	- integration programmes between schools, exchange programmes, cultural programmes
- socio-economic class barriers	
- racial prejudice	
- no social mixing	- multi-racial staff
- lack of communication	- multi-lingual educators
- language barriers	- shaping the conscience of a new nation
- no common multi-purpose facilities	- create an atmosphere, circumstances, options for people to develop towards integration
- lack of trained communicators	
- no motivation amongst teachers	
	- role models of the various cultural groups
- schizophrenia among students as a result of commuting between two worlds	- recognition, creating a sense of achievement

Factors that hinder integration	Factors that facilitate integration
	- economic growth
	- media
	- sport

The research conducted in the course of this study has shown that, under certain conditions, sport is a suitable medium for social interaction between population groups in South Africa. Multicultural sports programmes can help to reduce prejudices and build mutual acceptance, tolerance and understanding.

Mutual respect and tolerance may seem fairly modest aims in the light of the country's daunting problems, such as poverty, shortages and shortcomings in the health system, education, and housing, but they are effective because they can be instilled at "grassroots level", as the "Rainbow Paper" of the Western Cape Department of Sport puts it (cf. DSR, 1995b, p. 19). If certain conditioning factors (infrastructure, transport) are in place, contacts established in this way can continue and expand beyond the area of sport, and can thus lead to better co-existence. The educational value and advantage of sport only waits to be activated.

In this sense, sport can undoubtedly initiate the first steps towards social integration. However, this potential cannot be realised wherever prejudices, racism and intolerance abound and intimidate the disadvantaged population groups, or wherever the determining context and conditions do not allow for a multicultural sports programme. In other words, without comprehensive social changes, and especially without a solution to the problems of educational and sports policy, sport in South Africa will not be able to realise its potential as a tool for social integration.

Some readers may regard it as inappropriate to devote so much attention to sport, at a time when many members of the disadvantaged population groups still live under extremely harsh, even life-threatening conditions. However, the author is of the opinion that sport warrants this attention, not only because it can be a lifeline to many in conditions of economic, political and social insecurity, but also because, under certain conditions, it can make a valuable contribution to the process of nation-building. This is no attempt to divert the reader's attention from the acute problems besetting South Africa. On the contrary – as part of the determining context of any successful sports policy for the benefit of all South Africa's inhabitants, these very problems should remain the conscious and constant backdrop of any discussion on this topic.

BIBLIOGRAPHY

Abel, T. (1984). *Ausländer und Sport. Sportliche Aktivitäten als Freizeitinhalt ausländischer Familien in der Bundesrepublik. Mit einer Studie über Verhaltensdeterminanten und Strukturelemente im Ausländersport.* Cologne.

Adam, H. (1997). Africa's Nazis: Apartheid a Holocaust? *Indicator SA, Vol. 14* (1).

Ader, A. (1983). Zur Integration ausländischer Kinder durch Schulsport. *Sportpraxis, 24* (4), 76ff.

Adolph, H. & Böck, F. (1985). *Sport als Integrationsmöglichkeit ausländischer Mitbürger.* Kassel.

Adreses, R., Rieder, H. & Trosien, G. (Eds.). (1989). *Beiträge zur Zusammenarbeit im Sport mit der Dritten Welt.* Schorndorf.

Africa Institute of South Africa (Ed.). (1990). Reflections on Current Political Trends in South Africa *[Broschure] (pp.* 1-5). Pretoria.

Alexander, N. (1995). *The Great Gariep-Metaphors of National Unity in the New South Africa.* Cape Town.

Allison, M. T. (1979). On the Ethnicity of Ethnic Minorities in Sport. *Quest, 31* (1), 50-56.

Allison, M. T. (1982). Sport, Ethnicity and Assimilation. *Quest, 34* (2), 165-172.

ANC. (1994). *The Reconstruction and Development Programme. A Policy Framework.* Johannesburg: Umanyano Publications.

Archer, R. & Bouillon, A. (1982). *The South African Game: Sport and Racism* (2nd ed.). London.

Archer R. (1987). An Exceptional Case: Politics and Sport in South Africa's Townships. *In Sport in Africa* (p. 229ff). New York.

Asmal, K., Asmal, L. & Roberts, R. S. (1996). *Reconciliation through Truth. A Reckoning of Apartheid's Criminal Governance.* Cape Town.

Auswärtiges Amt. Referat für Öffentlichkeitsarbeit (Ed.). (1980). *Auswärtige Kulturpolitik im Schulwesen, Rahmenplan, 2,* 21.

Auswärtiges Amt (Ed.). (1990). *Rundbrief des Auswärtigen Amts an die Gremien der Schulgemeinschaft der Deutschen Schulen im südlichen Afrika, 20. August.*

Auswärtiges Amt. (1990). *Stand und Entwicklung der Deutschen Schulen im Ausland, Beschluß des Deutschen Bundestags, 7th March.*

Bahl, K. (1995). *Comparative Perspectives 1.* Paper presented at the IDASA Conference on National Unity and the Politics of Diversity in the Western Cape, Woodstock, Cape Town, 18-20 August.

Baker, W. J. & Mangan J. A. (Ed.). (1987). *Sport in Africa* (pp. 229). New York.

Bammel, H. & Becker, H. (1985). *Sport und ausländische Mitbürger.* (Ed.: Friedrich-Ebert-Stiftung) Bonn.

Banton, M. (1983). *Racial and Ethnic Competition* (pp. 32-59). Cambridge.

Becker, P. (Ed.). (1982). *Sport und Sozialisation.* Reinbek.

Bertelsmann (Ed.). (1977). *Das Moderne Lexikon* (Vol. 1, p. 363). Berlin.

Bingmer, K., Meistermann-Seeger, E. & Neubert, E. (Eds.). (1972). *Leben als Gastarbeiter. Geglückte und mißglückte Integration* (2nd ed.). Opladen.

Black, P. A. & Flangan, V. (1994). *Affirmative Action in South Africa: A Provisional Assessment.* Cape Town.

Boateng, F. (1983). African Traditional Education. A Method of Disseminating Cultural Values. *Journal of Black Studies, 13* (3), 321-336. Newbury Park. California.

Bogdan, T. & Taylor, R. S. (1975). *Introduction to Qualitative Research Methods. A Phenomenological Approach to the Social Sciences.* New York.

Bortz, J. (1984). *Lehrbuch der empirischen Forschung.* Berlin.

Bortz, J. (1989). *Statistik für Sozialwissenschaftler.* Berlin.

Braddock, J. H. (1980). The Perpetuation of Segregation across Levels of Education. In D. Chu & D. Griffey, *The Contact Theory of Racial Integration. The Case of Sport. Sociology of Sport Journal 1985, 2* (4), 323-333.

Brandt, H. (1984, February 21st). Die Angst vor den neuen schwarzen Bossen geht um. *Frankfurter Rundschau,* p. 21.

Breier, B. (1995, November 18th). Bosses May Have to Use Pencil Test. *Weekend Argus.*

Brockhaus Encyclopaedia. (1970). (Vol. 9, p. 162). Wiesbaden.

Brookes, E. H. (1968). *Apartheid a Documentary Study of Modern South Africa.* London.

Bröskamp, B. (1993). *Körperliche Fremdheit. Zum Problem der interkulturellen Begegnung im Sport.* Berlin.

Bydekarken, J. (1992, February 21st). Die neue Apartheid der Armut. *Deutsches Allgemeines Sonntagsblatt.*

CACE (1995, June 10th). Representations and Constructions of Race, Class, Gender and Culture in the Western Cape. *Conference Paper.* UWC. Bellville.

Chanaiwa, D. (1980). The Political Economy of Colonial Education in South Africa. In A. T. Mugomba & M. Nyaggrah (Eds.), *Independence without Freedom* (pp. 227-241). Santa Barbara, California.

Charney., C. (1991). Das Zünglein an der Waage. *Der Überblick, 4* (12), 27.

Christie, P. & Collins, C. (1982). Bantu Education: Apartheid Ideology or Labour Reproduction. *Comparative Education, 18* (1), 59-75. Carfax Publ. Oxford.

Chu, D. & Griffey, D. (1985). The Contact Theory of Racial Integration: The Case of Sport. *Sociology of Sports Journal, 2,* 4 Dec., 323-333.

Coakley, J. J. (1990). *Sport in Society. Issues and Controversies: Intergroup Relations. Is Sport a Model of Racial and Ethnic Harmony?* (4th ed.). (pp. 203-223). St. Louis.

Concise English Oxford Dictionary of Current English (8th ed.). (1990). (Vol. 1, p. 48). Oxford.

Day, R. D. (1981). Ethnic Soccer Clubs in London, Canada. A Study in Assimilation. *International Review for Sociology of Sport, 16* (1), pp. 37-52.

De Broglio, C. (1970). *South Africa: Racism in Sport.* London. IDAF.

DED (1991, June, 7/8th). Kapstadt schleift einen Stützpfeiler der Apartheid. *Handelsblatt.*

Deichmann, M. (1978). *Teilnahme und Beobachtung als soziologisches Basisverhalten.* Bern.

DE Lange-Report: see HSRC (1981).

Department of National Education (Ed.). (1993). *Education Realities in South Africa* (3rd ed.). Report: NATED 02-300 (93/12), Pretoria.

Der Spiegel (1993, December 20th, No. 51). *Stiefkinder Gottes. Südafrikas Mischlinge, einst Opfer der Apartheid, laufen zu den Weißen – aus Angst vor den Schwarzen.*

DET: *Annual Reports* (1980-1986). (Title changed: *Native Education to Bantu Education to Education and Training*). The Governament Printer. Pretoria.

Deutsche Sportjugend/Sportjugend. (1984). *Deutsch-Türkischer Kindertreff*. Berlin-Frankfurt.

Deutscher Sportbund (1972). *Sport für alle – Herausforderung an den Sport*. Frankfurt/Main.

Deutscher Sportbund (Ed.). (1990a). *Sport mit Aussiedlern. Experten-Hearing*. Frankfurt.

Deutscher Sportbund (Ed.). (1990b). *Sport mit Aussiedlern und Übersiedlern, Workshop II*. Frankfurt.

Deutscher Sportbund (Ed.). (1991). *Sport mit Aussiedlern. Workshop III*. Frankfurt.

Deutscher Sportbund (Ed.). (1992). *Sport mit Aussiedlern. Workshop IV.* Frankfurt.

Deutscher Sportbund (1994). Hilfe beim sozialen Aufbau des Sports – vorrangig Hans Hansen über Sportentwicklungshilfe nach Südafrikareise. *Circular for Members.* 10/94.

Dostal, E. & Vergnani, T. (1984). Future Perspectives on South African Education. *Occasional Paper, No. 4, October 1984. Business Series. Social Environment.* Institute for Future Research, University of Stellenbosch.

Draper, M. (1963). *Sport and Race in South Africa.* Johannesburg.

Drechsel, P. & Schmit, B. (1995). *Südafrika – Chancen für eine pluralistische Gesellschaftsordnung.* Opladen.

DSR (Ed.). (1995). *White Paper (Draft). Sport and Recreation in South Africa. A National Policy Framework.* Pretoria.

DSR Western Cape. (1995). *Rainbow Paper (Draft).*

Eiselen-Report. (1951). In *Union of South Africa. Report of the native education commission 1949-1951* (U.G. 53/1951). Pretoria.

Erbslöh, E. (1972). *Techniken der Datensammlung* (Vol. 1). Stuttgart.

Esser, H. (1980). *Aspekte der Wanderungssoziologie. Assimilation und Integration von Wanderern, ethnischen Gruppen und Minderheiten. Eine handlungstheoretische Analyse.* Darmstadt und Neuwied.

Flick, U. (Ed.). (1991). *Handbuch Qualitative Sozialforschung*. Munich.

Friedmann-Wittkowerw, E. D. (1971). The Influence of Movement on Culturally Deprived Children. *Gymnasium*, 9-13.

Frogner, E. (1984). Die Bedeutung des Sports für die Eingliederung ausländischer Mitbürger. *Sportwissenschaft, 14* (4), 348-361.

Frogner, E. (1985). Das „Integrationsmedium" Sport im Lichte einer sportsoziologischen Untersuchung bei türkischen Migranten. In H. Bammel & H. Becker, (pp. 34-50).

Germud, W. (1994, April 4th). Die ängstlichen Inder von Durban. *Die Tageszeitung*.

Giebenhain, H. (1995). Die gesellschaftliche Integration von Fremden durch den Sport. In *Müller et al. (Ed.), Fremde und andere in Deutschland. Nachdenken über das Einverleiben, Einebnen, Ausgrenzen* (pp. 165-178). Opladen.

Girtler, R. (1984). *Methoden der qualitativen Sozialforschung*. Wien.

Gomos, J. (1996). *100 Years "Emancipation of Slaves"*. Cape Town.

Grill, B. (1995, January 13th). Südafrikas Elite-Universität tut sich schwer mit dem Ende der Apartheid – „Oxford der Buren". *Die Zeit*.

GTZ (Gesellschaft für Technische Zusammenarbeit). (1986). *Nation-Building through Sports*. Eschborn.

Hagemann, A. (1995). *Nelson Mandela*. Reinbek.

Hain, P. (1971). *Don't Play with Apartheid*. London.

Hanisch, P. (1983). Der Sport – kein Allheilmittel für gesellschaftliche Probleme aller Art. In DSB (Ed.), *Akademieschrift 23: Der ausländische Mitbürger im Sport*. Berlin.

Harms, H. (1982). Die soziale Zeitbombe ist noch längst nicht entschärft, zur möglichen Funktion des Sports bei der Integration der ausländischen Arbeitnehmer und ihrer Familien. *Olympische Jugend, 12*.

Heckmann, F. (1985). Sport und die gesellschaftliche Integration von Minderheiten. In H. Bammel & H. Becker (Eds.), (pp. 21-33).

Heinemann, K. (1979). *Einführung in die Soziologie des Sports*. Schorndorf.

Heinemann, K. (1974). Sozialisation im Sport. *Sportwissenschaft, 1.*

Heinemann, K. (1988a). Einführung in das Tagungsthema „Sport und ausländische Mitbürger". In H. Bammel & H. Becker (Eds.), (pp. 5-11).

Heinemann, K. (1988b). Probleme und Entwicklungen im Sport für Ausländer – Schlußwort. In H. Bammel & H. BECKER (Eds.), (pp. 81-106).

Höhn, E. &. Seidel, G. (1976). *Das Soziogramm. Die Erfassung von Gruppen-strukturen.* Göttingen.

Holm, K. (Ed.). (1975). *Die Befragung 1. Der Fragebogen – Die Stichprobe.* Munich.

Howa, H. (1977). In A. Odendaal (Ed.), *Cricket in Isolation, the Politics of Race and Cricket in South Africa* (p. 277). Cape Town.

HSRC (Human Science Research Council). (1981). *Provision of Education in the Republic of South Africa.* Report of the Main Committee of the Human Science Research Council *(HSRC/RGN).* Investigation into Education. No. 1 (DE-LANGE-REPORT). Pretoria.

HSRC-Report (1982, April). *Sport in RSA. Main Committee Report. HSRC Sports Investigation.* Pretoria.

IDASA (1995a, August 19th). *Conference Paper: National Unity and the Politics of Diversity in the Western Cape.* Cape Town.

DASA. VIDEO. (1995b). *Now That We Are Free.* Cape Town.

James W. (1995, August 18-20th). *Making Sense of the Coloured Vote.* Paper presented at the IDASA-Conference on National Unity and the Politics of Diversity in the Western Cape. Woodstock, Cape Town.

Jansen, V. (1991). Daf-Unterricht im südlichsten Afrika. *Deutschunterricht im südlichen Afrika, 22* (2), 30+.

Jones, R. C. (1973). The Education of the Bantu in South Africa. In *B. Rose (Ed.), Education in Southern Africa* (2nd ed.). (pp. 40-92). London.

Karpen, U. (1996, March 10th). Die Mühen um die Einheit des Landes – Südafrika auf dem Weg zum demokratischen Verfassungsstaat. *Frankfurter Allgemeine Zeitung, 60,* S. 10.

Keim, M. (1992) DaF-Unterricht im südlichsten Afrika – Ich war in Mitchell's Plain ... *Deutschunterricht im südlichen Afrika, 23* (1), 18-26.

Keim, M. (1994, January). The Advantages of Sport and Physical Education in Open Schools. *Open Schools Association*, pp. 1-4.

Keim, M. (1996). The Value of Dance in the Integration Process. In *South African Federation for Movement and Leisure Science, Biennial Congress Report* (p. 26). Stellenbosch.

Keim, M. & Qhuma, W. (1996, November). Infrastructural Problems in Sports Promotion in Townships with Particular Reference to Women. *Agenda, 31*, 81-85.

King, D. (1990). Multiple Jeopardy, Multiple Consciousness. In *M. Malson et al., Black Women in America – Social Science Perpectives*. Chicago.

Kosel, H. (1981). Integration. In *K. A. Jochheim & P. van der Schoot, Behindertensport und Rehabilitation II* (Vol. 38, p. 234+). Cologne.

Kröger, C. &. Kemper, G. (Eds.). (1990). *Evaluierung von Sportprojekten*. Ahrensburg.

Lamnek, S. (1988). *Qualitative Sozialforschung* (Vol. 1, Methodologie). Munich.

Lamnek, S. (1989). *Qualitative Sozialforschung* (Vol. 2, Methoden und Techniken). Munich.

Landessportverband Baden-Württemberg (Ed.). (1996). *Jahresbericht. Sport für alle – Projekt: „Sport mit Aussiedlern"*.

Lapping, B. (1986). *Apartheid a History*. Glasgow.

Lewis, C. H. (1978). Ethnic Sport and Recreation. Participation: A View from the Middle of a Tightrope. In T. Abel, *Ausländer und Sport* (s. o.) (p. 8). Cologne.

Longman Dictionary of Contemporary English. (1981). (Vol. 1, p. 37). London.

Lucius von, R. (1994, August 18th). Hochstimmung, Versöhnung, Ineffizienz. Die ersten hundert Tage Präsident Mandelas. *Frankfurter Allgemeine Zeitung*.

Luhmann, N. (1995). *Soziologische Aufklärung* (pp. 235-265). Opladen.

Malherbe, E. G. (1977). *Education in South Africa* (Vol. II: 1923-1975). Cape Town.

Mandela, N. (1991a). *Mein Kampf gegen die Apartheid*. Munich.

Mandela, N. (1991b, November 21st). *Vision für Südafrika*. Rede von ANC-Präsident Nelson Mandela zur Eröffnung einer Konferenz von IDASA in Johannesburg. *Der Überblick 4/91*, p.12+.

Martenson, S. (1993). Mehr als nur ein Spalt – Die Öffnung der Deutschen Schulen im südlichen Afrika am Beispiel der DHPS Windhuk und der DS Kapstadt. *Begegnung, 1*, 29-33.

Mayntz, R., Holm, K. & Hübner, P. (3rd ed.). (1972). *Einführung in die Methoden der empirischen Soziologie* (pp. 9-31, pp. 68-134, pp. 189-230). Opladen.

Mc Cloy, M. (1997, May 30th-June 5th). A Dance Floor Divided. *Mail & Guardian 13* (21), p. 32.

Merkel, R. (1980). Initiative Drei-Vereine-Gesamtprojekt Wetzlar Konzeptionsentwurf für den Ländessportbund Hessen,. Unpublished. Manuscript. Frankfurt. In F. Heckmann. (1985), *Sport und ausländische Mitbürger* (p. 30).

Moreno, J. L. (1974). *Die Grundlagen der Soziometrie* (3rd ed.). Opladen.

Morgenrath, B. (1994). Wir sind nur mit dem Boss hier. 'Coloureds' wählen mehrheitlich Nationale Partei. *Afrika süd 4*, 8-10.

Moyo, B. (1994). Ich will nicht enden wie meine Mutter. *Informationsdienst südliches Afrika, 2*, 4-6.

Müller, A. (1990). In E. Dostal (Ed.), *Education for South Africa's Future. Institute for Future Research*. University of Stellenbosch.

Mummendey, H.-D. (1987). *Die Fragebogen-Methode, Grundlagen und Anwendung in Persönlichkeits-, Einstellungs- und Selbstkonzeptforschung.* Göttingen.

Munzinger Länderhefte (1991). Int. Handbuch Länder aktuell. Republik Südafrika. *Munzinger-Archiv 22, 3.*

Munzinger Länderhefte (1994). Int. Handbuch Länder aktuell. Republik Südafrika. *Munzinger-Archiv 41, 2.*

Natorp, K. (1995, December 19th). Im Jahre zwei nach der Apartheid. *Frankfurter Allgemeine Zeitung*, p. 12.

Niven, J. M. (1982). *The Educational Systems of the Republic of South Africa.* Occasional Paper No. 4, University of Natal, Dept. of Education, Pietermaritzburg.

NSC: National Sports Council. (no publ. date). *The Complete Guide to the NSC.* Johannesburg.

Nyaggrah, M. (1980). Apartheid and Second-Class Education in South Africa. In A. T. Mugomba & M. Nyaggrah (Eds.), *Independence without Freedom* (pp.59-78). Santa Barbara, California.

Oswald, W. D. (1977). *Grundkurs Soziogramm.* Paderborn.

Parson, T. (no publ. date). Commentary on Clark. In A. EFFRAT (Ed.), *Perspectives in Political Sociology* (pp. 299-308). Indianapolis.

Pooley, J. C. (1976). Ethnic Soccer Clubs in Milwaukee: A Study in Assimilation. In M. Hart (Ed.), *Sport in the Sociocultural Process.* Dubuque, Iowa.

Ramsamy, S. (1977). Racial Discrimination. *Non-racial Sport in South Africa, Centre Against Apartheid.* United Nations, New York.

Ramsamy, S. (1982). *Apartheid, the Real Hurdle: Sport in South Africa and the International Boycott* (pp.19-23). London International Defence and Aid Fund.

Räther, F. (1993, April 5th). Die Wunden der Apartheid werden noch lange bluten. *FOCUS 14,* S. 5.

Ribeiro, F. R. (1995) *Diversity and Assimilation in Brazil: A Difficult Interplay.* Paper presented at the IDASA Conference on National Unity and the Politics of Diversity in the Western Cape, Woodstock, Cape Town, 18-20th August.

Rieder, H. (1977). *Sport als Therapie.* Berlin.

Rigauer, B. (1982). *Sportsoziologie.* Reinbek.

Roberts, C. (1988). *SACOS 1973-1988: 15 Years of Sports Resistence.* Cape Town.

Roberts, C. (1992). *Don't Deny My Dream.* Cape Town.

Roosevelt Thomas, R. (1990). From Affirmative Action to Affirming Diversity. *Harvard Business Review, 3/4,* 107-113.

SACOS. (1975, October). *Report: SACOS Biennial Conference* (p. 70).

SACOS (1977, April 6th). *Statements on Double Standard. Issued by SACOS.*

SANEP Report. (1985). *South African National Education Policy. The Structure and Operation of the South African Education System, SANEP-170.* May 1985, Dept. of National Education. Pretoria.

Scheid, V. (1994). *Soziale Integration behinderter Menschen durch Bewegung, Spiel und Sport. Anthropologische Grundlagen – Ökologisches Rahmenkonzept – Empirische Analysen – Pädagogische Konzequenzen.* Habilitation. University of Würzburg.

Schlemmer, L. & Bot, M. (1987). Swart oder wys. Agter die Storm en Drang. *Die Suid-Afrikaan, 9,* 19-22.

Scholz G. & Olivier, J. L. (1984). Attitude of Urban South Africans toward Non-Racial Sport and their Expectations of Future Race Relations – A Comparative Study. *International Review for Sociology of Sport, 19* (2), 129-143.

Schulke-Vandre, J. (1992). Integrationssport als alltagskultureller Gesundheitssport für jeden. *Hochschulsport, 13,* 4-8. University of Bremen.

Seibert G. & Wendelberger E. (Ed.). (1984). *LEXIKON 2000.* (Vol. 3, p. 1232). Weinheim.

Sharp, J. (1994, August 31st). Magic of a Mix of Cultures. *Democracy in Action* (Vol. 8).

Sharp, J. (1995, August 19th). *Identitiy Politics and Cultural Differences: An Overview from Anthropology.* Conference Paper for IDASA-Conference on "Understanding National Unity and the Politics of Diversity". Cape Town.

Sheron, B. & Sheron, U. (1982). *Integration von Gastarbeiterkindern.* Frankfurt.

Simon, A. M. (1994). In the Mix: Remarking Coloured Identities. *Africa Insigh., 24 (3),* 161-173.

Singer, R. & Willimczik, K. (Eds.). (1985). *Grundkurs Datenerhebung 2.* (Vol. 3). Ahrensburg.

Snyder, E. & Spreitzer E. A. (2nd ed.). (1983). *Social Aspects of Sports.* (pp. 174-200). New York.

Sociology of Sports Journal (1985, December 4th). *Case of Sport.* p. 323.

South African Communication Service (Ed.). (1994). *South Africa Yearbook.* Pretoria.

South African Communication Service (Ed.). (1995). *South Africa Yearbook.* Pretoria.

South African Communication Service (Ed.). (1996). *South Africa Yearbook.* Pretoria.

Sparks, A. (1990). *The Mind of South Africa.* New York.

Standard Encyclopaedia of Southern Africa. (1970). (Vol I., p. 472). London.

Statistisches Bundesamt (Ed.). (1991). *Länderbericht Südafrika.* Wiesbaden.

Statistisches Bundesamt (Ed.). (1995). *Länderbericht Südafrika.* Wiesbaden.

Steinkamp, E. W. (1976). *Sport und Rasse – der schwarze Sportler in den USA.* Ahrensburg.

Stüwe, G. (1984). Sport. In G. Auernheimer (Ed.),. *Handwörterbuch Ausländerarbeit* (pp. 303-305). Weinheim.

Sunday Independent. (1996, May 19th).

South African Institute of Race Relations (Ed.). (1960-1994). *Survey of Race Relations in South Africa.* Johannesburg.

Taylor, P. (1993, May 11th). South Africa's 'Coloreds' Are Sliding with Whites. *Herald Tribune.*

Thieme, B. (1992). Integration Behinderter in den Hochschulsport an der FU-Berlin. *Hochschulsport im Wandel, Part 1, 1/23,* p. 4+.

Thirer, J. & Wieczorek, P. J. (1984). On and Off Field Interaction Patterns of Black and White High School Athletes. *Journal of Sport Behaviour, 7,* 3.

Tickly, L. (1993, Oct. 29th-Nov. 1st). *Levelling the Playing Fields whilest Moving the Goal Posts: Changing Discourses on 'Race' in Apartheid Education Policy.* Paper presented at Olwandle Conference.

TIME. (1994, April 24th). *Special Report: South Africa – The Second Struggle* (pp. 39-63).

UNESCO. (1972). L'Apartheid, ses effects sur léducation, la science, la culture et l'ínformation, Paris, (pp. 63-64). In *W. J. Baker & J. A. Mangan, (Ed.), Sport in Africa, Essays in Social History,* (p. 239). New York: 1987.

USSASA. (1994). *Working Document towards a New School Sports Structure in South Africa.* Johannesburg.

Uwechue, R. C. (1981). Nation Building and Sport in Africa. In B. Lowe, D. B. Kanin & A. Strenk, *Sport and International Relations* (pp. 538-550). Champaign/Illinois.

Volk, D. (1994). Das Erbe der Apartheid – Politische Gewalt seit der Wende. *Blätter des Informationszentrums Dritte Welt* 194 (93), 15-19.

WCED (Ed.). (1995, June, 15th). *Circular L.1/0/30/4.*

Weekend Argus. (1994, March 5/6th). (p. 16). Cape Town.

Weekend Argus. (1997, May 24th). (p. 20). Cape Town.

Weekly Mail & Guardian (1994 November 25th-December 1st). *Getting Schools Ready for the Children* (p.13). Cape Town.

Weische-Alexa, P. (3rd ed.). (1980). *Sozial-kulturelle Probleme junger Türkinnen in der Bundesrepublik Deutschland.* Cologne.

Weixlederer, M. (1990). *Die Leibeserziehung in der Republik Südafrika mit besonderer Berücksichtigung des schwarzen Bildungssystems.* Dissertation, University of Graz.

Wesgro (Ed.). (1996). *Report: Western Cape Economic Monitor.* Cape Town.

White Paper: (1983). *White Paper on the Provision of Education in the Republic of South Africa. Government Printer.* Pretoria.

Wilke-Launer, R. & Kühne, W. (1993). Südafrika. In Nohlen & Nuscheler (Ed.), *Handbuch der Dritten Welt.* Bonn.

Wohl, A. (1981). *Soziologie des Sports.* Cologne.

Zahn, I. (1992). Südafrika heute – Furcht vor dem anderen, der mir fremd ist. *Afrika Post, 10,* 6-10.

Zollschan, G. K. & Hirsch, W. (Ed.). (1976). *Social Change: Explorations, Diagnoses and Conjectures* (pp. 370-383). New York.

NEWSPAPERS AND JOUNALS
(INCL. PLACE OF PUBLICATION)

Cape Argus	Cape Town
Cape Times	Cape Town
Die Zeit	Hamburg
Frankfurter Allgemeine Zeitung	Frankfurt
Frankfurter Rundschau	Frankfurt
Handelsblatt	Düsseldorf
Harald Tribune	Johannesburg
Sunday Independent	Johannesburg
Time International	Johannesburg, Amsterdam, New York
Weekly Mail & Guardian	Johannesburg
Weekend Argus	Cape Town

ACKNOWLEDGEMENTS

When a PhD dissertation finally becomes a published book and years of research finds a home between two covers, the joy of seeing ones work made available to a wider readership is tremendous. The challenge arises, however, with the publisher waiting patiently for that last section, the acknowledgements. How can one ever sufficiently thank the large number of individuals and institutions without whom one's work could never have been carried out? It is a task as daunting as the original research itself. I will try here, knowing that failure is in part unavoidable.

I begin where one should in South Africa, by recognizing and giving thanks to the thousands of men, women and children who, over many decades, gave their lives in the struggle to create a nation that holds high the ideal of all people being equal regardless of differences in race, colour, gender, religion or sexual preference. I believe in that view for South Africa and for the world. It was the magnet which drew me to this corner of the world from my native Germany in 1991 and has kept me here ever since. And I give thanks to remarkable leaders like former president Nelson Mandela and Archbishop Desmond Tutu for continuing to lead South Africa and the world toward a greater humanness for all.

Drawing the circle a bit closer, I thank the South African and German students who formed the first multi-racial class at the German School Cape Town in 1991/2 who inspired me to write this book. My special thanks go further to the 1144 students, teachers, parents and representatives of religious and sporting organizations and the schools from Cape Town, Athlone, Langa, Khayelitsha, Pinelands, Mitchells Plain and Zonnebloem who form the backbone of this research. All of you "subjects" were wonderful and willing participants. I thank you for your openness, co-operation, the interesting talks and especially for your trust.

I thank all those I interviewed, particularly Archbishop Desmond Tutu, the late Minister of Safety and Security, Steve Tshwete, the Minister of Sport and Recreation, Ngconde Balfour and Dr. Neville Alexander for sharing their extensive knowledge, valuable insights and challenging views.

For their organisational assistance I thank Ms. Libby Burrell, University of the Western Cape, and the Sports Administration office of the University of Cape Town for providing me with the organisational framework for the project work. I also thank Ms. Dawn Langdown (Jazz Art), Ms Judith Wasserfall, Mr. Wilfred Allen (UWC), Mr. Nolen Charles (St. Raphael's Primary School), Mr. Wium Mostert, Mr. James Fraser (Western Province Athletics Association), Mr. Jermaine Boyle and Mr. Greg Willemburg (Western Province Baseball Association) for their dedication and practical assistance in the project. I further thank Mr. Klaus Althoff for his co-operation and ample time for numerous discussions.

Very special thanks go to the late German Consul General, Mr. Erich Urmoneit, for his support over many years and to the German Consulate itself, especially Mr. Jürgen Kurzhals.

At my home university, the University of Heidelberg, my sincere thanks go to Professor Dr. Herman Rieder for his support and encouragement for the research involved in this book. I also thank Professor Dr. Klaus Roth who was always motivating me in my work in South Africa.

The German Academic Exchange Service (DAAD) receives my thanks for a research grant which enabled me to conduct my research in South Africa. A special thanks to Martin Fritze and Jasmine Johnson for their assistance with the many statistics and tables presented in the book, and to Mr. Richard Bertelsmann for the translation into English.

A very special thank you goes to my friends who, throughout the years of research and writing, have always supported and encouraged me. To Dr. Günther Strobel, Birgit Arnold and the Fernandez family I give even more thanks for being the very special and close people they are, and for enduring me during hectic times. The friendship and patience they have shown me are invaluable.

So many thanks go to my husband, Jim, for his love, understanding, patience and support. Particularly important were his double batches of warm chocolate muffins which got me through the final stages of the book. You are a source of strength and inspiration.

Last but most importantly, I dedicate this book to my parents. This is only a little thank you for the endless love, support, patience and understanding you have show me for my entire life and for creating a secure foundation of love which made it possible for me to travel so far from home to this amazing land of South Africa in the first place.

Marion Keim
Cape Town
20 December 2002